SCIENCE-BASED BIBLE LESSONS

Exploring God's truth through science

ROSEKiDZ®

Top 50 Science-Based Bible Lessons

Copyright © 2020 Rose Publishing LLC.

Published by RoseKidz®
a division of Tyndal House Ministries
Rose Publishing, LLC
P.O. Box 3473
Peabody, Massachusetts 01961-3473 USA
www.hendricksonpublishinggroup.com

Managing Editor: Karen McGraw
Assistant Editor: Talia Messina
Editorial and Production Associate: Drew McCall
Cover & Interior Design: Drew McCall
Writer: Mary Gross Davis

Conditions of Use

Scripture quotations are taken from the Holy Bible, New Living Translation, copyright © 1996, 2004, 2015 by Tyndale House Foundation. Used by permission of Tyndale House Publishers, Inc., Carol Stream, Illinois 60188. All rights reserved.

R50022
ISBN: 978-1-62862-960-6
RELIGION/Christian Ministry/Children

Printed in United States of America
Printed August 2024

CONTENTS

INTRODUCTION

TOP 50 SCIENCE-BASED BIBLE LESSONS

Have you ever marveled at the wonders of creation? Explore God's creation through science! The *Top 50 Science-Based Bible Lessons* combines biblical truths with scientific laws. Too often, Christians think that science and faith are at war with each other. Yet, God is the creator of science! He wrote all the rules that govern our world. By looking at our world we find beauty, order, creativity, ingenuity, and care—all characteristics of our God. Teach children (ages five to ten) fifty important Bible truths in the context of God's abundant creation through lessons on light, air, earth, water, and more.

HOW TO USE THIS BOOK

The fifty Bible lessons are divided by the scientific principles they explore: light, air, earth, water, weather, laws of nature, plants, human body, sound, and electricity.

Each lesson includes:

- **Memory Verse**
- **Big Idea:** Bible truth emphasized in each activity.
- **Overview:** Guided conversation to introduce the lesson.
- **Bible Story:** God's Word
- **Opening Game:** Game related to the Bible story or the scientific law.
- **Object Lesson:** Use everyday objects to explain biblical truths through science.
- **Three Optional Activities:** Children with different learning styles will engage with the Bible truths through crafts, games, snacks, and more. Includes quick-reference materials lists, step-by-step instructions, and guided conversations.
- **Reproducible Activity Page:** Use as a take-home resource, time-filler, or in-class activity.
- **Plus!** Includes a Bible lesson index and a memory verse index at the back of the book!

See creation in a whole new light with the ***Top 50 Science-Based Bible Lessons!***

1. GOD CREATES LIGHT

GENESIS 1:1–5; JOHN 1:1–5,14,17

Jesus . . . said, "I am the light of the world. If you follow me, you won't have to walk in darkness, because you will have the light that leads to life."
John 8:12

BIG IDEA

JESUS IS THE LIGHT OF THE WORLD

OVERVIEW

Say: Let's all close our eyes tightly. Now that your eyes are closed, what can you see? (*Children respond.*) What would happen if we all got up and ran around the room with our eyes closed? (*Children respond.*) We need light to be able to see where we are going! You can open your eyes now!

What are some other reasons we need light? (*Children respond.*) Light is SO important. We could not live without it! That's one reason why the Bible tells us that **Jesus is the light of the world**. We'll talk more about that in a few minutes! (*Open with prayer requests, praises, and a time of prayer.*)

BIBLE STORY

Say: (*Read Genesis 1:1–5 aloud.*) When God made the world, what did he create first? (*Children respond.*) Light! God could have created everything at once. Why do you think he chose to make light first? (*Children respond.*) What do you think is the most important thing about light? (*Children respond.*)

There is another place in the Bible that describes creation. Listen to this! (*Read John 1:1–5 aloud.*) Wow! Who is the Word? (*Children respond.*) **Let's read verses fourteen and seventeen for clues!** (*Read John 1:14 aloud, pausing to let children guess who it is talking about. Then read verse 17 aloud.*) Jesus is the one John describes as the creator of the world.

Do you know what Jesus called himself? (*Read John 8:12 aloud.*) Jesus is the light of the world. What are some of the reasons we said we need light? (*Children respond.*) Without light, there is no life. If the sun were a little farther away from Earth, we'd freeze to death. If it were a little closer to Earth, it would be too hot for humans to live!

God made the world through Jesus. He gives us the light that gives life! Even people who don't know Jesus yet live in the light he gives us! Jesus wants us to understand that we need him for everything. I'm so glad that **Jesus is the light of the world.**

OPENING GAME
IN THE DARK

Optional Preparation: Set up an obstacle course in the playing area using tables, chairs, toys, or anything you'd like.

Directions: Children find a partner and stand in pairs at the outside edges of the playing area. One partner closes their eyes. On the leader's signal, the seeing partner guides the child who cannot see from one side of the playing area to the other. The goal is to get safely across without bumping into anyone or anything. Give children about a minute to move across, and then have partners switch assignments and move back to their original spot.

Say: When you were in the dark, who did you have to trust? (*Children respond.*) What would have happened if you had tried to cross the area without your partner guiding you? (*Children respond.*)

When we don't know what to do, or don't have light to see where to go, we can trust Jesus because **Jesus is the light of the world.** That means he shows us what to do. He is always ready to help us. Jesus' light is also inside anyone who believes in him. Like being guided by our partner who had the light, we can trust Jesus, instead of going our own way.

Tip: Some children don't like blindfolds. Let the child choose whether to wear a blindfold for this game.

> ### Optional
> - obstacles (tables, chairs, toys, etc.

OBJECT LESSON
THE NATURE OF LIGHT

Tip: Provide enough flashlights and hand mirrors that several teams of children can work to reflect the light onto the target.

Preparation: Tape the sheet of paper to the wall at chest height. This is the target for the light reflecting experiment.

Say: Let's take a vote. Who here thinks light travels in a straight line? (*Children respond.*) Who thinks light bends? (*Children respond.*) We're going to experiment to find out!

Directions: Give two or three children each a hand mirror. Darken the room. Shine a flashlight at the mirror of the child closest to you. Child angles their mirror so that the light hits another mirror. That child then angles their mirror so that it hits another mirror or hits the target paper.

> ### Materials
> - tape
> - paper
> - hand mirrors
> - flashlights

Try this several times with different children, so that everyone has the chance to participate. Or, let children work in teams (see tip).

Say: Now we can see that light moves in a straight line! We can bend the light by letting it reflect off our mirrors, but the light itself will travel only in a straight line. This is one of the reasons we can send different kinds of beams into space; we know that they will keep on going and going! Just like a beam of light that goes straight on forever, **Jesus is the light of the world.**

OPTIONAL ACTIVITIES

WHEN IT'S DARK

Directions: Children tell times they need light. Write the answers on the whiteboard.

Say: There are MANY things we can't do unless we have light. We need Jesus so we can have his light inside us and be part of his family. **Jesus is the light of the world.**

> ## Materials
> - whiteboard
> - dry-erase marker

SUN CATCHERS

Preparation: Punch two holes on either side of each deli lid. Cut yarn into 6-inch lengths, making one for each child.

Directions: Set markers where all children can reach. Give each child a deli lid to decorate. When child has finished, help child insert yarn through the hole and tie to make a hanger.

Say: We are making sun catchers today. When you take them home, hang them in a sunny window. You will get a colorful surprise! Our sun catchers can't make any pretty colors unless the light shines through them. In the same way, we need Jesus so his light is inside us. When we are part of his family, we can be like the sun catchers and shine his colors to the whole world! **Jesus is the light of the world.**

> ## Materials
> - hole punch
> - clear deli lids
> - permanent colored markers
> - scissors
> - yarn

SHADOW PLAY

Preparation: Photocopy the Shadow Animals on page 10, making one copy for each child.

Directions: Distribute Shadow Animals to children.

Depending on the size of your wall and the number of children, assign some children to hold flashlights while others make shadow shapes with their hands. Invite children to create a story about the shapes while they are making them.

Tip: Set a slide projector so it shines onto the wall instead of using flashlights.

Developmental Tip: For younger children, provide cardboard shapes to hold up and make shadows as well as using their hands.

Say: We're going shine light on our hands to make fun shadows! Look at the shapes on your page. See if you can make some of them. Or you can make your own shapes! Just like we need the light to make these shadow shapes, we need Jesus in our lives so we can live! **Jesus is the light of the world.**

Materials

- Shadow Animals, page 10
- flashlights

SHADOW ANIMALS

Jesus . . . said, "I am the light of the world. If you follow me, you won't have to walk in darkness, because you will have the light that leads to life."
John 8:12

rabbit

bird

eagle

flamingo

goat

lizard

dog

cat

deer

2. GOD CREATES STARS

GENESIS 1:14–19

Both day and night belong to you; you made the starlight and the sun.
Psalm 74:16

BIG IDEA

GOD SHOWS HIS LOVE IN HIS CREATION

OVERVIEW

Say: How many planets can we see in the night sky? (*Children respond.*) At different times of year, we may see several planets shining brightly. But which planets make their own light? (*Children respond.*) Today, we will find out the answer to this question! There is so much to discover about what God made! **God shows his love in his creation!** (*Open with prayer requests, praises, and a time of prayer.*)

BIBLE STORY

Say: We asked a question about the planets earlier. Which planet do you think makes its own light? (*Children respond.*) I have a surprising answer: NO planet makes its own light. When we see the light from Mars or Venus, or even from the moon, that light is all reflected light!

The only sources of light in our sky are stars—and the SUN is the closest star to us! (*Read Genesis 1:14–15 aloud.*) When God made the world, he made lights in the sky so that we would know day from night. A constellation is a group of stars that make a pattern. The constellations in the sky can tell us what season it is.

What were the two biggest things that light up the sky? (*Children respond.*) Yes! The sun and the moon. (*Read Genesis 1:16–18 aloud.*) God set the sun in just the perfect place so that we would have daylight. He made the earth spin so that part of the time, we are on the side of the planet that is in the shadow—we call that night!

What planet do we see at night that changes a little every night? (*Children respond.*) Yes! The moon sometimes looks like a tiny sliver of silver. At other times, it is big and round. Why do you think God made the moon to change? (*Children respond.*)

There are many reasons—but one is that the moon became a calendar for people. The moon goes from dark to full to dark again about every twenty-eight days. People counted the days, looked at the moon, and knew where they were in the calendar year! That's just one of the many ways **God shows his love in his creation!**

OPENING GAME
LIGHT SWEEPER

Directions: Dim the lights. Give a flashlight to a volunteer who will be the light bearer. Use more flashlights if you have a very large group. Light bearer stands at one side of the playing area, lit flashlight in hand, and back to the group.

Children start at the opposite side of the play area. Light bearer repeats the first part of the Bible verse: "Both day and night belong to you." Children may move while the light bearer's back is turned, until the word "you" is spoken. On "you," children must freeze and reply, "You made the starlight and the sun" as light bearer turns and sweeps the light across the playing area once.

Anyone touched by the light returns to the start area. Play continues until one child moves all the way across and then becomes the new light bearer.

Say: We're learning our Bible verse while we play! Who is "you" in this verse? (*Children respond.*) Yes! The "you" is God. God loves us. **God shows his love in his creation!**

Tip: For a greater challenge, place colored cellophane over the lit end of another flashlight and secure with a rubber band. Use this as the "unfreeze" light for one player to sweep one time as he or she repeats the second part of the Bible verse.

OBJECT LESSON
MOON SHADOWS

Tip: You may set up more than one experiment area for smaller groups of children.

Say: When the moon is full, what does it look like? (*Children respond.*) Some people look at a full moon and see a face. What causes this face? Is it really a face? (*Children respond.*) Let's try today's experiment to see how the face is made.

Directions: Set up six to eight dominoes in any way you like. Darken the room. Shine the flashlight at the dominoes from about 12 inches away.

Change the angle of the flashlight. Give children time to look at the change.

Invite a child to move the dominoes to make a different pattern.

Invite volunteers to work together to see if they can make a shallow pattern that looks like the "man in the moon."

Say: Don't look at the dominoes. Look at the pattern of the shadows they make. What happens when we change

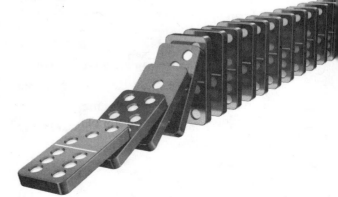

the angle of the flashlight? (*Children respond.*) When we move the dominoes into a different pattern? (*Children respond.*) Do you think the shadows look like a face? (*Children respond.*)

The moon has high areas that reflect the sun brightly. It has flat areas and craters that make shadows. Those shadows make the pattern we see on the face of the full moon.

What else do you think the shadows look like? (*Children respond.*) In some cultures, people see a rabbit. In other cultures, people see an old man carrying a bundle! But in every culture and to all people, **God shows his love in his creation!**

OPTIONAL ACTIVITIES
REFLECTION ACTION

Say: We know that there is only ONE source of light for the planets. What is it? (*Children respond.*) That's right. Even though the moon and other planets shine brightly at times, it is only because they reflect the light of the sun! The Bible tells us that when we're part of God's family, we reflect his light to other people. That's one way **God shows his love in his creation!** Let's find out what it takes to reflect light.

Directions: Children use their fingerprints, sticky notes, or tape, to cover the surface of the mirror. Children shine the flashlight at the mirror to see if the light reflects the same way.

Say: If the surface is covered, it doesn't reflect light as well. It's the same way with us. When we let other things get in the way of our relationship with God, we don't reflect his love as well. **God shows his love in his creation!** And we want to show that love, too.

Materials
- hand mirror
- sticky notes or tape
- flashlight

ECLIPSE

Say: When have you seen an eclipse? (*Children respond.*) What do you think causes it? (*Children respond.*) An eclipse is a shadow made on another planet. In a solar eclipse, a shadow cast by the moon shows on Earth. During a lunar eclipse, the Earth's shadow falls across the moon. Eclipses are another way **God shows his love in his creation!**

Directions: Set the larger ball on a table. This represents Earth.

Ask a child to hold the tennis ball with two fingers, away from their body.

Dim the lights, and then invite a volunteer to shine the flashlight at both the tennis ball and the larger ball. This is how a solar eclipse works.

Move the tennis ball around the larger ball until it is on the dark side, you'll see what a lunar eclipse looks like.

Materials
- basketball or playground ball
- tennis ball
- flashlight

MOON COOKIES

Preparation: Photocopy the Moon Phases on page 15, making one copy for each child.

Directions: Distribute Moon Phases to children. Children look at the phases of the moon. Children clean hands, and then break off parts of one side of their cookies to match the shapes they see. Children may lay their "moon cookies" on paper plates in a circle or on top of the examples on the page—and then, of course, eat their moon cookies!

Say: God made the moon to shine differently every night. It not only gives us a marker for the months but also affects the tides of the ocean! **God shows his love in his creation!**

Tip: Want kids to have fewer cookies to eat? Do this activity in pairs or trios.

Materials

- Moon Phases, page 15
- chocolate sandwich cookies
- wipes
- paper plates

MOON PHASES

Look at the phases of the moon. Break your cookies to match the moon phases.

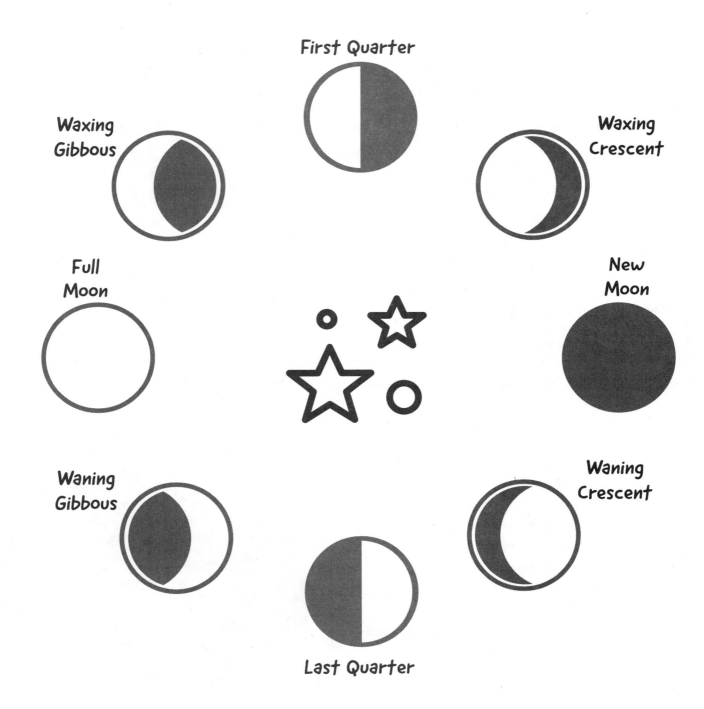

First Quarter

Waxing Gibbous

Waxing Crescent

Full Moon

New Moon

Waning Gibbous

Waning Crescent

Last Quarter

3. ALL CREATION IS GOOD

GENESIS 1

Everywhere—from east to west—praise the name of the LORD.
Psalm 113:3

BIG IDEA

WHAT GOD MADE IS GOOD

OVERVIEW

Say: Let's name twenty-six things God made, in alphabetical order. We'll start with **A!** (*Children respond.*) What did God make that begins with **B?** (*Continue until you reach Z.*) **Today we are going to look at EVERYTHING God made. We'll even discover how God felt about what he had made. We can praise him for what he made! What God made is good.** (*Open with prayer requests, praises, and a time of prayer.*)

BIBLE STORY

Say: We named some things God made when we used the alphabet. Did you know that there are over 45,000 species of spiders? There are more than 12,000 kinds of ants in the world. And there are more than 9,000 kinds of birds!

If we were to name EVERYTHING God made, we would never stop! Who remembers what God made first? (*Children respond.*) **That's right!** (*Read Genesis 1:3 aloud.*) **God made light first.**

What do you think he made next? (*Read Genesis 1:6 aloud.*) **God made the sky—the layers of gases that make up the air. When God separated the water from the dry ground, he called the ground** *land,* **and he called the waters** *seas.* **And let's read what he thought about it.** (*Read Genesis 1:10 aloud.*) **Let's say that together: "God saw that it was good."**

What do you think God made next? (*Children respond.*

Read Genesis 1:11 aloud.) God made all kinds of plants—from tiny flowers to towering trees. And what did he think about it? Let's say it together: "God saw that it was good."

After that, God put the planets and stars in the heavens so that people could keep track of the four directions, the seasons, and times. He made the sun and moon—and guess what God thought? Let's say it together: "God saw that it was good." Next, God filled the water with living creatures from tiny fish to great whales. He spoke, and the air was filled with those 9,000 or so kinds of birds!

And let's say it: "God saw that it was good." After God made all the animals that live on earth, from those tiny ants to the giant elephants, he made humans. He made humans in his own likeness. Humans would be creative and would be able to know God!

And what did God think of what he had made? Let's say it: "God saw that it was good." **What God made is good!**

OPENING GAME
FOUR DIRECTIONS

Directions: Play where you can designate four corners. For each round, name four creations (bluebirds, elephants, monkeys, sloths) and point to one corner for each. At your signal, children move to the corner that indicates their choice. Play as time allows; invite volunteers to name four creations or choose a way for others to move.

Tip: To increase the challenge, call out a way for players to move each time (hop, skip, hop on one foot, etc.)

Say: Our Bible story told how God made the stars and planets to help people find their way and to know what season it was. What four directions do we use? (*Children respond.*) Knowing north, south, east, and west helps us talk about where we are going. Where does the sun rise? (*Children respond.*) The sun rises in the east. Where does it set? (*Children respond.*) The sun sets in the west. Our memory verse tells us that God should be praised from the east to the west—that's all around the world! **What God made is good!**

Optional: Use the compass to discover which corner is the northernmost, southernmost, etc. Designate each corner as north, south, east, or west.

Optional Materials

• compass

OBJECT LESSON
SUNRISE, SUNSET

Preparation: Use a pen or pencil to punch a small hole in the center of the black paper. Secure paper to the lighted end of the flashlight with tape, centering the hole to make a narrow beam of light.

Say: What color is the sky? (*Children respond.*) Our Bible memory verse talks about the east and the west. These are the places where the sun rises and where it sets. What color is the sky when the sun rises and when it sets? (*Children respond.*) Let's find out the reason!

Directions: Volunteer holds a glue stick away from their body. Another volunteer turns on flashlight, aiming light through the glue stick to hit the wall or paper (taped to wall). Volunteer adds one or more glue sticks in front of the light beam.

Say: What color do you see? (*Children respond.*) Now let's add another glue stick. What changes do you see? (*Children respond.*) The sun's light has all the colors of the rainbow.

The colors travel from the sun to the Earth in waves. Imagine strings of color going from the sun to the Earth. Some colors have long waves and some have short waves. The color blue has short waves.

We usually see blue during the day. The angle of the sunlight changes at sunrise and sunset. At this time, the light has to travel through bits of dust in the air to reach the Earth. When light travels through those dust bits, some colors scatter. Colors with short waves, like blues and purples appear to disappear.

Red and yellow have long light waves so they are not easily scattered by the dust bits. This makes us see the sunrise and sunset as more red and yellow. God does so many amazing things! **What God made is good!**

Materials

- pen or pencil
- black paper
- flashlight
- tape
- glue sticks
- white wall or paper taped to wall

OPTIONAL ACTIVITIES
WHERE THE COMPASS POINTS

Directions: Children use the compass to find the four basic directions. Children tell where the sun rises and sets. They may also use the compass to determine in which direction other buildings stand, which direction a street runs, etc. Children repeat the Bible verse while facing the east and west.

Say: God made so many amazing things, we can never praise him enough! **What God made is good!**

Materials

- compass or compass app on phone

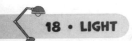

PLANET PLAY

Directions: Turn off overhead lights and darken the room. Turn on lamp. Give a few children balls to hold in front of them. Children take turns to move in a circle around the lamp and in front of each other.

Say: Every planet moves in an orbit, like a big circle, around the sun. This lamp was our sun and you all held the planets. What happens to the ball when the lamp lights the front side? (*Children respond.*) That's how day and night are made on our earth—but our little earth-ball is also spinning! What happens if one ball blocks the light on another ball? (*Children respond.*) That's a little like an eclipse. God made the sun, moon, stars, and planets to help us know where we are, and to know times and seasons. **What God made is good!**

Materials

- lamp (without shade)
- several balls of various sizes

SUNRISE DAY TIMER

Preparation: Photocopy the Morning Reminders on page 20, making one for each child.

Directions: Distribute Morning Reminders to children. Children use the page to plan the things they need to do every morning. Children decorate as desired.

Say: When you take your page home, put it where you will see it when you get up in the morning. It will remind you of the things you need to do every morning! God gave us the sunrise so that we can start our day. **What God made is good!**

Materials

- Morning Reminders, page 20
- crayons or markers

MORNING REMINDERS

Color the page. It will remind you of what you need to do every morning.

Get Up

Bathroom Time

Get Dressed

Time with God

Feed My Pet

Eat Breakfast

Pack My Backpack

4. GOD CREATES A RAINBOW

GENESIS 6—9:17

*Let us hold tightly without wavering to the hope we affirm,
for God can be trusted to keep his promise.*
Hebrews 10:23

BIG IDEA

GOD KEEPS HIS PROMISES

OVERVIEW

Say: Tell about a time when someone kept a promise to you. (*Children respond.*) Sometimes people don't keep their promises. They may forget. They may not be able to do what they said they would do. But who always keeps his promises? **God keeps his promises!** (*Open with prayer requests, praises, and a time of prayer.*)

BIBLE STORY

Say: Today we are going to learn about Noah and the flood. (*Read Genesis 6:13–14 aloud.*) God told Noah to build the boat because God was sending a HUGE flood. Was Noah going to be alone on the boat? (*Read Genesis 6:18–20 aloud.*) Noah would be surrounded by animals on the boat!

How long did it rain? (*Read Genesis 7:12 aloud.*) For forty days and nights that rain covered everything! And only Noah, his family, and the animals on the ark were alive. After a long, long time, Noah sent out a raven to see if there was any dry land, but the raven came back.

What bird do you think Noah sent out next? (*Children respond. Read Genesis 8:10–12 aloud.*) A dove! After Noah and his family and the animals left the boat, what promise did God make to them? (*Children respond. Read Genesis 9:11–13 aloud.*)

When we see a rainbow today, we can remember that God promised to never again send a flood so big to the earth. We can trust God to keep his promises. He is faithful—that means he does what he says he will do. Every day, all the time, **God keeps his promises!**

OPENING GAME
COLOR CODE

Preparation: Cut each sheet of paper into a bookmark-sized piece. Place all pieces in paper bag. Write out Bible memory verse where children can see it (whiteboard, etc.).

Directions: Children pass the bag and each one removes two papers. Each child holds a paper in either hand.

Children then move quickly to stand beside another child who is holding a matching color of paper in the hand next to that child's. For example, child holding red in left hand stands beside a child holding red in the right hand. The principle is like that of dominos. Play several rounds, replacing the colored papers and mixing them up between each round.

Children on the ends of the line at the end of each round repeat today's Bible memory verse or choose another child to repeat the verse.

Say: We made our own unique rainbow pattern. Real rainbows always follow the same color pattern. We can count on every rainbow to have red, orange, yellow, green, blue, indigo, and violet. In the same way, we can always count on God. God promised Noah that he would save him and his family from the flood. **God keeps his promises.**

Materials

- sheets of colored paper (at least six colors. See tip.)
- scissors
- paper bag
- whiteboard
- dry-erase marker

OBJECT LESSON
INDOOR RAINBOW

Say: Light seems to be clear or colorless. But let's see if our experiment can show us what is hidden in light!

Directions: Fill jar about halfway with water. In a room with white walls (or with a white surface nearby), set the mirror inside the jar of water. Lean the mirror at an angle against the inside of the jar so that the mirror is tilted slightly upward. Darken the room, and then shine the flashlight at the mirror. A rainbow should appear on the wall (move the white surface as needed). If no rainbow appears, change the angle of the light or the mirror.

Say: God makes his rainbows outdoors when it rains. But by using a mirror and some water, we were able to make an indoor rainbow! When we shine the flashlight at the mirror, the mirror reflects that light back through the water. The water acts as a prism. A prism bends the beam of light so that each color in the light can be seen! The rainbow reminds us that **God keeps his promises!**

Materials

- wide-mouthed glass jar
- water
- small mirror (small enough to fit inside jar)
- flashlight
- white surface (wall, whiteboard, etc.)

OPTIONAL ACTIVITIES

RAINBOW LIGHTS

Say: Here is another way to make a rainbow—we'll use the colors and let the sunshine through them.

Directions: Children fill each bottle with water, and then drop some food coloring into each bottle—red, orange, yellow, green, blue, and purple. An adult closes bottles and secures them with masking tape. Children take turns to shake the bottles so that the color mixes thoroughly. Set the bottles in rainbow order. When the sun shines through the bottles, it should create a rainbow.

Say: God used a rainbow to remind us of his promise to never again flood the whole world. **God keeps his promises!**

> ### Materials
> - 6 empty plastic water bottles
> - water
> - 6 colors of food coloring
> - masking tape

EAT THE RAINBOW

Directions: Give each child a paper plate. Children clean hands with wipes. Pour out fairly equal numbers of Skittles onto each plate. At your signal, children race to see who can put the Skittles on their plates in rainbow order—although not every color of the rainbow is represented. Children may eat candy and then play another round.

Say: Which color of the rainbow is missing? (*Children respond.*) I'm glad God didn't forget the blue! It's a very important color. God gave us the rainbow to remind us that no matter what, **God keeps his promises!**

> ### Materials
> - Skittles candy (or other colored candy)
> - hand wipes
> - paper plates

RAINBOW NUMBERS

Preparation: Photocopy Color the Rainbow on page 24, making one for each child.

Directions: Distribute Color the Rainbow to children. Children use the number key to color the rainbow in the correct order. Invite children to add birds, trees, etc. to make their pages unique.

Say: Can we say the colors of the rainbow in order together? (*Children respond.*) No matter what happens, we can know that **God keeps his promises**!

> ### Materials
> - Color the Rainbow, page 24
> - crayons or markers

COLOR THE RAINBOW

Let us hold tightly without wavering to the hope we affirm, for God can be trusted to keep his promise.
Hebrews 10:23

Color the sections of the rainbow according to this key:

1. Red
2. Orange
3. Yellow
4. Green
5. Blue
6. Indigo
7. Violet

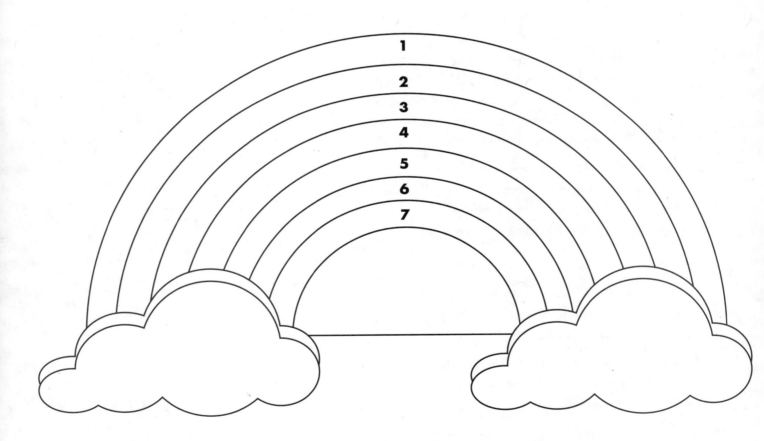

5. ABRAHAM AND THE STARS

GENESIS 15:1–6

[God] counts the stars and calls them all by name. How great is our Lord! His power is absolute!
Psalm 147:4–5

OVERVIEW

BIG IDEA

GOD KNOWS EVERYTHING

Say: Tell us an animal fact you think no one else might know. (*Children respond.*) I found a few animal facts myself:

- Did you know that a shrimp's heart is in its head?
- Did you know that a slug has four noses?
- Did you know that elephants cannot jump?

Those things are surprising and interesting! What's something you think no one might know about you? (*Children respond.*) Sometimes we think some things might be secrets. But there are no secrets to God. He is never surprised by anything. He is never worried about anything. Why? Because **God knows everything!** (*Open with prayer requests, praises, and a time of prayer.*)

BIBLE STORY

Say: Let's repeat our Bible memory verse together. (*Children respond.*) Did you know that God has a name for each star in the sky? Today we're going to learn about a starry promise God made to a man named Abraham. Abraham lived a very long time ago.

God had told Abraham that he and his wife Sarah would have a son. But years passed. There was no baby. Abraham became an older man. He was talking to God about not yet having a son. Listen to what God told Abraham! (*Read Genesis 15:5 aloud.*)

How many children did God promise to Abraham and Sarah? (*Children respond.*) How many stars do you think are in the sky? (*Children respond.*) Scientists GUESS that there are at least one hundred billion stars in the universe. But there could be more.

That is a LOT of stars. God told Abraham that he would have THAT MANY children! Wow! What do you think Abraham said about that? (*Read Genesis 15:6 aloud.*)

That number was WAY beyond anything Abraham could understand. It is WAY beyond any number WE could understand! But Abraham didn't try to figure it out. He didn't start counting stars.

The Bible tells us Abraham did something else. It says Abraham believed God. And to God, that was all Abraham needed! That's a good lesson for us. When we don't understand what is going on, we can always ask God.

Sometimes God will tell us what we need to know. But often, we can't understand, even if he DID tell us! So even if we don't understand, we can be like Abraham and trust God! Why? Because **God knows everything!**

OPENING GAME
TRUST ME RELAY

Preparation: Mark a start and finish line with masking tape. Lay two of each item you have chosen (newspaper, carpet square, etc.) at the starting line for each team to use.

Directions: Divide group into teams of evenly numbered players. If you have an odd number of children, join a team and play!

Each team forms pairs and lines up behind start line. One member of the first pair on each team moves across the room and back, stepping only on sheets of newspaper, carpet squares, or hand towels laid down by their partner. When they reach the finish line, pairs switch roles and return to start team, and tag the next pair who takes a turn. Play continues until all pairs have completed the relay.

> ### Materials
> - sheets of newspaper, carpet squares, or hand towels
> - masking tape

Say: That was fun! Was it easy or hard to wait for your partner to put down the next sheet? (*Children respond.*) What did you have to do? (*Children respond.*) Yes! You had to wait. And you had to trust your partner. You had to wait and trust, a little like Abraham. We can trust God when we don't understand things because **God knows everything!**

OBJECT LESSON
ALWAYS SHINING

Say: We know that there are over a hundred billion stars! But which star seems the brightest star by far? (*Children respond.*) That's right. The sun is the closest star to Earth. To us, it seems to be the biggest! We have all seen stars shine at night. But what happens to stars during the day? This experiment will help us figure that out!

> ### Materials
> - index card
> - hole punch
> - white envelope
> - flashlight

Directions: Punch ten to twenty holes randomly in an index card. Place the card in an envelope. Hold the envelope in front of you. Shine the flashlight onto the front of the envelope from about two inches away.

Move the flashlight behind the envelope. Shine the flashlight on the back of the envelope from about two inches away.

Alternate Idea: Divide children into groups of four. Give each group an index card, hole punch, white envelope, and a flashlight. Walk them through the steps of the object lesson.

Say: What do you see when you shine the light on the front of the envelope? (*Children respond.*) What can you see when you shine the light from behind the envelope? (*Children respond.*)

The holes in the card can't be seen when you shine light on the front. But when you shine light onto the back, you can easily see the light through the holes.

The light in the room is always passing through the holes in the card. But only when there is a light brighter than the room's light can you see the holes.

In the same way, the stars shine all the time, but sunlight is so bright that starlight is not visible. When the sky is dark, the stars shine brightly!

When the moon is full and bright, do you think you can see as many stars? (*Children respond.*) You're right. The moon reflects so much sunlight that it makes it harder to see the stars! And just think—God knows exactly how many stars there are, and he gives them each a name! Even when we can't see them, God knows them! **God knows everything!**

OPTIONAL ACTIVITIES

WHAT CAN YOU TRUST?

Say: We talked today about Abraham, who trusted God. What are some other things we trust?

Directions: Draw simple pictures of items like a bike, an airplane, a car, a foot, etc. As children call out what you are drawing, ask them to tell what they have to trust about the thing you have drawn (trust that my bike tire is not flat, trust that the pilot knows how to fly the plane, etc.)

Say: We have to trust a LOT of things, don't we! Unless we trust, there is not much we will be able to do. God is always worthy of our trust because **God knows everything!**

> ## Materials
> - whiteboard
> - dry-erase marker

CONSTELLATION CREATION

Directions: Children look at constellation images. Children may either make a recognized constellation, using the marshmallows as stars and the toothpicks as connectors, or may make constellations of their own design.

Say: Constellations are groups of stars. Often people have connected those stars to make a pattern, kind of like when we look for pictures in cloud shapes. Until there was GPS, many people used the constellations to know where they were and where they needed to go. Especially on the ocean, sailors used the North Star and the constellations to steer by. God made the stars—but it was people's imaginations that gave us constellations! **God knows everything!**

GOD'S PROMISE TO ABRAHAM

Preparation: Photocopy the Star Maze on page 29, making one copy for each child.

Directions: Distribute Star Maze to children.

Say: People have always used the constellations, or groups of stars, to help guide them. Abraham looked at the stars to remember God's promise. Help Abraham get through the star maze to his promised son, Isaac! Remember, if you ever feel lost you can turn to God. **God knows everything.**

STAR MAZE

[God] counts the stars and calls them all by name. How great is our Lord! His power is absolute!
Psalm 147:4–5

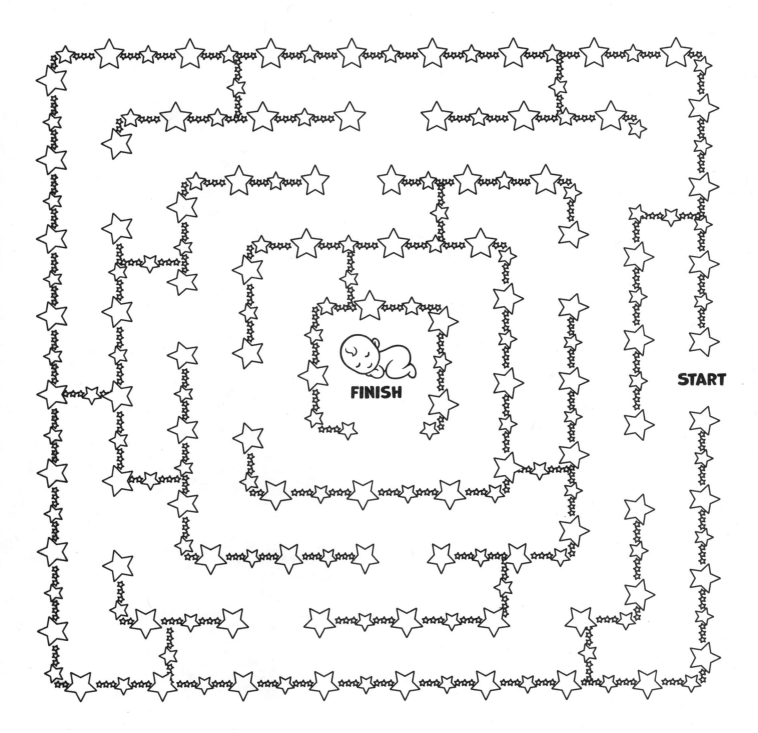

FINISH

START

6. DAVID ADMIRES THE STARS

1 SAMUEL 17:34–35; PSALM 19:1–4

For ever since the world was created, people have seen the earth and sky. Through everything God made, they can clearly see . . . his eternal power and divine nature.

Romans 1:20

BIG IDEA

GOD SHOWS HIS CHARACTER THROUGH CREATION

OVERVIEW

Say: What are some things you think everyone knows? (*Children respond with answers like dogs bark, sun shines, ice is cold, etc.*) We already see and know many things about what God made. Each thing he made shows us something about God—that he is creative, he is powerful, he is good, he loves us, and many other things. Can you name some things that might show us God's greatness? (*Children respond.*) **God shows his character through creation!** (*Open with prayer requests, praises, and a time of prayer.*)

BIBLE STORY

Say: What are some things you see in the sky? (*Children respond.*) In Bible times, there were no electrical lights, so you could see the stars really well. Today, we are going to learn about a famous shepherd who lived a long time ago. He spent many days and nights taking care of his father's sheep.

The shepherd's name was David. David spent a lot of time outdoors, making sure the sheep were eating the right things. He had to make sure no sheep got lost or hurt. What else do you think he had to do? (*Children respond.*)

Listen to this! (*Read 1 Samuel 17:34–35 aloud.*) **David had to chase the wild animals away and protect his sheep!** He often spent the night outdoors, too. Listen to the way he described the sky at night. (*Read Psalm 19:1–4 aloud.*)

David loved to watch God's beautiful creation. He knew that when people saw what God made, it showed them God's character—what he's like. How would you describe what God

is like? (*Children respond.*) **The stars and the heavens are like a message about God. We feel small in comparison because creation shows how great and amazing God is. Everyone can understand it!**

This was always true, from the very beginning of creation. (*Read Romans 1:20 aloud.*) God certainly has great power. He put the sun and moon and stars in the sky! God created an amazing world. No one can say that they didn't know God exists. Everyone knows about it! **God shows his character through creation!**

OPENING GAME
I SPY

Directions: Play a game in which you describe something in plain sight which everyone can see—if they look carefully. Children may ask questions that can only be answered "yes" or "no." Winner is the child who guesses the item correctly. That child leads the next round.

Say: Today, we are talking about seeing God's greatness in his creation. This is something that EVERYONE can see, but sometimes you are not aware of it.

This game reminds us that some things are obviously right in front of us, but we miss them if he are distracted. Let's not be distracted by the things around us. Let's focus on God. **God shows his character through creation!**

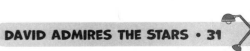

OBJECT LESSON
RAINBOW DENSITIES

Tip: This can all be done by one person, but if you have the materials, children will enjoy doing this themselves in groups of four.

Preparation: Fill each of the five cups halfway with light corn syrup glycerin, water, cooking oil, and rubbing alcohol.

Say: We've been talking about things God made that everyone can see. Let's do something that will show us something about the way God made the sky. (*Point to the cups.*) Liquids are made up of tiny molecules. Each of these liquids is a different density.

Density measures how close the molecules are in that liquid. Some of these are not very dense. Others are denser. What do you think will happen when we put them together? (*Children respond.*)

Directions: Show and tell what each liquid is. Children add food coloring to each cup. Children take turns to tilt the jar and then pour the contents of one cup down the inside of the jar so that it doesn't mix too much. If time allows, stir the liquids to see them separate again.

Say: Now that we have put the liquids in the jar, what has happened to each liquid? (*Children respond.*) Why do you think that has happened? (*Children respond.*) Which liquid is the least dense (the one on top)? Which one is the densest (the one on the bottom)? How can you tell? (*Children respond.*)

The atmosphere of our planet is something everyone sees. Everyone lives inside it! If we could stand outside of it, it would look a little like our jar. There are layers of density. God created a layer of air that is less dense than water and denser than the gases in our upper atmosphere. It's just right for us to breathe! God knew exactly what we needed. **God shows his character through creation!**

OPTIONAL ACTIVITIES
MESSAGE WITHOUT WORDS

Say: David said that the sky tells everyone about God without using words. (*Read Psalm 19:1–4 aloud*) Do you think you can send messages without using words? (*Children respond.*) Let's see what we can tell each other without using words! **God shows his character through creation!**

Directions: Children make signs or motions for others to guess the meaning. Start by doing one or two motions that children will easily understand (tap your watch for "it's time," make eating motions for "food," etc.)

SNOWY SURPRISE

Preparation: Lay drink mix powders across the pan or tray. Sprinkle baking soda over the colors so that no color is seen. It should look like a field of snow. Fill a shallow container with vinegar.

Materials

- variety of powdered fruit-flavored drink mixes
- plastic pan or tray
- baking soda
- eyedroppers
- vinegar
- shallow container

Directions: Children use an eyedropper to drop vinegar onto the baking soda. If time allows, drop other liquids onto baking soda to see if they work in the same way.

Say: What happened when we dropped vinegar over the baking soda? Why? (*Children respond.*) Everyone could see the surprising color when the baking soda and vinegar combined and made gas bubbles. We didn't have to say what color it was. We could see the color in the chemical reaction. God made so many wonderful and surprising things! Everything that he made reminds us who he is. **God shows his character through creation!**

GOD MADE GREAT THINGS

Preparation: Photocopy the Scavenger Hunt on page 34, making one copy for each child.

Materials

- Scavenger Hunt, page 34
- crayons or markers

Say: Today we talked about things everyone can see that God made. **God shows his character through creation!** We can see his greatness in the things around us. Let's have a scavenger hunt to find things colors, textures, and shapes! Then, let's give glory to the creator! God shows his character through creation.

Directions: Distribute Scavenger Hunt to children. Children fill in blanks as they find items that meet the color or shape criteria.

SCAVENGER HUNT

For ever since the world was created, people have seen the earth and sky. Through everything God made, they can clearly see . . . his eternal power and divine nature.
Romans 1:20

Fill in the blanks with the name of something you see that fits the description.

_____ something red

_____ something that is wet

_____ something triangle shaped

_____ something brown

_____ something that makes a circle

_____ something that is flat

_____ something that is shiny

_____ something fuzzy

_____ something that is the same color as your shoes

_____ something that makes noise

_____ something that is shiny

Which of these things in list are things God made?

_____

Which are things humans made?

_____

God shows his character through creation! What can you learn about God by looking at his creation?

_____

7. ELISHA AND THE BLIND ARMY

2 KINGS 6:8-23

So we don't look at the troubles we can see now; rather, we fix our gaze on things that cannot be seen.
2 Corinthians 4:18

BIG IDEA

GOD IS DOING MORE THAN WE CAN SEE

OVERVIEW

Say: Imagine you are playing in the ocean. Now imagine you see a fin sticking out of a wave near you. What do you think it might be? (*Children respond.*) It's funny, but most people think of sharks when they see a fin sticking out of the water! But what else could it be? (*Children respond.*) Yes, it could be a dolphin! If we could see both a shark and a dolphin side by side, we could easily tell whose fin was whose! That's just one example of what we'll talk about today. Often, we see something and we think we know what it is. But there is more to see. And **God is doing more than we can see!** (*Open with prayer requests, praises, and a time of prayer.*)

BIBLE STORY

Say: Now we know that a fin in the ocean might NOT be a shark. What are other times you've seen something but found out that there was more to see? (*Children respond.*) Listen to this account of how things LOOKED and what more God was doing!

Elisha was a prophet in Israel. He gave people messages from God. Now, a nearby king kept trying to surprise and attack Israel. But every time he tried, the Israelites were READY!

The king was VERY angry about this! He asked his advisors why this kept happening. (*Read 2 Kings 6:12 aloud.*) The king decided Elisha had to be STOPPED! So he sent a big army to Elisha's town. When Elisha's helper saw the soldiers and horses and chariots, he was TERRIFIED!

He said to Elisha, "OH NO! What shall we DO?" Elisha was not worried. Why do you think he wasn't worried? (*Children respond.*) Here's the reason! (*Read 2 Kings 6:16–17 aloud.*) GOD had a BIGGER and STRONGER angel army protecting Elisha's town!

When the enemy army came toward him, listen to what Elisha prayed.

(*Read 2 Kings 6:18 aloud.*) **God made the whole army blind!** Then Elisha led them all the way to a big walled city—and he SHUT the gate behind them all. Now the big army was trapped!

Elisha's helper thought Elisha did this so that they could kill the enemies. But you know what Elisha did? (*Read 2 Kings 6:23 aloud.*) After that, the enemy raiders didn't come back and bother the Israelites! What do you think the enemy army must have thought? (*Children respond.*)

It LOOKED like the army could make Elisha their prisoner. It LOOKED like they had a big, strong army. It LOOKED like they could all have died inside the walled city. But **God was doing MORE than anyone could see!** And that has not changed.

When we see something, and we think we know what we are seeing, we're always smart to ask God, "What else do I need to see?"

OPENING GAME
SNOWBALL RELAY

Preparation: Crumple up at least two or three paper balls for each child. These will be "snow balls." Store balls in a large trash bag. Mark a start line with masking tape at one side of the play area. Set a bucket or can where each team will line up. At the other side, lay a masking-tape line behind which you place the "snow balls."

Tip: If you don't have time to prepare the paper balls, simply spill out a container of craft pom poms behind the masking-tape line.

Directions: Children form pairs; equal numbers form teams for a relay race. One member of each pair closes eyes (or uses blindfold). At your signal, first pair moves together to the "snow ball" line. Only the "blind" player may pick up balls. Partner gives verbal instructions, but may not touch the balls. When at least one ball has been picked up, pair returns to tag the next pair.

Play continues until all pairs on one team have gone. Now teams count the number of balls in their bucket or can.

Team that finished first answers this question: When have you seen something happen that was confusing? What helped you to see more?

Team that had the most balls answers this question: What are some words a person could pray when they see something scary or confusing? What are some words a person could pray when they see something that they're sure is clear?

Alternate Idea: Play the game in the same way, but give each "blind" child enough masking tape to wrap around their hand to help pick up the "snow balls."

Materials

- crumpled paper balls or craft pom poms (See tip.)
- large trash bag
- masking tape
- bucket or can (one per team)

Optional

- blindfold

Say: What made our game harder? (*Children respond.*) How did the players who couldn't see find the balls? (*Children respond.*) Yes! ONE partner could see MORE than the other! We can't always see everything, but God can! In the same way, **God is doing more than we can see!** He is always doing a million more things than we can see!

OBJECT LESSON
MORE KINDS OF LIGHT

Directions: Set cups in a sunny place. Children watch as you fill one cup with tonic water and the other cup with tap water.

Invite a volunteer to hold the sheet of black paper behind the cups. Children take turns to look through the sides of the glasses to view the top surface of both kinds of water.

Say: Did you know that there are kinds of light that we can't see? God made MANY kinds of light besides the light we can see with our eyes! Who thinks they know the name of any of those other kinds of light? (*Children respond.*) Some of them are called x-rays and gamma rays and ultraviolet rays. This experiment should make us able to see the reflection of one kind of light we usually cannot see.

(*Point to the filled cups.*) What do you see? We know that water is clear. But which cup of water looks blue on the surface? What do you think makes it blue? (*Children respond.*)

The cup that holds the tonic water contains a chemical called quinine. When the sunlight shines on the tonic water, the quinine makes it possible for our eyes to see the ultraviolet light that we normally don't see! In the same way, **God is doing more than we can see!**

Tip: You may wish to do several setups of this experiment to make it easier for children to see the ultraviolet reflection.

> ## Materials
> - clear plastic cups
> - bottle containing tonic water
> - bottle containing tap water
> - black construction paper

OPTIONAL ACTIVITIES
FULL SPECTRUM

Preparation: Open laptop to web page illustrating the spectrum of light. Set your laptop so that the page you choose displays continuously. Set books where children may look at them.

Directions: Children do independent research (reading!) about light and waves.

> ## Materials
> - laptop
> - children's books about light and electromagnetic waves

Say: I didn't know that there were so many kinds of light. I didn't know that electromagnetic waves were related to light. What is something you learned that surprised you? (*Children respond.*) There is so much more to creation than what we can see. **God is doing more than we can see!**

LOOK CLOSER

Directions: Children look at nature items, and then look at the same item with a magnifying glass.

Optional: Children use paper and crayons or markers to write or draw the details they see with their eyes. Then, they write or draw what they see with the magnifier.

Say: When you pick up a leaf, what do you notice? (*Children respond.*) What more did you notice when you looked at that same leaf with a magnifying glass? (*Children respond.*) It's easy to miss the details unless you have a way to see better—like the magnifier. It's the same thing in life.

It's easy to miss the great things God is doing because we're not really noticing. But **God is doing more than we can see!** That's why it's always a good idea to ask him, "What do I need to see here? What do I need to know?" He loves us and wants us to be part of what he is doing!

> **Materials**
> - magnifying glasses
> - small nature items (leaves, seashells, etc.)
>
> **Optional**
> - paper
> - crayons or markers

WHAT DO YOU SEE?

Preparation: Photocopy the Robot Visions on page 39, making one copy for each child.

Directions: Distribute Robot Visions to children. Children color page as desired. As children work, read aloud each question on the page. Invite volunteers to answer according to what they see.

Say: When we all look at the same thing, do we SEE the same thing? As you colored, what other details did you notice that you didn't see at first?

Just like one of us may see one part clearly, another person may notice something else and think it is more important. Even on this page, there is more going on than we can tell. And in real life, it's good to remember that **God is doing more than we can see!**

> **Materials**
> - Robot Visions, page 39
> - crayons or markers

ROBOT VISIONS

So we don't look at the troubles we can see now; rather, we fix our gaze on things that cannot be seen.
2 Corinthians 4:18

1. How many robots do you see? _____
2. Which robot(s) looks upset? _____
3. Which robot(s) is waving? _____
4. Which robot(s) has more than two arms? _____
5. Which robot(s) has more than two legs? _____
6. Which robot looks the smartest? _____
7. Which robot looks the friendliest? _____
8. Which robot would you want at your house? Why? _____
_____

GOD IS DOING MORE THAN WE CAN SEE

8. JESUS AT CREATION

JOHN 1:1–3; HEBREWS 1:1–3

The Son radiates God's own glory and expresses the very character of God, and he sustains everything by the mighty power of his command.
Hebrews 1:3

OVERVIEW

Say: Let's do a survey. Raise your hand if you have ever tried to:

- carry all the bags from the car into the house at one time.
- hold more than three tennis balls in one hand.
- hold ten grapes in your mouth.
- carry five basketballs in your arms.

What is the same about all those things? (*Children respond.*) **Yes! It doesn't matter how strong or smart we are, there are things we just can't carry. We can't hold those things together for very long! But today, we're going to find out what it takes to hold everything in this whole universe together. Jesus holds everything together!** (*Open with prayer requests, praises, and a time of prayer.*)

BIBLE STORY

Say: In the book of John, Jesus is sometimes called the Word of God. (*Read John 1:1–3 aloud.*) Who does this passage say made everything we see? (*Children respond.*) **Jesus even said he is the light of the world! But did you know that God's Son Jesus did more than CREATE the universe along with God the Father and God the Holy Spirit? Listen to this!** (*Read Hebrews 1:1–3 aloud.*) **So the Bible tells us that God spoke to us by sending Jesus, his Son. It tells us that Jesus MADE the things we see in our universe. But he also keeps all those creations going and keeps them together!**

Atoms are the smallest pieces of things. In the center of every atom, there are protons. Protons are supposed to push away from other protons, but they don't. Why? Because there is a force that holds them together. Scientists call it the "strong force." The Bible calls it Jesus' power!

There is no job too big for Jesus—and nothing too small for him, either! The best part is Jesus paid the price for our sins so that we could be forgiven. Because of his great power, **Jesus holds everything together.**

OPENING GAME
HOLD IT TOGETHER

Directions: Children stand in a circle, arm's distance apart. Toss one ball into the circle. Children must kick the ball back and forth without letting it get out of the circle. After a short time, add another ball. To increase the challenge, add a third ball. Play as time and interest allow. If a ball escapes the circle, simply toss it back in and play continues.

Say: We talked about how **Jesus holds everything together**—but how good do you think we might be at keeping something simple together? The goal of this game is to keep kicking the ball or balls so they keep on moving, but don't let a ball escape the circle. Are you ready? Remember, keep the circle closed and keep the balls inside the circle!

> **Materials**
> • several soccer or playground balls

Tip: If your group is mostly younger children, don't use more than two balls. To Increase the challenge for older children, use several different kinds and sizes of balls for this game.

OBJECT LESSON
SUN POWER

Say: We know that Jesus is the SON of God. And the power of the sun in the sky can remind us of Jesus' power to keep everything going! The power of the sunlight gets the seeds to sprout. And our experiment today will show us another kind of power the sun has.

Directions: Show the sprouted seeds. Invite children to inspect the sprouts as you prepare the experiment. Talk about what it takes for the seeds to sprout (light, water, etc.). In a very sunny spot outdoors, set out two cups, and fill each halfway with water. Set one cup in the black pan and cover it with the lid.

> **Materials**
> • sprouted seeds in a jar
> • clear plastic cups
> • water
> • black metal pan with lid (cast iron works well)

Say: Let's see if we can turn solar power into heat. When it's a sunny day, do you walk on the black part of the street barefooted? Why or why not? (*Children respond.*) When you want to stay cool in the summer, do you wear dark-colored clothing or light-colored clothing? Why? (*Children respond.*)

(*Test the water in each of these two cups to see if they are the same temperature. You can check it with your fingers.*) We'll set one cup inside the dark colored pan and cover it with a dark-colored lid. Which cup of water do you think will heat up the fastest in the sun? We'll check it in about twenty minutes!

(*After another activity, come back to the experiment. Children take turns to touch the water in both cups to see if their predictions were correct.*) Just like the sun has the power to make things hot, **Jesus has the power to hold everything together!**

OPTIONAL ACTIVITIES

MOLECULAR MODELS

Tip: Show images of molecular models and explain how some kinds of atoms combine better with others to make something new. For instance, two hydrogen atoms combine with one oxygen atom to make a molecule of water.

Directions: Children use toothpicks or pretzels to connect the fruit pieces. Then they eat their models!

Say: We talked about how Jesus' power holds the atoms together. Let's make our own edible models of atoms that are connecting with each other to make molecules. **Jesus holds everything together!**

Materials

- small pieces of fruit (strawberries, apple chunks, grapes, melon balls, etc.)
- stick pretzels or toothpicks
- paper plates

HOLDING TOGETHER

Preparation: Lay strips of masking tape, sticky-side down, on the table so that they appear to be in a pile like a pile of pick-up sticks. Note: Don't press the tape strips down hard!

Directions: Children take turns to decide which piece of tape to pull up first, then second, etc. without disturbing the other pieces, as in a game of pick-up sticks.

Say: This game takes some looking and thinking! Just like these pieces of tape are all held together, **Jesus holds everything together!**

Materials

- masking tape
- table

JESUS IS THE CENTER

Preparation: Photocopy the Jesus Nut on page 43, making one copy for each child.

Say: We know that **Jesus holds everything together**. But did you know that on a helicopter, the part that holds those big rotors in perfect balance is called the "Jesus nut"? It's true! That piece is so important that if it broke, the helicopter would fall to the ground. Whoever named it knew our Bible memory verse that tells us how Jesus holds everything together by the word of his power.

Directions: Distribute Jesus Nut to children. Children write or draw on each rotor blade something that seems strong or scary to them. Lead children in prayer. Thank God that Jesus holds everything together, even big things that seem too strong or scary for us.

Materials

- Jesus Nut, page 43
- crayons or markers

THE JESUS NUT

The Jesus nut holds the propellers in place. Write something that scares you on the blades. Draw a picture of it between the blades.

JESUS HOLDS EVERYTHING TOGETHER

9. GOD LAYERED THE AIR

GENESIS 1:6–8,11–12; 2:7

I am the one who made the earth and created people to live on it. With my hands I stretched out the heavens.
Isaiah 45:12

BIG IDEA

GOD GIVES US WHAT WE NEED

OVERVIEW

Say: How many of you have climbed up a big mountain? (*Children respond.*) How many of you have camped at a high elevation? (*Children respond.*) What did you notice about breathing? (*Children respond.*) Yes! Up high in the mountains, the air is different!

The air is made up of many tiny things called molecules. When there are many molecules in the air, we say the air is more dense. When there are fewer molecules, we say the air is less dense. At high elevations, the oxygen molecules that we need for breathing are not as close together as they are when we are at sea level. Up high, our bodies must work harder to get the oxygen we need. Today we'll find out more about that! God made this world to be the right place for us to live. **God gives us what we need!** (*Open with prayer requests, praises, and a time of prayer.*)

BIBLE STORY

Say: We talked a little about what the air is like when we are high up in the mountains. What do you know about the air outside when we are flying in an airplane? (*Children respond.*) It is even less dense—and VERY cold! Airplanes have special air equipment so that people can easily breathe inside them.

What do you know about being in outer space? Is there oxygen out there? (*Children respond.*) There is very, very little. We can see that God gives us what we need.

God made gravity so we would stick to Earth. Then, he made the air nearest Earth the most dense—the easiest for us to breathe. The oxygen molecules are closer together. (*Read Genesis 1:6–8 aloud.*)

On the second day, God made layers of air that we now call the atmosphere. What would make it hard to live on another planet? (*Children respond.*) Yes! We are air-breathers. When astronauts go into space, they can't live unless they take air to breathe!

(*Read Genesis 2:7 aloud.*) What did God do so that the man came to life? (*Children respond.*) Yes! Breathing made him live. What do you think makes oxygen on our planet? (*Read Genesis 1:11–12 aloud.*)

God made the trees and plants. They make food for us, but here's another thing they do—every one of them gives oxygen that we can breathe! God made our planet unique—it's perfect for us to live on. **God gives us what we need!**

OPENING GAME
THIN AIR

Preparation: In the center of the playing area, mark a line of masking tape. Place and keep inflated balloons in the ice chest for at least an hour before playing the game.

Directions: Children form two teams; teams stand on either side of masking-tape line. Remove a cold balloon and bat it to one team. Team tries to get the balloon batted by each member before sending it over the line. Once the balloon begins to expand, toss out a second cold balloon. Play continues, with children using up to four balloons at one time.

Say: When I put these balloons into the ice chest, they were full and round and light. When we added a second balloon, and then a third, what did you notice about the balloons? (*Children respond.*) The balloons expanded. Why do you think that is? (*Children respond.*) Air expands when it heats up. What do you think will happen to the balloons if we put them back into the ice chest? (*Children respond.*) The balloons will shrink. God made the air so cool! **God gives us what we need.**

Optional: Purchase a helium balloon and place it in the ice chest as well. Try playing the game using the helium balloon! Then, ask children what they noticed about it.

OBJECT LESSON
BUBBLES UP

Tip: This experiment can easily be set up for small groups of about four children.

Say: In our game, we saw what happens when air inside a balloon gets cold. The molecules get closer together. The Bible says that God separated the waters (oceans) from the gases in sky (see Genesis 1:6–8). This experiment will show us how God made some gases more dense than others.

Directions: Set a plastic cup in the bowl. Place about ¼ cup of baking soda in the cup. Pour about a cup of vinegar into the cup.

Once the bubbles are foaming, use the bubble solution to blow bubbles over the bubbles coming from the cup.

Say: We breathe out a gas called carbon dioxide. The bubbles made by the vinegar and baking soda are filled with carbon dioxide. Now, let's blow some bubbles with our bubble solution. What happens? (*Children respond.*) Why don't the bubbles we blew fall down? (*Children respond.*) Why don't the baking soda and vinegar bubbles rise up? (*Children respond.*)

The carbon dioxide inside the baking soda and vinegar bubbles is denser than the air in the room. That means the molecules inside the bubbles are closer together. The air in the room is less dense than the carbon dioxide. We are breathing the air in the room. So when we blow bubbles, the air in the bubbles is the same as the air in the room. Our bubbles float above the carbon dioxide bubbles because the air is less dense.

When God made the atmosphere—the air, the sky, all the way up to outer space—he made it just right for us to breathe! We couldn't live on any other planet because there is not any oxygen! **God gives us what we need!**

OPTIONAL ACTIVITIES
WIND WATCHING

Directions: Turn on warming tray and set it where children may watch but not be burned. While children watch, sprinkle talcum powder onto the tray.

Say: Imagine that the tray is Earth. The talcum powder will show us what happens when the land warms up.

(*Sprinkle the talcum powder on the tray.*) What happens when the powder hits the warm tray? (*Children respond.*) Yes. The powder rises. This shows us what happens when the sun warms up the land. The warmth causes the air to rise. When the warm air rises, cooler air rushes in beneath it. Talcum powder helps us to see the way wind moves on Earth! **God gives us what we need!**

Materials

- warming tray
- talcum powder

COLOR DENSITY

Say: We talked today about how God separated the less dense atmosphere from the more dense seas. Which do you think is more dense—shaving cream, water, or food coloring? (*Children respond.*) **Let's test them.**

Directions: Fill container halfway with water. Set the container of water at children's eye level. Cover the surface of the water with the shaving cream. Use eyedroppers to squirt several drops of food coloring into but not through, the layer of shaving cream. Children watch as color drops through the cream and down into the water. Use other colors to watch them mix in the water.

Say: Which is denser, the water or the shaving cream? (*Children respond.*) Water! Which is most dense, the food coloring or the water? (*Children respond.*) Food coloring!

Because the food coloring is the densest, it falls through both the shaving cream and the water. God made things with different densities so that we would have what we need. **God gives us what we need!**

Materials

- wide clear container
- water
- shaving cream
- eyedroppers
- food color

COLOR THE SKY

Preparation: Photocopy Earth's Atmosphere on page 48, making one copy for each child.

Directions: Distribute Earth's Atmosphere to children. Children color the page, using ever darker colors for the higher layers of atmosphere. Name the layers with them.

Say: These are the layers of Earth's atmosphere. Each one is less dense than the one below it. God made things perfect for us to live here! **God gives us what we need!**

Materials

- Earth's Atmosphere, page 48
- crayons or markers

EARTH'S ATMOSPHERE

Color the page, using ever darker colors for the higher layers of the atmosphere.

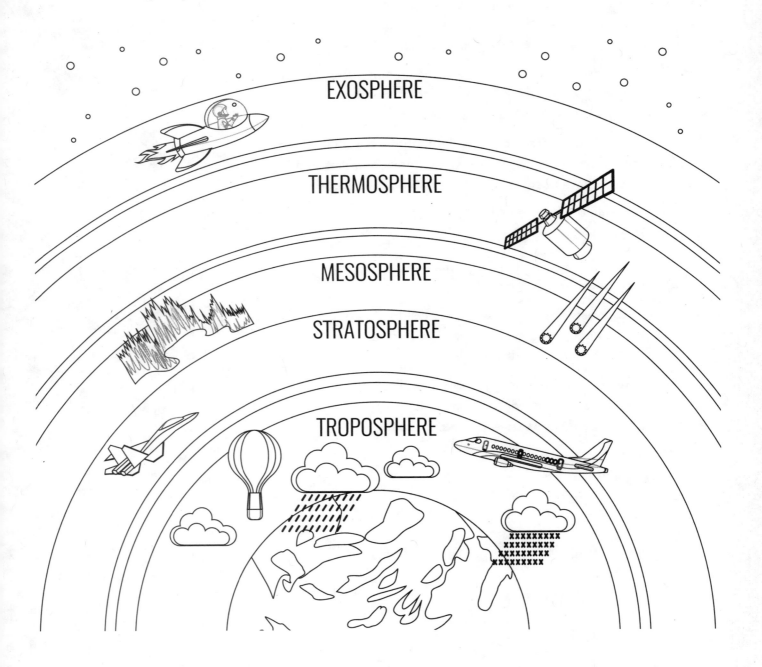

EXOSPHERE

THERMOSPHERE

MESOSPHERE

STRATOSPHERE

TROPOSPHERE

10. GOD BREATHES LIFE

GENESIS 2:7; LUKE 23:46; JOHN 20:19–22; 2 TIMOTHY 3:16–17

Let everything that breathes sing praises to the LORD.
Psalm 150:6

BIG IDEA

GOD GAVE US BREATH TO PRAISE HIM

OVERVIEW

Say: How long do you think you can hold your breath? (*Invite several volunteers to try while you use your phone or watch to time them.*) Describe how it feels when you stop breathing. How does your body tell you that it needs to breathe? (*Children respond.*) God made us to live in the bottom of an ocean of air!

So unless we hold our breath, the air pressure around us is usually higher than it is in our lungs. This causes air to rush into our lungs when we breathe in. The air is pushed out when we breathe out. When we push out our breath, we might sing, talk, yell, or laugh—our breath has a purpose! And the best purpose is this: **God gave us breath to praise him!** (*Open with prayer requests, praises, and a time of prayer.*)

BIBLE STORY

Say: Adam was the first human that God created. What did God make Adam out of? (*Read Genesis 2:7 aloud.*) God made the first human out of DIRT! But what else does this verse tell us? (*Children respond.*) Yes! God did something besides make a person's body.

There was no life in Adam's body until God breathed life into him. The Bible says that God's breath is the breath of life! That means when God breathes, LIFE happens.

When Jesus lived on Earth, did he breathe? (*Children respond.*) Yes! He breathed just like everyone else. When he died, it says he "breathed his last" (Luke 23:46). When Jesus came back to life again, he appeared to some of his friends.

Let's find out what happened.(*Read John 20:19–22 aloud.*) Jesus came to his closest friends, his disciples. He showed them that he was alive again! They were SO HAPPY!

But Jesus was different after he died and rose again. How do we know that? What did Jesus do in the story we just read? (*Children respond.*) First, he didn't knock on the door; he just showed up!

Second, Jesus BREATHED on his friends. He said, "Receive the Holy Spirit " (John 20:22). Now that he is alive again, his breath is the breath of God's Spirit. When Jesus breathed on them, new LIFE happened inside them!

Here is one more thing to know about God's breath. (*Read 2 Timothy 3:16–17 aloud.*) **What do these verses tell us about the Scriptures?** (*Children respond.*) **It is more than nice stories or interesting stuff. It is useful! Reading the Bible teaches us to do what is right with our lives.**

- God breathed LIFE into Adam. He became a living being.
- Jesus (God in a human body) breathed God's HOLY SPIRIT on his friends.
- The Scriptures are God-breathed. God spoke them into existence—so those words are FULL of his life!

Who knew? Breath introduces us to God the Father, God the Son, and God the Holy Spirit! And that breath can go back to God, too. **God gave us breath to praise him!**

OPENING GAME
BREATHE IN, BREATHE OUT RELAY

Preparation: Mark a start and finish line with masking tape.

Directions: Children form two even teams and line up at the start line. Players take turns to run to the finish line and then repeat the words of the Bible verse in this fashion: On each word, player speaks one word while breathing in or breathing out. "Let (while breathing out) everything (while breathing in) that (breathing out again) breathes (breathing in again) . . ." and so on until the sentence is completed. Player then runs back to the line to tag the next child. Game continues until all have gone on one team.

> ### Materials
> - masking tape

Say: Let's all repeat the verse together in the same way! God's breath is life-giving. He created humans from dirt and breathed life into us. We can praise God for our lives in many ways—singing, dancing, praying, and more! **God gave us breath to praise him!**

Alternate Idea: If you have many children who can't breathe in and out easily, have them turn around once between speaking each word of the verse.

OBJECT LESSON
BREATHING BALLOON

Say: We talked a little about holding our breath and how the air pressure around us helps us to breathe in. Watch this to see how a change in air pressure affects this balloon!

Preparation: Boil water. Store water in thermal container.

> ### Materials
> - 2–3 ounces of very hot water
> - thermal container
> - funnel
> - clear glass bottle with a narrow neck
> - balloon

Directions: Use the funnel to pour the very hot water into the bottle. Quickly slide the neck of the balloon over the mouth of the bottle, sealing it completely.

Say: Wow! We can see the steam inside the bottle, which is rising. What is happening to the balloon? (*Children respond.*) It gets bigger, or inflates. Do you think the steam is making the balloon bigger? (*Children respond.*)

Keep watching! What do you see on the inside of the bottle? What is the balloon doing NOW? (*Children respond.*)

Why do you think the balloon is doing this? (*Children respond.*) Remember how we talked about air pressure and density? The steam, or water vapor, rises when it is hot. But as it cools, it condenses into liquid water again.

This creates lower pressure on the inside of the bottle. Since the air pressure is now higher outside the bottle, air rushes into the bottle and takes the balloon with it. The more the bottle cools, the more air rushes in from the outside, and the more the balloon expands inside the bottle.

The balloon experiment reminds us that **God gave us breath to praise him!**

OPTIONAL ACTIVITIES
UPSIDE-DOWN WATER

Tip: This can be set up for small groups of several children around one dishpan.

Directions: Fill a glass to the very top with water. Make sure the rim is wet. Slide the index card over the top of the glass. Holding the card in place, flip the glass upside down over the dishpan. Wait a moment, and then remove hand from the card. The index card should remain stuck to the glass for a few moments.

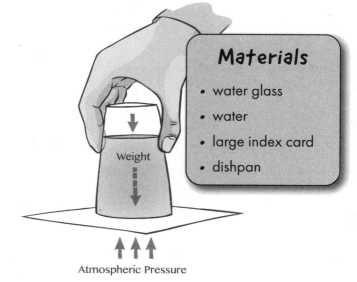

Materials
- water glass
- water
- large index card
- dishpan

Weight

Atmospheric Pressure

Say: What is happening? (*Children respond.*) **Why do you think it is happening?** (*Children respond.*) This shows that air pressure is all around us. This pressure in the room pushes up on the index card as the water in the upside-down glass pushes down. The pressures hold the card still for a short time. When water begins to seep out, then the air in the glass pushes out the rest of the water. Gravity pulls the water downward. God made us to live in this place that is perfect for us—at the bottom of an ocean of air! **God gave us breath to praise him!**

WHO'S BREATHING?

Directions: Children take turns to run to the whiteboard and write or draw something that "has breath" as in the Bible verse. See if you can fill up the entire board with names and drawings (which can lead to a guessing game!).

Say: We don't always think about what has breath—monkeys and marmots, cows and capybaras. Did you know that plants breathe, too? **God gave us breath to praise him!**

Materials

- whiteboard
- dry-erase marker

RESPIRATIONS

Preparation: Photocopy the Breath-O-Meter on page 53, making one copy for each child.

Say: In medicine, counting respirations (breaths in and out) is an important measurement. When people are in the hospital, their respirations are counted all the time. How many times do you breathe in a minute? Let's find out!

Materials

- Breath-O-Meter, page 53
- watch or phone with stopwatch app
- crayons or markers

Directions: Distribute Breath-O-Meter to children. While you use the watch or phone to time a minute, each child counts the number of respirations (breaths in and out) that they take. Record the number of respirations on the worksheet. Do this three times, inviting older children to average the numbers together to find their average respiration rate. Have adults in the room try it, as well. Do they breathe more slowly or more quickly?

Children color the picture.

God gave us breath to praise him! Let's all name a reason to praise God!

BREATH-O-METER

Let everything that breathes sing praises to the LORD.
Psalm 150:6

Respiration Test! Count how many breaths you take in a minute. If it helps, close your eyes to concentrate.

Minute 1: _____

Minute 2: _____

Minute 3: _____

Color all the things in the picture that have God's "breath of life."

11. ON WINGS LIKE EAGLES

ISAIAH 40:28–31

Those who trust in the LORD will find new strength.
They will soar high on wings like eagles.
Isaiah 40:31

OVERVIEW

Say: What does the word "powerful" make you think of?
(*Children respond.*) What are some powerful animals?
(*Children respond.*) What abilities do these animals have
that make them powerful? (*Children respond.*) Powerful
animals can fly really high, swim or run fast, and kill their prey with
their strength. Other animals give them space because they fear them.

Does that mean that weak animals are not important? (*Children respond.*)
No! All animals are important—whether strong or weak. God cares for us
even more than the animals. When we feel weak, we can turn to him. **God will give
us strength.** (*Open with prayer requests, praises, and a time of prayer.*)

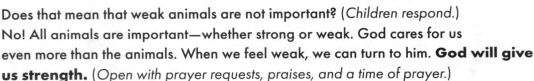

BIG IDEA

GOD WILL GIVE US STRENGTH

BIBLE STORY

Say: Have you ever been really tired? (*Children respond.*) What happened?
(*Children respond.*) When we get tried we can't focus. Easy tasks seem
complicated. We get mad over little things. Nobody likes to be tired.

People in Bible times were often tired. They had much
harder lives than we have today. If they wanted
to see a faraway friend, they had to walk or ride
an animal. They had to grow their own food and
livestock. They had no television to entertain them
or heaters to keep them warm at night. They were
used to being exhausted at the end of the day.

It's hard to be hopeful when you're always tired. Life can
bog you down sometimes. God sent prophets to his people
to give them hope. God sent Isaiah to tell his people
about the Messiah many years before Jesus was born.

Isaiah also reminded them to turn to God when they were tired (*Read Isaiah 40:28 aloud.*) God is never weak or weary. He lives forever and has great power. What does God do with his power? (*Children respond. Read Isaiah 40:29–30 aloud.*)

God gives power to the weak and powerless. He shares it with them. Whoever believes in God will have strength. Even young people get tired. But God gives new strength and energy every morning. He built our bodies so he knows exactly what we need.

But strength doesn't have to mean physical strength. What are ways that we can be strong as Christians? (*Children respond.*) God can give us strength to avoid sin and temptations. He can give us hope in times of trouble. He can give us strength to do his will.

(*Read Isaiah 40:31 aloud.*) If we put our trust in God we will be like eagles that have great strength to fly high in the sky. What do you know about eagles? (*Children respond.*) Eagles are huge birds of prey. They can fly up to 10,000 feet high using wind currents. By trusting in God, we will not get tired. He will be our wind current and lift us up like the eagles. **God will give us strength.**

OPENING GAME
BIRD OF PREY RELAY

Preparation: Mark a start and finish line for the relay with masking tape. Where each team will line up, place a bath towel.

Directions: Children form teams of three. Each person must take three turns, twice to pull the towel and once to sit on the towel. Children pull teammate to the finish line, switch "sitters", and turn back. First team to finish repeats the memory verse or shares a fun fact about eagles.

Alternate Idea: Older children might try this by carrying the third person low to the ground.

Say: How many of you were tired after that game? (*Children respond.*) It takes a lot of effort to carry someone. Eagles are birds of prey. They have to carry their prey high up into their nest to feed their babies. Luckily, they have powerful wings and big talons. But it's still hard work.

When work is hard, it feels less fun, but God has important work for us to do every day. What are some things that are good for us to do every day, even if we are tired? (*Children respond.*) Good ideas! Just like the eagles, **God will give us strength!**

Materials

- masking tape
- large bath towel (one per team of three)

OBJECT LESSON
WIND RESISTANCE

Tip: Set up at least two stations where small groups of children may experiment with the materials after you demonstrate.

Materials
- paper

Say: We learned that eagles are powerful creatures. They use the wind currents to fly super high. Without the wind currents, it would take a lot of effort for the eagles to get up high. Why? Because of something called wind resistance.

Wind resistance is a force that an object needs to overcome as they move through the air. Imagine you are walking down the street on a really windy day. The wind is blowing so strong, that you have to push against it to move forward. The wind is resisting your motion. Let's try an experiment that will help us see what wind resistance is.

Directions: Show two sheets of paper that are exactly the same. Crumple one into a small ball. Invite children to tell which piece of paper is the heaviest. Have them predict which piece of paper will hit the ground first. Drop both pieces from the same height. Children tell which piece hit the ground first. Children tell why they think the ball hit the ground first.

Say: Who can tell me why the sheet went slower than the ball? (*Children respond.*) The sheet of paper has more wind resistance than the ball. When we crumpled up one sheet of paper, we only changed the shape of the paper, not the weight of the paper. But the ball has less wind resistance than that big, flat sheet.

Even powerful birds like eagles have to deal with wind resistance. It can be very tiring. What did God promise he would give us if we are tired and weary? (*Children respond.*) **God will give us strength!**

Alternate Idea: Use three sheets of paper. Set up a target. Crumple one into a ball and turn one into a paper airplane. Leave the last one as is. Throw the paper, paper ball, and paper airplane at the target. Talk about which one went the farthest.

OPTIONAL ACTIVITIES
PARACHUTES

Preparation: Cut four 8-inch lengths of string for each child.

Directions: Children decorate their coffee filters with crayons or markers. Tape string to four sides of the coffee filter. Children tie all four strings together and attach the toy person. Child tosses up the parachute and then watches how it uses wind resistance to slow down the person's fall.

Materials
- string
- scissors
- coffee filter (one per child)
- crayons or makers
- tape
- toy people (or small objects)

Say: Why does a parachute work? (*Children respond.*) When the parachute opens, it creates wind resistance. In this case, we use wind resistance to slow down the person falling. The wind resistance slows the person more than the pull of gravity. Then they land safely.

Still, jumping out of a plane with a parachute sounds scary! Remember if you are ever afraid to turn to God in prayer. **God will give us strength!**

TUG OF STRENGTH

Preparation: Lay a strip of masking tape in the center of the room. Lay the long, sturdy rope (or jump rope) across the tape. There should be an equal length of rope on both sides of the tape. Mark the center of the rope with masking tape.

Directions: Choose four volunteers. Assign two volunteers to each side of the rope. Children pick up the rope and pull in opposite directions. The goal is to get the center of the rope to their side.

Materials

- masking tape
- long, sturdy rope (or jump rope)

Say: You needed a lot of strength and determination to pull the rope onto your side. Remember that **God will give us strength**! Remember there are all kinds of strength. Self-discipline is strength. It means you don't eat all the cookies at once. Forgiveness is strength. It means you don't hold grudges. God is always our source of strength.

SOAR LIKE EAGLES

Preparation: Photocopy Eagle Strength on page 58, making one copy for each child.

Directions: Distribute Eagle Strength to children. Children draw lines from the words in clouds to the corresponding question. Children may write or draw more answers to the questions.

Materials

- Eagle Strength, page 58
- crayons or markers

Say: Eagles are often called the "Kings of the Birds." Because they are a symbol of power, they can be found on many country emblems (including the USA). We know God is more powerful than eagles. God is always with us.

He makes it possible for us to accomplish tasks that we never knew were possible. He helps enemies become friends. He heals the sick. He comforts the lonely. If we are ever tired, sad, or lonely, we can turn to him in prayer. **God will give us strength!**

EAGLE STRENGTH

Draw lines from the words in the clouds to the corresponding question. Add your own ideas in their own clouds.

HOW DO WE GET PHYSICALLY STRONG?

HOW DO WE GET SPIRITUALLY STRONG?

go to church

memorize Bible verses

read the Bible

exercise

sleep

ask questions about God

pray

wash hands

eat healthy

drink water

12. GOD LOVES US MORE THAN BIRDS

MATTHEW 6:25–34

Don't worry about anything; instead pray about everything. Tell God what you need, and thank him for all he has done.
Philippians 4:6

BIG IDEA

WE CAN TRUST GOD AND NEVER WORRY

OVERVIEW

Say: What are some things you already did today? (*Children respond.*) Some of you ate food. It looks like all of you got dressed! Most of you live in a house or apartment. What things might you do later today? (*Children respond.*) Will you eat again? (*Children respond.*) Will you need a sweater or a jacket later today? (*Children respond.*) How many of those things have you worried about today? (*Children respond.*)

For some people, many of those things are a worry. Will I have warm clothes? Will there be food for me to eat? Will I be able to pay for my house this month? These are all things most people need. But here is the good news about things we need. **We can trust God and never worry!** (*Open with prayer requests, praises, and a time of prayer.*)

BIBLE STORY

Say: One day, Jesus was talking to a crowd of people sitting on a hillside on a beautiful day. But not all of them were thinking about the beautiful place or the lovely day. They were worried. They worried about food and clothes and a place to live, just like we do today.

Listen to what Jesus told them. (*Read Matthew 6:25 aloud.*) Why did Jesus say we don't need to worry? (*Children respond.*) Yes. Life is more than just what we eat and what we wear. Jesus went on to point out some creatures who DON'T worry.

(*Read Matthew 6:26 aloud.*) God loves the birds. He makes sure the birds have food. They don't worry about it! God knows what we need, too. We are more important to God than the birds.

(*Read Matthew 6:28–32 aloud.*) God gives the wild flowers beautiful clothes—petals

in every color and green leaves. Even though they die quickly and are burned up, he makes them beautiful. God thinks we're more important than the flowers.

God doesn't want us to worry like the people who don't know him. Jesus tells us what to do instead of worrying. (*Read Matthew 6:33 aloud.*) **What do you think it means to seek God's Kingdom?** (*Children respond.*)

It means to want God to be first in our minds instead of worries. It means wanting what God wants for us and being thankful for what he gives us. He loves us and will take care of us! **We can trust God and never worry!**

OPENING GAME
BIRD BEAK RELAY

Preparation: Mark a start and finish line with masking tape. Set the bowl over the finish line. Set a pair of chopsticks and a bag of marshmallows at the start line.

Directions: Children form even teams and line up behind the start line. First child in line picks up chopsticks, uses both chopsticks to pick up and hold a marshmallow. No spearing of marshmallows! Child goes to the bowl at the finish line and drops the marshmallow in. Child returns to give chopsticks to next player. Play continues until one team has completed the task.

Say: We're going to play a game where you will pretend to use your "bird beaks" to carry the marshmallow back to your nest! God cares for the birds. He feeds them what they need—not marshmallows! He cares for us even more. When we worry about anything, we can turn to him. We can ask him for what we need. **We can trust God and never worry!**

> **Tip:** If players are older, increase the challenge by having them use only one hand to hold the chopsticks.

Materials

- masking tape
- plastic bowl
- chopsticks (pair per team)
- bag of marshmallows (one per team)

OBJECT LESSON
UP AND AWAY

> **Tip:** If you don't have enough funnels for each child to have one, small groups can share. Provide sanitizing wipes to use between each child's turn. Sanitize the Ping-Pong ball as well.

Say: How is it that birds are able to fly? (*Children respond.*) Most people think that the air pushes them up. God made an amazing law related to air resistance. It is called LIFT. Lift is what makes it possible for birds and airplanes to lift off the ground and fly. Let's see how it works!

Materials (one per child)

- plastic funnel
- Ping-Pong ball

Directions: Hold the funnel upside down. Place the small end of the funnel into your mouth, bending over so that the funnel is upside down when you blow through it.

Practice blowing steadily through the funnel. Put your hand beneath the funnel so you can feel the air going straight down.

When you have a good flow of air going, lay a Ping-Pong ball in your open hand. Hold your hand flat under the airflow from the funnel.

Continue blowing, and then take your hand away. The Ping-Pong ball should float in the air.

Say: Why do you think the ball floats inside the end of the funnel? (*Children respond.*) It's because the air passing through the funnel is moving quicker than the air around and below it. There is less pressure above the ball than below the ball. Since the air pressure is greater below the ball, the ball is held in the air. We call this LIFT. Lift makes a bird fly! And we can be as free as birds, too. **We can trust God and never worry!**

OPTIONAL ACTIVITIES
BIRD CALLS

Directions: Children take turns to make a bird call for others to guess the kind of bird.

Say: Does anyone know how to sound like a bird? (*Children respond.*) What kinds of birds can we imitate the calls of? (*Children respond.*) God cares for the birds. He ensures they have twigs for their nests and seeds for their food. Birds have far fewer needs than humans. God cares for us even more than birds. What are some human needs? (*Children respond.*) **We can trust God and never worry!**

Optional: Set laptop or phone to play bird calls or sounds. Children identify sounds that they recognize.

> **Optional Materials**
> - laptop or phone

CHICKEN CLUCKER

Preparation: Poke hole in bottom of the paper cup with a pencil, one for each child. Cut string into 2-foot lengths, one for each child. Fill shallow container with water.

Directions: Pull length of string through the hole in the bottom of cup. Make large knots in the end outside of the cup. Turn cup upside down. String should hang inside the cup.

Dip the hanging string into the water. Hold the cup in one hand. Use your thumb and forefinger to pull on the wet string, a little at a time.

Say: Let's make the sound of one bird we all know well—chickens! What happens when we pull on the wet string between our thumb and forefinger? (*Children respond.*) What does it sound like? (*Children respond.*) When the wet string stops our fingers, it makes a vibration in the string that sounds like a chicken clucking.

God cares for chickens. God loves us even more. Whenever we are worried we can turn to God in prayer. **We can trust God and never worry**!

Materials (one per child)

- paper cup
- pencil
- scissors
- cotton string
- ruler
- water
- shallow container

AVOID WORRY

Preparation: Photocopy the No Worries Maze on page 63, making one copy for each child.

Directions: Distribute No Worries Maze to children. Children follow the Bible verse (and avoid dead-end temptations) to complete the maze. Children write the completed Bible verse on the lines provided.

Say: What are some things that you or people you know worry about? (*Children respond.*) These worries can stop us from trusting God. But if we do what our Bible verse says, **we can trust God and never worry!**

Materials

- No Worries Maze, page 63
- crayons or markers

Answer Key: Don't worry about anything; instead pray about everything. Tell God what you need, and thank him for all he has done.

NO WORRIES MAZE

Follow the Bible verse to complete the maze. Write the completed verse on the lines provided.

Start

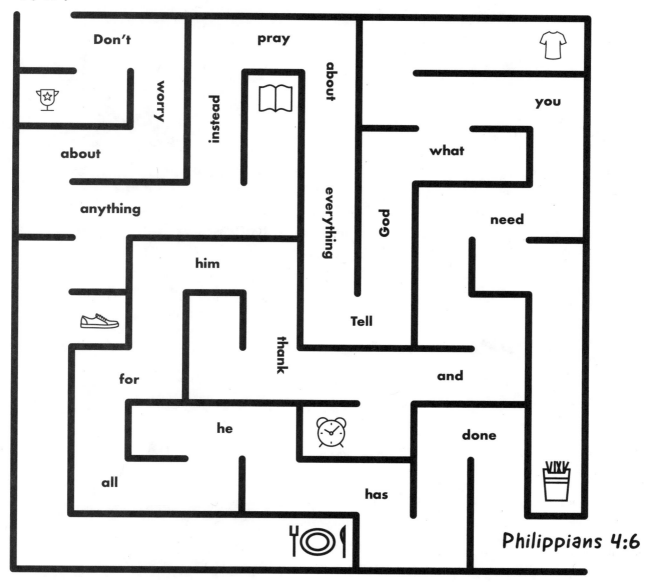

Don't   pray

worry   instead   about

about

anything   everything   God   you   what   need

him   Tell

thank   and

for   he   done   has

all

Philippians 4:6

_____

_____

_____

13. JESUS CALMS THE STORM

MARK 4:35–41

*God elevated [Jesus] to the place of highest honor and
gave him the name above all other names.*
Philippians 2:9

BIG IDEA

JESUS IS
STRONGER
THAN ANYTHING

OVERVIEW

Say: Let's look outside. Let's see if there is any wind today. Is it a big wind
or a breeze? (*Children respond.*) Can we control where the wind goes?
(*Children respond.*) What is the biggest kind of wind called? (*Children
respond.*) Tornados are huge winds that circle around themselves. Hurricanes
are big winds that also have heavy rain. Big winds can be scary and can cause a lot of
damage! But do you think the biggest wind could stop Jesus? (*Children respond.*) No! Because
Jesus is stronger than anything! (*Open with prayer requests, praises, and a time of prayer.*)

BIBLE STORY

Say: There was a time when Jesus and his friends were sailing across the lake
called Galilee. There were quite a few boats going across the water and things
seemed fine. Jesus went to the back of the boat and laid down to take a nap.

What do you think happened? (*Read Mark 4:37 aloud.*)

Wow! This wasn't any ordinary breeze. This wasn't even a STIFF
breeze! This was such a big wind that the waves were suddenly huge.
They were breaking over the boat. It was filling with water!

What happens to a boat if it gets full of water? (*Children respond.*) Yes! A boat
full of water will SINK! Jesus' friends were TERRIFIED! What do you think they could
do about their problem? (*Children respond. Read Mark 4:38 aloud.*)

Jesus' friends were SURE they were going to drown! They had done all the things good sailors can
do—and it wasn't enough! So they woke Jesus! What do you think Jesus did? (*Children respond.*) Did
he take a bucket and start to bail? Did he try to take over the rudder and steer the boat? NO! (*Read
Mark 4:39 aloud.*) And JUST LIKE THAT, the wind stopped. The waves settled down to a glassy calm.

Jesus looked at his friends. He asked them, "Why are you afraid? Do you still have no faith?" (Mark 4:40).

The friends looked at each other—they were AMAZED! They had seen Jesus heal sick people and cast out demons. They knew Jesus was powerful. But they asked each other, "WHO is this man? Even the WIND and waves obey him!" (Mark 4:41). Now they could see that there is nothing Jesus can't do. **Jesus is stronger than anything!**

OPENING GAME
AIR FORCE

Preparation: Mark start and finish lines about eight feet apart with masking tape. Set out the packages of straws and a packing peanut where each team will line up. (Keep extras on hand.) Set a chair at the opposite side of the playing area from where each line will stand.

Directions: Children form two teams. Teams line up at start line. First child in line takes a straw from package. Child uses the straw to blow the packing peanut around the chair and back to the start line. (If your group is younger, make this a shorter distance.)

Play continues until all players have gone. First team to finish repeats the memory verse, or chooses someone to repeat it. Players may keep their straws to play another round.

Say: What did you use to get the packing peanut around the chair and back? (*Children respond.*) Our lungs can take in air and push it out very well! Air can move things—and can even pick up houses and cars sometimes! But who is stronger than the strongest wind? Yes! **Jesus is stronger than anything!**

Materials

- masking tape
- 2 packs of straws
- packing peanuts
- 2 chairs

OBJECT LESSON
AIR-POWERED HOVERCRAFT

Directions: Use scissors to make a hole in the center of each item you have (paper bowls, cups, or plates). Turn items facedown.

Choose an item. Plug in the dryer and blow air (on cool setting) through the hole. Children take turns to experiment with the items they choose. Children talk about the shape of the items and the weight of the item versus the power of the air.

Say: What happens when you blow a stream of air through the hole? (*Children respond.*) Can you move the item around by moving the hair dryer? (*Children respond.*) Which shape seems to move best? (*Children respond.*) Does blowing in the hole make any of these move a little bit? (*Children respond.*)

Materials

- scissors
- paper bowls
- cups
- plates
- hand-held blow dryer

Hovercrafts are a real invention! They use a strong stream of air to keep the craft off the water. Fans blow a stream of air under the craft to make a cushion of air. It can move faster than a boat of the same size, because it is floating on air, not water. It's powered by a strong wind—but not too strong for Jesus. **Jesus is stronger than anything!**

OPTIONAL ACTIVITIES
COMPRESSED AIR

Say: Air is everywhere. How strong can air be? (*Children respond.*) When we talk about compressed air, that means the air can't escape from a space. Let's see how compressed air works.

Directions: Try to push the straw into the potato. Place a thumb over the top of the straw and try again. Children take turns to experiment with this as time and interest allow.

Say: The open straw doesn't go very far into the potato, does it? But when we close off the top of the straw, we trap a column of air inside the straw. That is compressed air. The compressed air made the closed straw strong enough to drill deeper into the potato. Many power tools use this principle. Drills that use compressed air can break rock! But **Jesus is stronger than anything!**

> ### Materials
> - plastic straws
> - 2 raw potatoes

JET PROPULSION BALLOON RACE

Preparation: Mark a start line with masking tape at one end of the playing area.

Directions: Give each child a different colored balloon (for identification). Standing on a line, children all inflate their balloons as far as they can. At your signal, they release balloons to see which one goes farthest straight ahead. Notice which ones go crooked or make spirals. Talk about why this might be. Pick up the used balloons, pass out new ones, and try again!

> ### Materials
> - masking tape
> - small balloons in various colors (water balloons work well)

Tip: If desired, use masking tape to note where the farthest balloon lands with each round.

Say: There are huge jets and rockets that use the principle of jet propulsion, just like our little balloons do. When you let go of your balloons, the air that escaped pushed the balloon away from you. Those big jets and rockets are very powerful and can go fast and far. But **Jesus is stronger than anything!**

JESUS SOARS

Preparation: Photocopy Paper Airplane on page 68, making one copy for each child.

Say: Jesus' power is stronger than the wind and the waves. Today we're going to make paper airplanes to remind us that Jesus is above these forces of nature.

Directions: Distribute Paper Airplane activity to children. Invite children to make paper airplanes in any way they like, or use the activity page as a guide. Children test different models and observe which ones fly best.

Say: When we folded our planes according to the instructions on this page, they fly well. Why do you think that is? (*Children respond.*) The planes glide on the air better when they are made a certain way. The air holds up the planes. Air can move fast and make tornados and hurricanes. It can make sandstorms and storms on the water, like our story today. But **Jesus is stronger than anything!**

Materials

- Paper Airplane, page 68
- paper

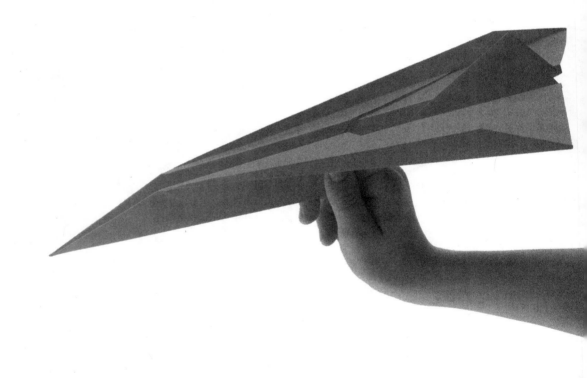

PAPER AIRPLANE

God elevated [Jesus] to the place of highest honor and gave him the name above all other names.
Philippians 2:9

Jesus is stronger than anything! He commands the wind and the waves. Follow the instructions below to make a paper airplane as a reminder that Jesus soars above the forces of nature.

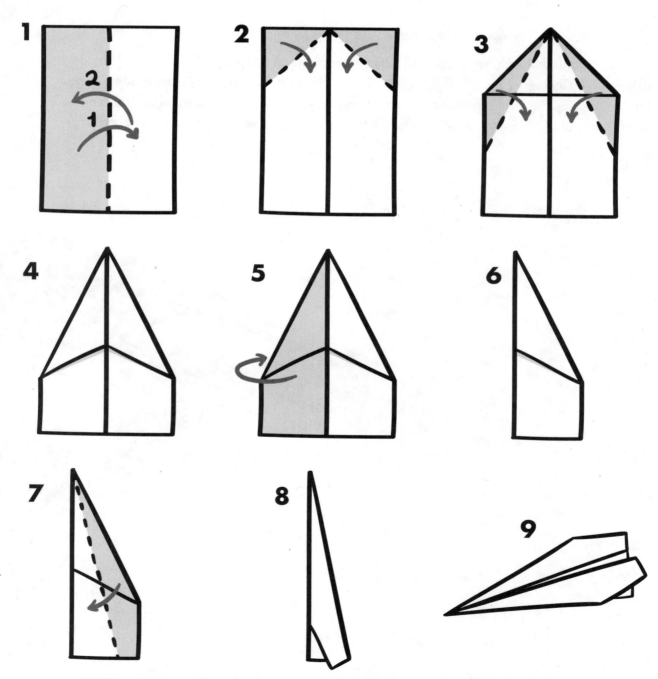

14. ABRAHAM AND LOT SPLIT

GENESIS 13:1–18

Trust in the LORD and do good. Then you will live safely in the land and prosper.
Psalm 37:3

BIG IDEA

GOD MADE THE LAND IN AMAZING WAYS

OVERVIEW

Say: What did you eat today? (*Children respond; list the foods on the whiteboard.*) Where did each of these foods come from? (*Children respond; continue to ask questions until children see that all food grows from the ground.*) We don't usually open a bag of potato chips and think about where they came from, or eat a grilled cheese sandwich and think about how the cheese got to us. But without the land there wouldn't be much growing. What do you think there would be to eat if we didn't have land? (*Children respond.*) The land is important. **God made the land in amazing ways!** (*Open with prayer requests, praises, and a time of prayer.*)

Materials

- whiteboard
- dry-erase marker

BIBLE STORY

Say: Humans rely on food that can be grown in the soil, the Earth's crust. Land is very important! Some people who live where there is nothing but ice and snow survive on fish and animals. Those animals and fish live on plants that grow under the sea in another part of the Earth's crust! So one way or the other, people live on plants that grow in soil—like the foods we put on our list.

Today we're going to talk about a faithful man named Abraham. God had promised Abraham that there was a special land for him and his family. When Abraham and his family traveled through the land God gave them, they had to decide how to use it. They weren't yet settled in one place, so they were not growing plants, but they were growing animals.

What do you think those animals needed to eat? (*Children respond.*) Yes, they need plants to eat. Listen to what happened when there were too many animals and not enough grass. (*Read Genesis 13:5–7 aloud.*)

Abraham and Lot's herdsmen, who took care of the animals, were ready to beat each other up! What do you think Abraham and Lot could do about this problem? (*Children respond. Read Genesis 13:8–9 aloud.*)

By moving away from each other, there would be enough pasture for their animals. Abraham gave Lot the first choice. Lot looked around. He saw the lush, green grass down in the flat area. It was beautiful—and it looked like a good place for many animals! He chose that part.

Abraham took the high hills, with less grass and more bushes. Do you think it would be easier or harder to feed the animals in the hills or in the green pasture? (*Children respond.*) Listen to what God told Abraham. (*Read Genesis 13:14–17 aloud.*)

God had a bigger plan, a different way to help Abraham. Even though it LOOKED like Abraham got less USABLE land, God promised to give Abraham much MORE land— land that would belong to his family forever. By being kind to Lot, Abraham pleased God. God gave him what he needed! **God made the land in amazing ways!**

OPENING GAME
OPEN SPACE

Preparation: Use masking tape to create at least three large open spaces on the floor—they can be square, triangle, rectangle, etc. Make shapes large enough for five children to stand inside. (Make more shapes if you have more children, so that at any time, there is space for at least five children to stand.)

Alternate Idea: Play this game outdoors and mark the shapes in chalk on the playground.

Directions: Ask a volunteer to be "It." Children form groups, each of which stands in one of the shapes. One at a time, call out descriptions such as "kids with black shoes" or "kids wearing red." Whoever fits that description must move to a new shape while "It" tries to tag them before they are safe in the new shape. Children who are tagged become "It" also. Continue play until nearly all have been tagged. Begin a new round as time allows.

Tip: For more challenge, shout "Run to a new land!" at times. All children then run to a new space—even the "Its," beginning a new round.

Materials
- masking tape

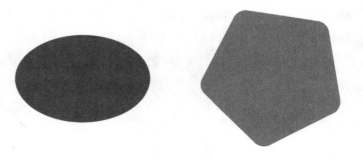

OBJECT LESSON
VOLCANO

Tip: Bring lava rock for children to explore.

Say: Abraham and Lot split up their land to feed their flocks. Today, we are going to split up Earth and learn about what makes the land so special. Think about Earth like a hard-boiled egg. (*Draw the three layers of an egg on the whiteboard.*) Like an egg, it has layers. Who can tell me what the three layers of an egg are? (*Children respond.*) Yes, the yolk, the egg white, and the egg shell.

The center of Earth is called the core. The middle layer is called the mantle and the outer layer is called the crust. The core is like the egg yolk, the mantle is like the egg white, and the crust is like the egg shell. Compared to the mantle and core, the crust is very thin.

The crust is where we live! It is mostly solid rocks and minerals that allow plants to grow for our food. The mantle is also mostly solid rocks and minerals, but there are also pockets of hot magma. The core, at the center of Earth, is hot, dense, molten metal. When the crust cracks, and pressure builds up in the hot magma, it explodes through the crust. Let's see how that works!

Directions: Set bottle (cap loosened) in the center of the box. Children help you pour potting soil over the bottle and pat into a mound. Open the bottle cap. Place the funnel into the mouth. Children put about a tablespoon of baking soda into the bottle. Drop in a little red food coloring. Add a tablespoon of liquid dish soap. Pour about a cup of vinegar through the funnel into the bottle and remove the funnel. Watch and talk about what happens.

Materials

- whiteboard
- dry-erase marker
- empty half-liter bottle with cap
- large shallow cardboard box
- small bag of potting soil
- funnel
- measuring spoons
- baking soda
- red food coloring
- liquid dish soap
- vinegar

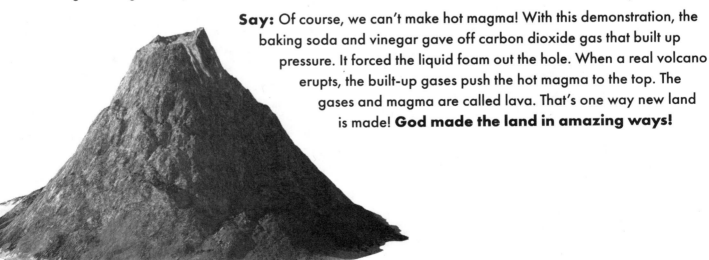

Say: Of course, we can't make hot magma! With this demonstration, the baking soda and vinegar gave off carbon dioxide gas that built up pressure. It forced the liquid foam out the hole. When a real volcano erupts, the built-up gases push the hot magma to the top. The gases and magma are called lava. That's one way new land is made! **God made the land in amazing ways!**

OPTIONAL ACTIVITIES

BIRTH OF AN ISLAND

Directions: On a laptop, show children videos of a volcano erupting. Or show children books with images of volcanos. Discuss how the new land is created. Discuss what makes land good.

Say: Today we learned that a healthy land produces healthy crops for people and animals. Abraham and Lot needed more land to feed all their livestock. What happened because they didn't have enough land? (*Children respond.*) They split up the new land. How is new land created? (*Children respond.*) Volcanos produce new land after the lava cools. **God made the land in amazing ways!**

Materials

- laptop
- books showing images of volcanos

ROCKSPLORATION

Preparation: Cover the surface with newspaper or trash bags or do this activity outdoors.

Directions: Children participating don glasses and gloves. Using one rock, children hit rocks together to see them break. Notice which ones are harder and which are softer.

Say: How could you tell which rocks are softer? (*Children respond.*) What do you think this pile of leftover rock bits looks like? (*Children respond.*) Some rocks break more easily and wear down faster. Others are harder and last longer in the weather over thousands of years. **God made the land in amazing ways!**

Tip: Save the rock dust for later soil explorations.

Materials

- newspaper or trash bags
- safety glasses
- work gloves
- rocks

EARTH'S STRUCTURE

Preparation: Photocopy One Hot Mass on page 73, making one copy for each child.

Directions: Distribute One Hot Mass to children. Children discuss what they've learned as they color. Children label the layers of Earth.

Say: Our planet is one hot mass! It is molten rock at the center. It gets cooler as it moves out to the crust—until it is under our feet as the land. You can color it any way you like, but remember that it is hot in the center and cools as it moves away from the core. **God made the land in amazing ways!**

Answer Key: 1. Crust; 2. Mantle; 3. Outer Core; 4. Inner Core

Materials

- One Hot Mass, page 73
- crayons or markers

ONE HOT MASS

Trust in the LORD and do good. Then you will live safely in the land and prosper.
Psalm 37:3

God promised good land to Abraham. Good land is found on the outer-most layer of Earth, but God made Earth special. He created layers inside Earth. Color the layers of Earth below. Label the layers. Remember that God cares about Earth and all that he created.

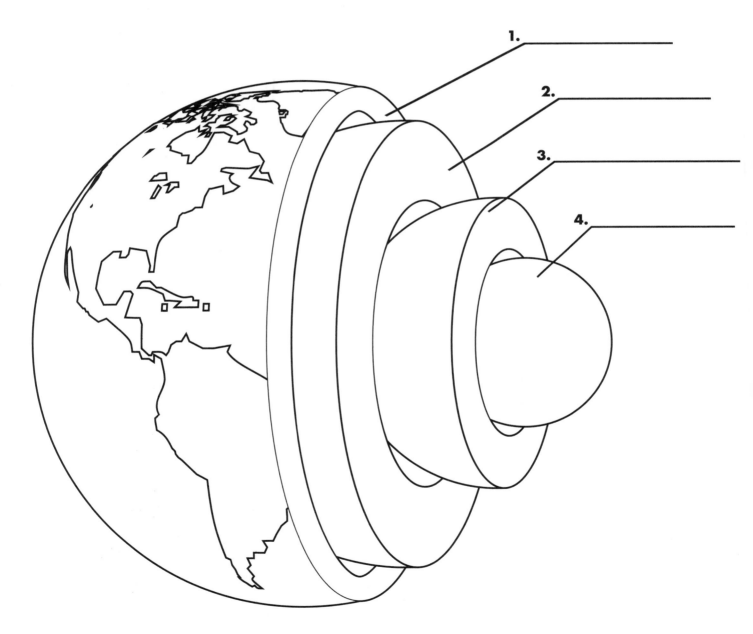

1. _____

2. _____

3. _____

4. _____

15. MINING FOR WISDOM

JOB 28

The fear of the Lord is true wisdom; to forsake evil is real understanding.
Job 28:28

BIG IDEA

GOD TEACHES US HIS WAYS

OVERVIEW

Directions: Show a compass or a compass app on your phone.

Say: Why do you think this compass works? (*Children respond.*) How do you think ancient people—way back in early Bible times—knew the directions north, south, east, and west? (*Children respond.*) All through the Bible, God taught people his ways. And even knowing which way to go is part of that! I'm glad God doesn't wait for us to figure everything out on our own! He loves us and wants us to understand. **God teaches us his ways!** (*Open with prayer requests, praises, and a time of prayer.*)

Materials

• compass or compass app on a phone

BIBLE STORY

Say: God made the world a perfect place for us to live! Let's talk about some of the amazing things God has taught people, even long ago! In Bible times, people mined for precious jewels and stones, just like we do today. (*Read Job 28:1–4,10–11 aloud.*)

Mining looked a little different in Bible times. Today, mines have big elevators that lower people down into the earth. Back then, they lowered people down into the darkness on ropes (See Job 28:4). What do you think it was like down in the mines? (*Children respond.*)

It was probably scary, and very dark! But the gems that they searched for were so precious that it was worth their while. How do you think people figured out that by digging up certain rocks, and MELTING those rocks, they got gold, silver, copper, and iron? (*Children respond.*)

There must have been WISE people who figured out how to get the jewels safely. Where do you think wise people get their wisdom? (*Children respond.*) Let's read what the Bible says about searching for wisdom. (*Read Job 28:12–15,21–24 aloud.*)

Human beings are good at searching for things. They discovered jewels inside of mountains! But for all that searching, God says people can't find wisdom—not on their own, at least.

Have you ever tried to search for something you couldn't find? What was that like? (*Children respond.*) I bet it was pretty frustrating. Trying to find wisdom on our own is frustrating, too.

Thankfully, we can pray to God and ask him to give us wisdom. (*Read Job 28:28 aloud.*) Wisdom is not found on Earth or even inside Earth. True wisdom comes from God. No mining needed. **God teaches us his ways!**

OPENING GAME
MINER'S BLUFF

Directions: This game is played like Blind Man's Bluff. Designate one player as "It." Blindfold that player. "It" must try to tag the other players, who are moving about and hiding in plain sight around the room.

Say: This was a wild game! There is so much to learn about God's world. He hides all kinds of wonderful things—but it's like an Easter egg hunt. He hides things so that we can find them! He wants us to learn his ways and be wise. I am so glad that **God teaches us his ways!**

Materials
- blindfold

OBJECT LESSON
CRYSTAL-CLEAR WISDOM

Tip: Each child may make one of these if you have enough materials.

Directions: Pour Borax and hot water into the glass jar. Stir to dissolve.

While mixture is dissolving, twirl a pipe cleaner around a pencil to form a spiral. Slide the pipe cleaner off the pencil. Tie a piece of string at the top of the pipe cleaner to create a loop.

Place a pencil through the string loop. Lay the pencil horizontally over the mouth of the jar so that the pipe clearer is fully immersed in the water.

Let the pipe cleaner sit in the water for about an hour, until you see crystals form. You can even leave the mixture overnight.

Let the crystallized pipe cleaner dry. You can now hang it as an ornament or decoration, just like a beautiful crystal.

Materials
- 9 tablespoons Borax
- 3 cups hot water
- glass jar
- spoon
- pipe cleaner
- pencil
- string

Say: Many beautiful things have formed deep below Earth's surface. That's the way God created it! What do you think is below the earth? (*Children respond.*) We read in Job that people go down into the earth to search for precious stones and minerals. But no matter how hard we search, we can't find wisdom on our own. That only comes from God! Remember the beauty of God's wisdom with these crystal ornaments. **God teaches us his ways!**

OPTIONAL ACTIVITIES
IRON OR NOT?

Say: Job 28 tells us that humans can discover things under Earth's crust that no other creature has seen! One thing people mine for is iron. What are some things that have iron in them? (*Children respond with answers like vehicles, appliances, utensils, etc.*) **Great ideas!**

We know that only iron or iron-containing items respond to the magnetic fields. Why? Because there is a giant molten iron river that flows under Earth's crust. The flow of the iron river makes an electric current that creates a magnetic field around Earth. So if we want to know if something has iron, we can test it with magnets.

Let's test to see what things contain iron and which ones don't. I'm glad that we can explore because **God teaches us his ways!**

Directions: Give each child a magnet. Child tests a variety of materials around the room to see which ones contain iron. For older children, have them make a list of those items.

Alternate Idea: Set up a tray of various items, some magnetic and some not.

> ### Materials
> - variety of items (some magnetic and some not)
> - magnets

WHERE IS WISDOM?

Preparation: Use rope or masking tape to make a line in the center of the playing area. Print "LAND" on one sheet of paper and "SEA" on the other. Place Land paper on one side of the rope and Sea paper on the other side.

Directions: Begin by having all players stand beside the prepared line. Call out one of the three locations: land, sea, or air. If you call out "land,"

> ### Materials
> - rope or masking tape
> - marker
> - 2 sheets of paper

children jump to the other side of the rope with the Land paper. If you call out "sea," children jump to the side of the rope with the Sea paper. If you call out "air," children jump straight up in the air.

You can try to confuse the players by calling out the same location twice or calling out locations super fast. Whenever someone jumps the wrong way, they are out. Play until one or two players are left. Remaining players repeat the memory verse.

Say: There are many places in the world that have beautiful things that God created. People have discovered jewels inside of mountains, special light-up fish in the depth of the ocean, and fascinating facts about the layers of the sky. But wisdom is not something that we can find by ourselves. If we want to be wise, we need to turn to God in prayer. Let's be thankful that **God teaches us his ways!**

ABOUT THE EARTH WORD SEARCH

Preparation: Photocopy the About the Earth activity on page 78, making one copy for each child.

Say: Miners search for rocks and minerals underground, and God can help us search for WISDOM. You can search for these words all on your own! **God teaches us his ways!**

Directions: Distribute About the Earth activity to children. Children circle the words from the word bank. Words can be found up, down, and across.

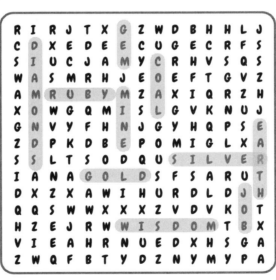

R I R J T X G Z W D B H H L J
C D X E D E E C U G E C R F S
S I U C J A M Y C R H V S Q S
W A S M R H J E O E F T G V Z
A M R U B Y M Z A X I Q R Z H
X O W G Q M I S L G V K N U J
G N V Y F H N J G Y H Q P S E
Z D P K D B E P O M I G L X A
S S L T S O D Q U S I L V E R
I A N A G O L D S F S A R U T
D X Z X A W I H U R D L D J H
Q Q S W W X X X Z V D V K O T
H Z E J R W W I S D O M T B X
V I E A H R N U E D X H S G A
Z W Q F B T Y D Z N Y M Y P A

Materials

- About the Earth, page 78
- crayons or markers

ABOUT THE EARTH

The fear of the Lord is true wisdom; to forsake evil is real understanding.
Job 28:28

WORD BANK

COAL	EARTH	GOLD	MINE	SILVER
DIAMONDS	GEM	JOB	RUBY	WISDOM

```
R  I  R  J  T  X  G  Z  W  D  B  H  H  L  J
C  D  X  E  D  E  E  C  U  G  E  C  R  F  S
S  I  U  C  J  A  M  Y  C  R  H  V  S  Q  S
W  A  S  M  R  H  J  E  O  E  F  T  G  V  Z
A  M  R  U  B  Y  M  Z  A  X  I  Q  R  Z  H
X  O  W  G  Q  M  I  S  L  G  V  K  N  U  J
G  N  V  Y  F  H  N  J  G  Y  H  Q  P  S  E
Z  D  P  K  D  B  E  P  O  M  I  G  L  X  A
S  S  L  T  S  O  D  Q  U  S  I  L  V  E  R
I  A  N  A  G  O  L  D  S  F  S  A  R  U  T
D  X  Z  X  A  W  I  H  U  R  D  L  D  J  H
Q  Q  S  W  W  X  X  X  Z  V  D  V  K  O  T
H  Z  E  J  R  W  W  I  S  D  O  M  T  B  X
V  I  E  A  H  R  N  U  E  D  X  H  S  G  A
Z  W  Q  F  B  T  Y  D  Z  N  Y  M  Y  P  A
```

16. GOD NEVER CHANGES

PSALM 46

Jesus Christ is the same yesterday, today, and forever.
Hebrews 13:8

BIG IDEA

EARTH CHANGES BUT JESUS STAYS THE SAME

OVERVIEW

Preparation: Wear the wearable items.

Say: Let's play a game. Take a good look at me while I count to ten. Now close your eyes while I count to ten again. (*During that time, remove or change one of the items you are wearing.*) Ten seconds is up! Open your eyes and tell me what changed. (*Children respond. Repeat this as children show interest.*) Today we're going to talk about some ways Earth's crust can change, and what that causes. **Earth changes but Jesus stays the same!** (*Open with prayer requests, praises, and a time of prayer.*)

Materials
- wearable items you can easily change (watch, pin, scarf, hat, etc.)

BIBLE STORY

Say: Sometimes, we don't notice small changes, like me moving my watch from one hand to the other. When God made the world, he created layers within Earth. We live on the outermost layer called the Crust. God set things in motion so that Earth's Crust would change a lot! What are some ways that the land can change? (*Children respond.*)

In Psalm 46, we can read a description of one way the land changes. (*Read Psalm 46:1–2 aloud.*) What kinds of things can make mountains slide off into the ocean? (*Children respond.*) Earthquakes! The good thing is that even when a change as big as that comes, we can trust God to protect us, because he doesn't change. He always loves us!

God planned for the crust of the earth to be changing all the time. Wind, rain, earthquakes, floods—all make changes in the land. (*Read Psalm 46:3,6 aloud.*) Wow! What kinds of changes are described here? (*Children respond.*)

The mountains can shake from the pounding of the waves. And it says that God's voice is so powerful that it can make mountains melt! Still, no matter how exciting it gets to see mountains move or oceans roar and foam, God is always our safe place. This is what we read in Hebrews 13:8. (*Read Hebrews 13:8*

aloud.) It's good to know that Jesus is the same yesterday—when he made the world and today—when he holds everything together and forever! **Earth changes but Jesus stays the same!**

OPENING GAME
EROSION MATCH

Preparation: Write each of the following words twice on two separate index cards: yesterday, today, forever, wind, rain, crack, freeze, earthquake, boulder, Jesus.

Mark a start line with masking tape at one side of the playing area. Scramble each set of cards and lay them in a grid pattern facedown about ten feet from the starting line.

Directions: Children form two teams. Children take turns to run to the grid and choose one card to bring back to the team. Play continues until all cards are taken. Children now find the person on the other team whose word matches theirs. Direct as pairs take turns to talk about and then describe their words, or if it is a word of the Bible verse, everyone repeats the Bible verse together.

Say: Earth constantly changes around us. That can make us feel small and unsafe. But God has promised to protect us. He is the creator of the whole world and nothing surprises him. **Earth changes but Jesus stays the same!**

> **Materials**
> - index cards
> - crayons or markers
> - masking tape

OBJECT LESSON
NEVER THE SAME

Say: In our game, we learned some words about ways Earth's crust changes. Wind, water, freezing, cracking—all are ways to change what looks to us like solid, unchanging mountains of rock! Because we are so small compared to the landforms, we can't see the changes very well. But what if we make the landforms small so that we can see what happens? Let's try a few of these so we can watch what happens!

Directions: Mound up sand in one end of a plastic box to represent a beach. Pour some water into the box and invite children to move the box back and forth. **What happens to the beach? How does the form change due to the wave action and the shaking?** (*Children respond.*)

Mound sand into a tall ridge. Add several small rocks that stick out of the top.

> **Materials**
> - shallow plastic boxes or dishpans
> - sand
> - water
> - pitcher
> - variety of small rocks
> - spray bottle
> - sugar cubes
> - jar with lid

Use the spray bottle to "rain" over the ridge to see how it erodes. **What happens to the rocks that were on top? Where does the rock go when it is rained on in real life?** (*Children respond.*)

Show the sugar cubes to children, noting the sharp edges of the cubes. Put the cubes into a jar and shake them vigorously for thirty seconds. Remove the cubes to see how they have been weathered by abrasion—just rubbing and bumping into each other.

To show wind erosion, invite children to blow at the level of the sugar cubes from one side. **What do you see coming off the cubes? How is that like what happens when rocks weather and then the wind and water carry the bits into streams and rivers?** (*Children respond.*)

Say: These are all ways that rocks and mountains wear down. When that happens, the pieces of rock fall down and wash into the valleys where the rivers flow. All these changes make a difference in the landform! **Earth changes but Jesus stays the same!**

OPTIONAL ACTIVITIES
WHAT'S IN A ROCK?

Preparation: Lay out the rocks where children can see and touch.

Say: These rocks all look different. That's because they're made in different ways. Some rocks are called igneous because they came out of heat. They are hardened magma with bubbles that came from volcanos.

Some are called sedimentary because they are made of layers of sediment. Sediments are bits of rocks, shells, and sand.

The third kind of rock are metamorphic— that means they changed form. They were once another kind of rock, but high heat and pressure made them change into something else! **Earth changes but Jesus stays the same!**

Directions: Children sort rocks by what type they think each rock might be. Children line up the rocks by how hard each rock is, softest to hardest. They may also sort them by color, shape, size, etc. as time allows.

Materials
- a variety of rocks

Igneous

Granite   Basalt   Obsidian

Sedimentary

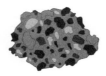 

Conglomerate   Mudstone   Limestone

Metamorphic

Gneiss   Schist   Slate

EDIBLE ROCKS

Directions: Empty the cookies into the resealable plastic bag. Be sure it is sealed well. Children use the rolling pin or their hands to smash the "rock material" until all pieces are pea-sized. Open the bag. Children clean their hands with wipes. Children eat rock snack.

Say: These look like rocks, don't they! We did a process that is a lot like extreme weathering! We changed the cookies into rocks—I guess that makes them metamorphic! **Earth changes but Jesus stays the same!**

Materials

- chocolate sandwich cookies
- resealable plastic bag
- rolling pin
- wipes

HOW ROCKS CHANGE

Preparation: Photocopy the From Rock to Soil activity on page 83, making one copy for each child.

Directions: Distribute From Rock to Soil activity to children. Children color and discuss the contents.

Say: Let's talk about the ways the huge rocks of Earth become tiny bits in the soil! As you color, think of the kinds and colors of dirt you have seen. The dirt doesn't look like those huge rocks anymore. **Earth changes but Jesus stays the same!**

Materials

- From Rock to Soil, page 83
- crayons or markers

FROM ROCKS TO SOIL

Jesus Christ is the same yesterday, today, and forever.
Hebrews 13:8

Color the rock cycle.

Rocks are weathered by sun, wind, rain, freezing, and other elements.

Bits of rock are washed and blown down into valleys.

Over time, bits of rock mix with dead plant matter. Rock becomes soil!

EARTH CHANGES BUT JESUS STAYS THE SAME

17. HOUSE ON SOLID GROUND

MATTHEW 7:24–29

Don't just listen to God's word. You must do what it says.
Otherwise, you are only fooling yourselves.
James 1:22

BIG IDEA

DO MORE THAN LISTEN—DO WHAT GOD SAYS

OVERVIEW

Say: Jesus told his friends—and us—that it's not enough to hear things from the Bible. Jesus said that if anything important was going to happen, people had to do something with the words they heard. What do you think it means to put something into practice? (*Children respond.*)

When we learn to do something, say tie our shoes, it's good to get information. We might watch a video about tying our shoes. We might have another person show us how. We could read instructions all about tying your shoes. What would happen if you KNEW in your head how to tie your shoes, but you never tried it? (*Children respond.*) If we're going to grow, we have to **do more than listen—we must do what God says!** (*Open with prayer requests, praises, and a time of prayer.*)

BIBLE STORY

People loved to listen to Jesus. They loved to crowd around and hear him teach and watch him heal people. But Jesus knows how we humans are. We listen to things—even important things—and then, we often forget them. We don't DO anything about the things we hear. Jesus understands what we are like, because he made us human beings!

Jesus knew that the best way for us to be happy is for us to live in ways that make God smile. And God wants us to DO what he says, not just LOOK like we're paying attention. So Jesus told a short story with this message: it is much more important to DO what God tells us than it is to only hear those things.

(*Read Matthew 7:24–25 aloud.*) Jesus said that when we practice what we hear, we are like a wise man who built his house on the rock. That doesn't sound easy, does it? What might make it harder to build on a rock? (*Children respond.*) Why do you think it might be a good thing to build on a rock? (*Children respond.*) This man knew that things might change. It might not always be sunny and bright. One day, a storm might come. So he built his house in a way that would make it ready for whatever happened—rain, wind, earthquakes—he was ready!

Jesus told about another builder, too. (*Read Matthew 7:26 aloud.*) This man did what was easier. He built his house on the sand area. It was flat, and easy to bring materials there. He probably had a nice view of the water, too!

Both houses had to stand when a storm came. What do you think happened to the house on the sand? (*Children respond.*) Let's find out. (*Read Matthew 7:27 aloud.*) What made the difference in how the houses weathered the storm? (*Children respond.*) The houses' foundations mattered! Rock is stronger than sand.

Everyone has hard times. Jesus even told us that in this world, we'll have troubles. Those times are like storms in our lives. When hard times come to us, it's important that we are ready. How do you think you can be ready for hard times? (*Children respond.*) When we have listened to what God says, and we have DONE the things God says, it makes us strong! During those hard times, we will remember God is with us. We'll be stronger. We won't be knocked down by the hard times. We'll be like the house built on the rock! Jesus told us to **do more than listen—do what God says!**

OPENING GAME
SIMON SAYS

Directions: A volunteer commands the group to do various actions. Children must obey the commands only if the command begins with the phrase, "Simon says." Include actions such as: lift your knees to your chin, run in place, pretend to be an elephant, act like a monkey, etc.

Say: When your mom tells you to do something like feed the cat, do you do it or not? (*Children respond.*) When your dad tells you to take out the trash, do you do it or not? Why? (*Children respond.*) When you read something in the Bible that God says to do, do you do it or not? (*Children respond.*) Why? What do you think might happen? (*Children respond.*) God always tells us to do things that are for our good—and make him happy! Hearing what God says and then doing what he says is always the best thing to do. Our Bible verse tells us to **do more than listen—do what God says!**

Tip: If playing with younger children, begin with simpler actions (turn around, jump once, shake your head, etc.). If they do something Simon "didn't say," don't eliminate them from the game. Simply say, "That's an oops!" and keep going.

OBJECT LESSON
SINKING SAND

Tip: If you have space, make several setups so that each child can try this experiment.

Preparation: Fill the pan about halfway with sand. Pour enough water into the pan to fill it to just below the surface of the sand.

Say: Today we learned about two men who built homes. One chose a strong foundation and one did not. What makes rock a stronger foundation than sand? (*Children respond.*) This experiment will show us how it works.

Directions: A volunteer pushes the brick into the sand so that it stands on its end.

This brick is going to be our tall building. When a building is built on loose soil, it may look as if the weight of the building would keep it standing. But watch what happens when there is water involved.

Children use cups to make "rain" over their dishpan. **What do you think will happen when it rains really hard?**

Remove the brick. Pour the water out of the dishpan until none is visible on the sand. Push the brick into the sand so that it stands on its end. Watch what happens to this if the ground shakes. Hit the end of the dishpan with the mallet or drum stick to see how the vibrations affect the "building." Try it again.

Say: When soil is added at the edge of water, like a river bottom or lakeshore, it's called terrace fill. The terrace fill has water molecules in the spaces between the bits of soil. The soil looks and acts like it is solid. But if something happens to make the earth shake, the waves of shaking squeeze the soil particles together. The water can't flow away, so for just a moment, the water pushes the soil particles apart from each other. That is called liquefication. The solid becomes liquid! When the soil particles or grains of sand aren't touching anymore, the building is floating for a second—then it falls!

Jesus' story says that the house on the sand will collapse. Maybe that's what happened! When we face hard times, we need to be ready. We need to practice what God says. **Do more than listen—do what God says!**

OPTIONAL ACTIVITIES
BUILDING STRONG

Preparation: Soak dried peas overnight in enough water to cover. Keep the peas covered so they won't dry out.

Materials

- loaf pan or small dishpan
- sand
- water
- thin brick
- cup
- rubber mallet or drumstick

Materials

- whole dried peas
- water
- bowl
- round toothpicks
- paper plates

Directions: Put some peas on one plate, and use another plate as the base for your building.

Push the toothpicks into the peas gently to make shapes and build a building. Let dry.

Say: Does it work better to make a building out of squares or out of triangles? (*Children respond.*) **Can you build a bridge?** (*Children respond.*)

As the peas dry, they will make your building stronger! What does Jesus say we need to do to be strong on the inside when trouble comes? (*Children respond.*) **Do more than listen—do what God says!**

WISE OR FOOLISH?

Preparation: Draw a line down the center of the whiteboard. At the top of one side, write "WISE" and at the other side, write "FOOLISH."

Directions: Form teams; players choose a team color of marker. At your signal, players take turns to run to the board. Children write or draw either a wise or a foolish choice on the appropriate side of the board. Children run back to pass the marker to next player on team. Play continues until one team has completed the relay.

First team to finish chooses to tell a reason why one choice on the board is wise or foolish. Continue to discuss the answers on the board, inviting teams to take turns choosing which one to answer.

Say: Some of these are funny. Others are kind of sad! But which of these wise choices do you think would help you be strong on the inside when trouble comes? (*Children respond.*) **Do more than listen—do what God says!**

Materials
- whiteboard
- dry-erase markers in several colors

GET STRONG CHALLENGE

Preparation: Photocopy the Get Strong Challenge on page 88, making one copy for each child.

Say: This week, let's take the "Get Strong Challenge!" Let's make a list of ways we could **do more than listen—do what God says!** Write or draw inside the circles. Maybe you would like to draw pictures of yourself doing these things. They will help you get strong on the inside.

Directions: Distribute Get Strong Challenge to children. Brainstorm together ideas children could do in each of these locations that would help them to do what God says. In each circle, children write or draw something that they can do to please God in each location.

Materials
- Get Strong Challenge, page 88
- crayons or markers

GET STRONG CHALLENGE

Write or draw things that you can do in each location to please God.

DO MORE THAN LISTEN—DO WHAT GOD SAYS

Home

School

Church

18. GOOD SOIL, GOOD FRUIT

LUKE 8:5–15; GALATIANS 5:22–23

The Holy Spirit produces this kind of fruit in our lives: love, joy, peace, patience, kindness, goodness, faithfulness, gentleness, and self-control.
Galatians 5:22–23

BIG IDEA

BE LIKE GOOD SOIL—FULL OF GOOD FRUIT

OVERVIEW

Say: What's your favorite fruit? (*Children respond.*) **Where does your favorite fruit grow?** (*Children respond.*) **What kinds of weather does it need?** (*Children respond.*) **What is one more thing besides weather and rain that we need if we want to grow good fruit?** (*Children respond.*) **The thing that is needed is good soil.**

Today, we're going to talk about how those rocks and mountains become good soil that grows good fruit! Jesus told a story about good soil because God wants us to **be like good soil—full of good fruit!** (*Open with prayer requests, praises, and a time of prayer.*)

BIBLE STORY

Say: How would you describe dirt that is good for growing plants? (*Children respond.*) **Listen to this story that Jesus told about good soil.** (*Read Luke 8:5–8 aloud.*) **Not many seeds can grow on footpaths, on rocks, or in thorns. They need good soil to prosper.**

Jesus' friends and disciples knew the story was about MORE than just good farming or the quality of the soil. So they asked him what the story meant.

Jesus was talking about people's hearts—who they are on the inside. He first described people who HEAR something God says but don't really pay attention. (*Read Luke 8:11–12 aloud.*) **Because they don't pay attention, the devil takes the good seed—the same way a bird steals seeds off the footpath.**

What was the second kind of soil? (*Children respond.*) **It was rocky. Here is what Jesus said about that kind of soil.** (*Read Luke 8:13 aloud.*) **Sometimes, people decide to follow Jesus, but then they give up when it gets hard for them. The roots of God's word couldn't go deep inside.**

There were two other kinds of soil. Both kinds grew plants—but listen for what the difference is between them! (*Read Luke 8:14–15 aloud.*) **What is the difference between the seed that fell into thorny soil and the seed that fell into good soil?** (*Children respond.*) **It wasn't about how pretty the**

plants were. It wasn't about how nice and straight the stems grew. The important thing was whether or not there was fruit! People with good-soil hearts patiently grow the good fruit of the Holy Spirit!

What are the fruits of the Spirit? (*Read Galatians 5:22–23 aloud.*) These aren't fruit like apples and bananas. But just like an apple tree expresses its full ability by producing apples, so God's Spirit produces fruit inside us. God expresses himself through US when we show love, joy, peace, patience, kindness, goodness, faithfulness, gentleness, and self-control. God wants us to **be like good soil—full of good fruit!**

OPENING GAME
FRUIT BASKET UPSET

Preparation: Set chairs in a circle, one for each child (except for "It"). Write out Galatians 5:22–23 on a whiteboard where children can easily see it.

Directions: Place a volunteer to be "It" in the middle of the circle. Children play a game like Fruit Basket Upset. Children count off by fives. The number ones are given the name of love, number twos are joy, threes are peace etc. (Feel free to switch up the fruits with each round.)

"It" calls out a fruit of the Holy Spirit—or a combination of fruits. Children with that fruit name must get up and switch seats, while "It" tries to steal one of their seats. Players may not keep the same seat. The person in the center can also yell "fruit basket upset," at which point everyone gets up and switches seats. Person left without a seat becomes the new "It."

Say: This game should help us remember what kinds of fruit our lives should grow if our hearts are like that good soil in Jesus' story. God wants us to **be like good soil—full of good fruit!**

OBJECT LESSON
MAKING GOOD DIRT

Say: I hope all of you have played in the dirt before! Dirt is AMAZING! It's the thin layer of Earth's crust on which EVERYTHING depends. It holds water. It holds air. It is full of living molds and microbes—and without it, food doesn't grow! So it's good to know what is in it, and how to take care of it.

Directions: Fill each of the three jars half full of dirt. Add just enough water to each jar to make mud. Tap the jar and let the mud settle. Mark the level of the soil on each jar.

Add a teaspoon full of water softener salts to each jar. Fill each jar the rest of the way with water.

Children shake the jars until the soil, salts, and water are well mixed. Wait at least forty seconds. Mark where the bottom level of the soil is layered. Keep watching to see the other layers settle out. (This may take some time, so children may wish to check it before they leave or even keep it until next lesson.)

Say: Do you know what is in soil? (*Children respond.*) Let's find out! This soil came from three different areas—so we'll see if the soils have different mixtures. When we add the salts or water softener, they separate the clumps of soil into the small particles, so that the particles can settle by size.

Soil is made up of three parts. We can see three layers in the settled soil in each jar: sand at the bottom, silt in the middle, and clay on top. Anything floating on the top is organic matter (the remains or waste of plants and animals.)

The thickest layer in your jar determines your soil type. You can measure the thickness of these layers to calculate the percentage of sand, silt, and clay in your soil. Ideal garden soil has some of each type.

- Sand helps with drainage. Too much sand, and the soil doesn't hold the water.
- Silt is decomposing organic matter. It boosts the minerals.
- Clay traps moisture and keeps nutrients from washing away. But too much clay closes up air gaps in soil. Then, plant roots and beneficial microbes suffocate.

So with a fairly equal mix of these three elements, plus organic matter, we get GOOD SOIL! And what does good soil grow? (*Children respond.*) Yes! Good fruit! God wants us to **be like good soil—full of good fruit**!

OPTIONAL ACTIVITIES
DIRT CUPS

Note: Feeds ten children.

Preparation: Measure out milk required by pudding mix directions (usually 2 cups) into the jar. Close jar and refrigerate until time for use. Place cookies in resealable plastic bag, pressing out most of the air.

Directions: Add pudding mix and shake ingredients together in the jar. Pour out some pudding into each of the ten cups. Meanwhile, children crush the cookies into small bits by using a rolling pin over the bag of cookies. When this layer is ready, pour a little over each cup of pudding. Add a gummy worm and eat!

Materials

- 1 package chocolate pudding mix (large size)
- milk
- large jar with lid (32-ounce size)
- cooler
- about 15 chocolate sandwich cookies
- resealable plastic bag
- small cups (4-ounce size)
- rolling pin
- gummy worms
- spoons

Say: Real dirt has layers like our dirt cups do. What shows us that there is good dirt? (*Children respond.*) Yes! It's good fruit! God wants us to **be like good soil—full of good fruit!**

PLANT EXPLORING

Preparation: Gather a variety of plant pieces from different kinds of plants—stems, leaves, flowers, small fruit, etc. and seal each different kind into a resealable plastic bag.

Directions: Children explore the plant materials and talk about what plants smell like, look like, what plants need, etc. Have the children each choose one of the plants to sketch or draw and color. Children write the memory verse below the picture. Display the plant art.

Say: Some of these plants grow food we use. But every plant grows some kind of fruit. We don't grow edible fruit, but we can grow spiritual fruit. Can you name one of the fruits of God's Spirit? (*Children respond.*) **The fruit of the Spirit shows others that God's Spirit is inside us! God wants us to be like good soil—full of good fruit!**

> ### Materials
>
> - a variety of plant pieces
> - resealable plastic bags
> - paper
> - crayons and markers

WHAT'S IN YOUR SOIL?

Preparation: Photocopy Good Soil Puzzle on page 93, making one copy for each child.

Say: Let's name the four kinds of soil Jesus talked about. (*Children respond.*) How do we know the soil is good? (*Children respond.*) **Yes! Good fruit! God wants us to be like good soil—full of good fruit!**

Directions: Distribute Good Soil Puzzle to children. Children fill in the code. The first number below each blank refers to the numbers on the horizontal axis. The second number refers to the number on the vertical axis. Write the letter found at the intersection of these two numbers on the blanks. The first one is done for you.

> ### Materials
>
> - Good Soil Puzzle, page 93
> - crayons or markers

Answer Key: GOOD SOIL GROWS GOOD FRUIT

GOOD SOIL PUZZLE

Fill in the code using the garden grid. The first number below each blank refers to the number at the top of the garden grid. The second number refers to the number on the left side. Write the letter found at the intersection of these two numbers on the blanks.

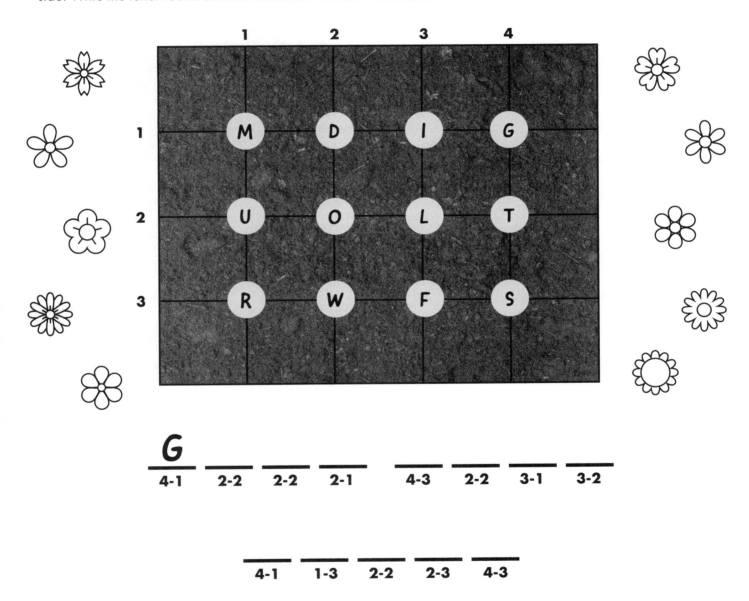

$$\underline{G} \quad \underline{} \quad \underline{} \quad \underline{} \qquad \underline{} \quad \underline{} \quad \underline{} \quad \underline{}$$

4-1   2-2   2-2   2-1   4-3   2-2   3-1   3-2

4-1   1-3   2-2   2-3   4-3

4-1   2-2   2-2   2-1   3-3   1-3   1-2   3-1   4-2

19. MOSES AND BITTER WATER

EXODUS 15:22–27

As the deer longs for streams of water,
so I long for you, O God.
Psalm 42:1

BIG IDEA

WE NEED GOD EVEN MORE THAN WATER

OVERVIEW

Say: What are reasons we need water? Let's see how many we can list. (*Children respond. Use a whiteboard and dry-erase marker to note children's answers.*) Look at our list. It is easy to see that we need water for MANY reasons! Water is the basis for everything that is alive on our planet. Without water, no food can grow. Without water, we will die! It's the most important thing we can get—except for God! **We need God even more than water!** (*Open with prayer requests, praises, and a time of prayer.*)

Materials

- whiteboard
- dry-erase marker

BIBLE STORY

Say: Tell me about a time when you were VERY thirsty. (*Children respond.*) We don't always think about water until our bodies tell us that we NEED water! After God got his people, the Israelites, out of slavery in Egypt, they had to walk through a DESERT to get to the land God had promised to them.

There was many THOUSANDS of people—and all their animals, too! What might be a problem for them if they were traveling through a desert? (*Children respond.*) There were SO many people; it was like a whole CITY was moving across the desert! And these people needed water EVERY day!

They were THIRSTY! Their animals were thirsty! They hadn't found any water for three days. Their leader, Moses, lead them to an oasis, and listen to what happened. (*Read Exodus 15:22–24 aloud.*) The water didn't taste good!

Can you imagine finally finding water in the desert and then not drinking it? Crazy! What do you think Moses did? (*Children respond. Read Exodus 15:25 aloud.*)

What did Moses do? (*Children respond.*) **Yes! He PRAYED!** He needed GOD even more than he needed water. God told Moses what to do. And what God told Moses didn't make sense to Moses—but Moses knew that obeying God is ALWAYS the smartest thing to do! God loved and cared for these people. And he wanted them to listen to him and do what he told them, because God ALWAYS knows much, much more than any human being! We know water is IMPORTANT! But **we need God even more than water.**

OPENING GAME

WATER UP

Preparation: Mark a start line with masking tape for a two-team relay. About eight feet away, lay a tarp or towel. Tape down the tarp or towel. Fill glasses with water (both nearly full). Set glass of water on either side of tarp or towel.

Directions: Children form two equal teams and line up at start line. At your signal, children take turns to run to the team's glass and insert a penny into the water. After one glass overflows, play stops. Children notice how the water has risen above the rim of the glass that has not overflowed. Dump water into bucket and then count pennies to declare a winner. Winning team repeats the memory verse.

Say: How can you make a glass of water more than full, without adding water? (*Children respond.*) **Let's play a game to find out!**

> ### Materials
> - masking tape
> - tarp or towel
> - 2 clear glasses
> - water
> - pennies
> - bucket

Why do you think we could put so many pennies into a glass of water that is already nearly full? (*Children respond.*) **Water is made up of tiny bits called molecules. The molecules form strong bonds on the surface. Some people describe it as holding hands. The molecules keep on holding hands even as the water rose above the rim of the glass. Water has many different properties; our game just showed us one of them! God's gift of water is amazing—but we need God even more than water!**

OBJECT LESSON
SKINNING WATER

Tip: This experiment can easily be set up for small groups of four or more, making a set for each group.

Preparation: Fill plastic bowl halfway with water. Fill shallow container with a small amount of dish detergent.

Directions: Lay two toothpicks side by side in the water. Notice what they do.

Take a third toothpick and pick up a drop of detergent on its end. Touch the soapy toothpick tip between the floating toothpicks.

Say: Our game showed us how water has this amazing ability to stick together on its surface—the molecules seem to "hold hands." But what does it take to make the molecules STOP holding onto each other? (*Children respond.*) **Let's find out!**

Because water molecules hold on to each other, some people call them sticky molecules. It is like a thin skin on the surface of the water. This is called surface tension. It is that tension that keeps the toothpicks floating on top.

When the detergent touches the water, it breaks the molecular bonds on the surface between the toothpicks. This makes the water molecules move outward—and take the toothpicks with them! We used detergent to break the skin of the water.

There are so many ways we rely on water: we need it for washing things, and detergent helps that process! But **we need God even more than water!**

Materials

- plastic or paper bowl
- water
- toothpicks
- shallow container
- dish detergent

OPTIONAL ACTIVITIES
SEED SPROUTING

Preparation: Several days ahead, lay some dry seeds between layers of paper towel and pour a little water into the tin. Take photos of the daily progress to show children.

Directions: Give each child a paper towel, clear cup, and several dry seeds. Children observe your sprouted seeds and your photos. Children make their own "sprouters" to take home.

Say: What do we need to change these dry seeds into living sprouts? (*Children respond.*) Yes! Water! We need water for MANY things! Moses and the Israelites needed water to survive the desert and God provided for their needs. But **we need God even more than water!**

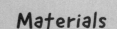

Materials

- dry seeds
- paper towels
- water
- pie tin
- camera or phone with camera
- photos of the plant progress
- clear plastic cups

EDIBLE SILLY PUTTY

Directions: In the bowl, children help you to mix cornstarch with the sugar-free gelatin mix. Add water a little at a time, while children stir. When mix reaches a dough-like consistency, stop adding water. Add a little more cornstarch if mixture becomes too wet. Children clean hands with wipes before taking a sample of putty to play with.

Say: Water is a powerful element of nature. It can be a rushing river that cuts through rock or it can be a calm lake. Water has the ability to change landscapes. In today's activity, we'll see water's ability to change something from a solid to a liquid and back again.

- What do you see when we mix the cornstarch with the gelatin mix? What changes?
- When we add water, what changes do you see? Why do you think this happens?
- What do you notice about the putty as you squeeze it, mold it, and roll it?

To make this fun putty, we needed water! But **we need God even more than water!**

Tip: Because someone will (of course) taste this, putty can be eaten and is non-toxic.

Materials

- bowl
- ½ cup cornstarch
- ½ large package sugar-free gelatin (half of a 1.55-ounce package)
- water
- spoon
- wipes

HOW MUCH WATER?

Preparation: Photocopy the Amazing Water Facts on page 98, making one copy for each child.

Directions: Distribute Amazing Water Facts to children. Children draw a line from each water fact to the referenced body part and color page.

Say: Wow! What amazing things water does for every single human that is alive! What percentage of water did you think your body is? (*Children respond.*) You're VERY full of water! We need water ALL of the time! But **we need God even more than water!**

Materials

- Amazing Water Facts, page 98
- crayons or markers

AMAZING WATER FACTS

As the deer longs for streams of water, so I long for you, O God.
Psalm 42:1

An average human drinks about 13,000 gallons of water in a lifetime. What does water do for us? Draw a line from the water fact to the body part it helps.

Helps joints move

Cools us down with sweat

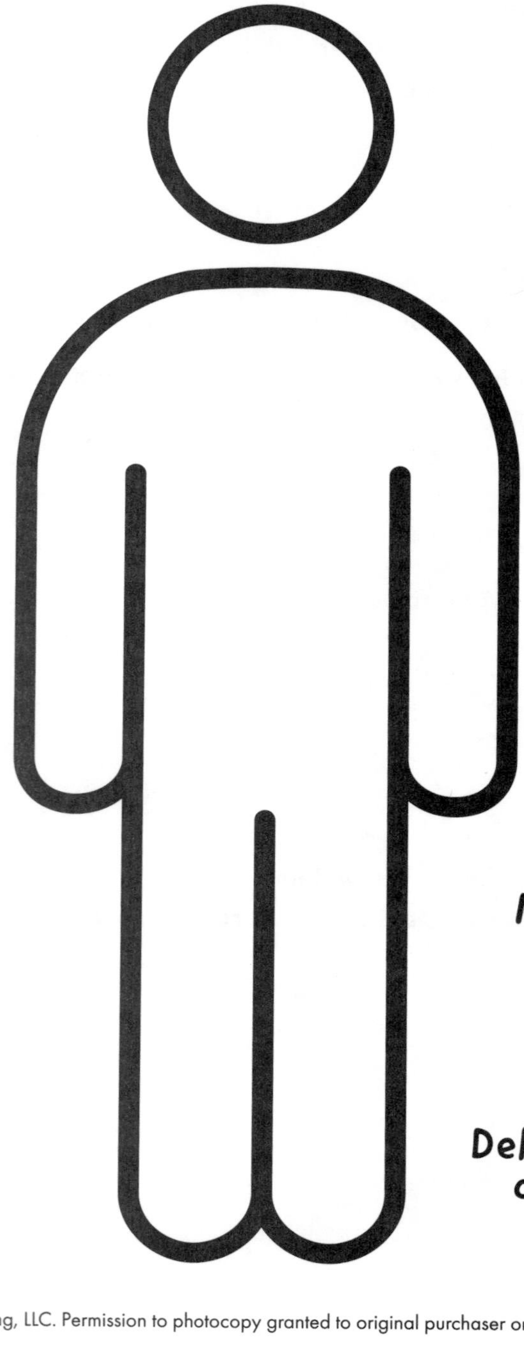

At different ages, people have different percentages of water in their bodies. Newborn babies have about 75%. By one year of age, kids have about 65%. Men have about 60% and women about 55%. Fill the body with how much water you think you have based on your age.

Makes up 75% of muscles

Gets rid of body waste

Makes saliva so we can digest food

Helps hormones so our brains work

Delivers oxygen all over the body

20. DAVID AND BATHSHEBA

2 SAMUEL 11—12:26

Create in me a clean heart, O God. Renew a loyal spirit within me.
Psalm 51:10

BIG IDEA

GOD WANTS US TO BE PURE

OVERVIEW

Say: (*Show children the jar of muddy water you brought for today's experiment.*)
Who would like to drink this water? (*Children respond.*) Who would like to take
a bath in this water? (*Children respond.*) How about washing your clothes?
Who would like to wash their clothes in this water? (*Children respond.*)

Why don't you want to use this water for drinking or bathing or washing
clothes? (*Children respond.*) Why do you think it is important to have
pure water? (*Children respond.*) We can't do much with dirty water, can
we? It needs to be made pure! It is the same with people. **God wants us to be pure!** We'll
talk more about that later. (*Open with prayer requests, praises, and a time of prayer.*)

Materials

- large jar of muddy water

BIBLE STORY

Say: When we looked at our jar of water, we knew that it needed something. What does
it need? (*Children respond.*) Yes! It needs to be clean and pure before we can use it.

What is sin? (*Children respond.*) Sin is separating ourselves from God. It isn't
just doing something wrong on the outside. It is turning away from God in our
minds and hearts. Soon, we're not pure and clean on the inside.

One time, King David decided to turn from God
and do what HE wanted. He was supposed to be
out with his soldiers, but he decided to stay home
instead—and he got into a lot of trouble! David had
a great and strong soldier on the battlefield named
Uriah. While Uriah was out fighting the enemy and
protecting his people, King David STOLE Uriah's wife.

And THEN, listen to what he did. (*Read 2 Samuel 11:14–16 aloud.*) **Wow. King David wanted Uriah to be KILLED! What do you think happened?** (*Children respond. Read 2 Samuel 11:17 aloud.*)

God was NOT pleased with what David had done! He had turned away from being close to God. Then he stole. Then he killed. And he did it because he was king. So he also disrespected the important job God had given him.

God sent a man named Nathan to David. Nathan was a prophet. He had a message from God for David. First, he told David about a rich man who stole a poor man's only little lamb. David was angry! (*Read 2 Samuel 12:5–9.*) When Nathan told David, "YOU are that man!" David realized that God knew EVERYTHING he had done—even his selfish heart attitude.

The good news is, David asked God to forgive him. **Do you think God could forgive David? Why or why not?** (*Children respond.*) God wants us to confess our wrong doings, but also our heart attitudes. God promises to forgive us when we confess our sins. **God wants us to be pure!**

OPENING GAME
VERSE VOLLEY

Preparation: Write the Bible memory verse where it is easily seen. Set a few chairs in a row across the playing area to represent "the net." Blow up balloons.

Directions: Children form even teams. Teams stand on either side of the row of chairs. Child bats the balloon across the chairs to the other team while saying the first word of the verse. Child who receives the balloon, bats it back across while repeating the second word of the verse. Volley continues with the goal of repeating the entire verse while volleying the balloon back and forth. If balloon pops, use an extra one—or increase the challenge by using several balloons and forming smaller teams.

Materials
• whiteboard
• dry-erase marker
• chairs
• balloons

Say: We're learning the words of our verse while we play our game! **What do you think sin is?** (*Children respond.*) Those are all good ideas. **But what happens in our hearts when we ask for forgiveness?** (*Children respond.*) I'm glad that God promises to forgive us when we confess our sins. **God wants us to be pure!**

OBJECT LESSON
NO MORE MUD

Preparation: Fill one clean jar halfway with water. Stretch cheesecloth over the mouth of the empty clean jar so that it sags a bit in the center. Secure cloth with the rubber band.

Say: (*Hold up jar of muddy water.*) Earlier, we saw this jar of muddy water. What do you think could be done to make this water usable again? (*Children respond.*) Today, let's make some more muddy water, and we'll find a way to make it more pure!

Directions: Volunteer adds some soil to the jar half-filled with water. Put the lid on tightly. Another volunteer shakes the jar to make muddy water. A third volunteer spoons sand onto the cheesecloth.

Say: When King David sinned his heart became like this muddy jar of water. When he asked for forgiveness, look what happened.

Children take turns to pour water slowly through the sand. Others observe what is happening.

- What happens when we pour the muddy water through the sand?
- How does the water in the second jar look?
- How is it different from our big jar of muddy water?
- What is happening to change the water?

This water is more pure than it was, but it is not perfectly pure yet. When we sin and ask for forgiveness, we can become more pure, but we can't be completely clean without God's help. Jesus died so that when God looks at us, he doesn't see the muddy water, he sees the purely clean water. I'm glad that when we confess our sins, God promises to forgive us completely! **God wants us to be pure!**

Tip: If time allows, try filtering the jar of muddy water you brought. Is it harder? Easier? Why or why not?

Materials
- 2 clean jars with lids
- water
- 8-inch square of cheesecloth
- heavy rubber band
- large jar containing muddy water
- large spoon
- soil
- sand

OPTIONAL ACTIVITIES

GOD ERASES SINS

Directions: Give each child a sheet of paper and a prepared pencil. Child uses the pencil to color over the page, and then uses the eraser to "erase write" a message about forgiveness (such as, "God's forgiveness makes me pure inside" or "God forgives me!" etc.)

Say: What are pencils made from? (*Children respond.*) Graphite and clay! Graphite is a kind of soft rock. It leaves a dark mark. But even when the paper is gray with graphite, the rubber in an eraser rolls that soft graphite off the page. When God forgives us, it's even better than erasing—God forgives us and forgets our sin! **God wants us to be pure!**

Materials

- paper
- sharpened pencils (#2 pencils work best)
- new pencil-top erasers

CLEAR AGAIN

Directions: While children watch, add red food coloring to the clear water. After discussion, pour the bleach into the red water to see the color disappear.

Say: The Bible says that when we sin, it's like a big red stain. I made the water red. Do you think that it can be made clear again? (*Children respond. Pour the bleach into the red water.*)

After I poured bleach into the water, what happened? (*Children respond.*) The water cleared up! When our sin makes a mess of our hearts, Jesus' forgiveness is like that bleach. God's forgiveness takes it all away. **God wants us to be pure!**

Materials

- red food coloring
- jar or glass
- water
- bleach

SQUEAKY CLEAN

Preparation: Photocopy Pure Water on page 103, making one copy for each child.

Directions: Distribute Pure Water to children. Children color the steps of the purifying process and discuss the page.

Say: We have talked about filtering water to make it more pure. But what else needs to happen for water to be safe to drink? (*Children respond.*) Yes. Like sin other people can't see, there are sometimes bacteria or viruses in water that looks pure. God doesn't want us to LOOK pure, he wants us to BE pure, even where no one else can see. **God wants us to be pure!**

Materials

- Pure Water, page 103
- crayons or markers

PURE WATER

Create in me a clean heart, O God. Renew a loyal spirit within me.
Psalm 51:10

1. **River:** they are full of dirt, sand, and bacteria. *Draw a river.*

2. **Coagulation:** chemicals are added to make the particles in the water clump together. *Draw clumps in the water.*

3. **Sedimentation:** the clumped up stuff settles to the bottom. *Draw clumps at the bottom.*

4. **Filtration:** the water is filtered, sometimes several times. *Draw a mesh screen.*

5. **Disinfection:** the water has chemicals like chlorine added. These chemicals kill the bacteria and viruses we can't see. *Draw soap.*

6. **Clean water:** water is ready to drink. *Draw a glass of water.*

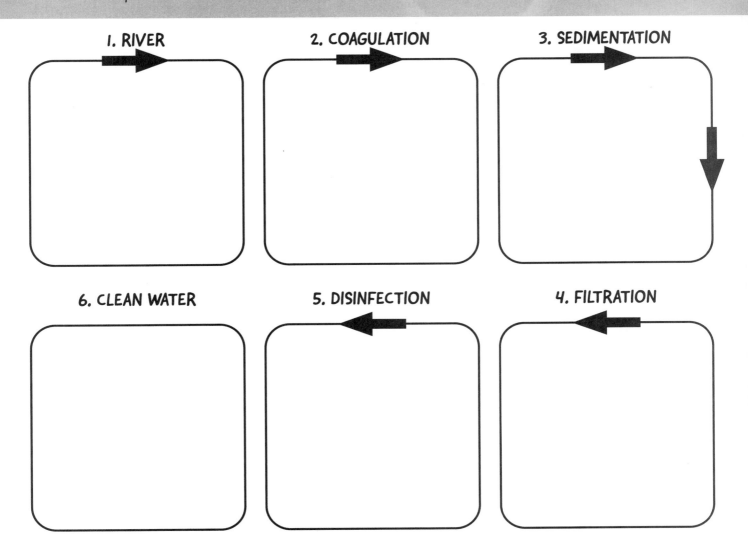

21. JESUS' FIRST DISCIPLES

LUKE 5:1–11

All glory to God, who is able, through his mighty power at work within us, to accomplish infinitely more than we might ask or think.
Ephesians 3:20

BIG IDEA

GOD DOES MORE THAN WE CAN IMAGINE

OVERVIEW

Say: Have you ever felt like you were having a bad day that was just going to get worse? (*Children respond.*) How do you feel when you're having a bad day? (*Children respond.*) Sometimes people want to curl up in their bed and disappear. Other times, they want to run or play games to keep their mind off things. No matter how you are feeling, you can always turn to God. **God does more than we can imagine.** (*Open with prayer requests, praises, and a time of prayer.*)

BIBLE STORY

Say: One day, when Jesus was teaching people beside the Sea of Galilee. Some fishermen were washing out their fish nets. Their day had already gone badly. They'd been up all night trying to catch fish. But guess what happened? (*Children respond.*) NOTHING. They had not caught a single fish!

When they looked up from their nets, they saw the crowd of people around Jesus. The crowd kept pushing closer and closer so they could hear and see him. Jesus was about to step into the sea! (*Read Luke 5:1–3 aloud.*)

Jesus wanted to use Simon Peter's boat to preach to the crowds. Simon Peter was glad for Jesus to use his boat. After all, there was no reason to go fishing again! Jesus got into the boat and they pushed it out from shore a little ways. Now, Jesus could talk without everyone standing so close.

After Jesus had finished talking, he asked Simon Peter to pull the boat back to land. Then Jesus asked him to do something more. What do you think Jesus asked him to do? (*Children respond. Read Luke 2:4 aloud.*)

Jesus told him to go fishing. WHAT? Simon Peter was washing his nets. He was finished with fishing! But there was something about Jesus' request that made Simon Peter hopeful!

Listen to how Simon Peter responded. (*Read Luke 2:5 aloud.*) Simon Peter was willing to give it one more try—just because Jesus said to! Can you guess what happened? (*Children respond.*) Listen to see if your predictions are correct! (*Read Luke 2:6–7 aloud.*)

Simon Peter caught so many fish that the nets began to rip! He was struck with amazement. He fell on his knees in front of Jesus and said, "I'm a sinner! You shouldn't stay around me!" But Jesus WANTED to be with Simon Peter. He WANTED Simon Peter to do something different with his life! (*Read Luke 2:9–11 aloud.*)

Jesus' plan for Simon Peter and his friends was to follow Jesus. They were to bring people to Jesus! They didn't need to worry about providing for their families for a while. There was SO MANY FISH! Now Simon Peter and his friends could follow Jesus and know their families would be taken care of. **God does more than we can imagine!**

OPENING GAME
FISH TOSS

Preparation: Mark a start and finish line with masking tape. About four feet behind the finish line, set the basket or bucket for each team.

Directions: Children form even teams, and line up at the start line. Children remove one shoe. This is the fish each one will toss. At your signal, first child in line runs to finish line with shoe in hand, tosses it into the basket or bucket and returns to tag the next player.

Play continues until all have put their "fish" in the bucket. If a child misses the bucket, they must go to the back of the line and try again.

Say: When we played this game, those who missed the basket the first time got more chances to get it in. That's the way God's goodness works in our lives, too. Today, we're going to learn about some fishermen who had a really bad day. Then, Jesus gave them some advice that changed everything! When we follow Jesus, we can trust him to do much more than we ask. **God does more than we can imagine!**

Materials

- masking tape
- 1 shoe from each child
- large basket or bucket (one per team)

OBJECT LESSON
FISH FLOATING

Preparation: Fill large bowl two-thirds full with water. Fill soda bottles nearly full with water.

Say: What did Simon Peter and his friends use to fish? (*Children respond.*) Fishing nets! Why didn't they just pick fish off the top of the water? (*Children respond.*) The fish didn't float on top of the water. The fishing nets fell deep into the water to pull up the fish. Have you ever wondered why fish can swim up and down, but don't float on top of the water? This will help us to see how fish swim!

Directions: Drop some condiment packets into the bowl of water. Select a packet that floats. Place this packet into one of the bottles and screw the lid on tightly.

Grab the bottle with both hands and squeeze the bottle tightly. Observe, and then release the bottle. Place a different packet inside the bottle and try again.

Say: Which way does the packet move when I squeeze the bottle? (*Children respond.*) Which way did it move when I released the bottle? (*Children respond.*) Did the second packet move in the same way? (*Children respond.*)

Materials

- large bowl
- water
- several 2-liter soda bottles with caps
- condiment packets (ketchup, mustard, soy sauce, etc.)

A bubble of air is sealed inside each of these packets. The bubble of air acts like a fish's swim bladder—an air-filled sac inside the fish's body. When the packet is inside the bottle, there is no pressure on the packet. It floats higher because the air bubble is larger. When I squeeze the bottle, the pressure on the air bubble increases. The packet gets denser and sinks.

This is the way some fish control the way they move. Their swim bladders can squeeze the air inside so they go down. They can relax the bladders so they go up. God is so creative. **God does more than we can imagine!**

OPTIONAL ACTIVITIES
UNDERSEA WONDERS

Preparation: Cue up laptop to show a short video about undersea life.

Directions: Children watch the video about undersea creatures. Children draw pictures with watercolor art materials based on what they viewed. Children use brushes dipped in water to create an undersea effect on their papers.

Materials

- laptop
- watercolor pencils or pastels
- paper
- cups of water
- paint brushes

Say: Jesus knows everything. When Simon Peter and his friends had a bad night for fishing, Jesus knew exactly what to do. What was Jesus' advice? (*Children respond.*) Jesus said to go into deeper water. There are many wonderful and amazing creatures that live underwater. Scientists discover new ones all the time. There is much more under the ocean than we know about. **God does more than we can imagine!**

MUCH MORE PRAYER

Preparation: Glue paper to the lid of the shoebox. Label it, "Much More Prayer."

Directions: Children write or draw something they believe Jesus can do in their lives or in their families. Children fold and place their papers in the Much More Prayer box. Keep the box for several weeks. Children revisit their prayers to see how Jesus has answered them.

Say: Sometimes life can seem hopeless. Simon Peter and his fisherman friends had tried all night to catch fish. They did everything they could think of and they were tired! When we feel tired and hopeless, we can turn to God in prayer. He knows much more than us. **God does more than we can imagine!**

Tip: Instead of a box, begin a class prayer journal with a notebook. You can revisit later to see how Jesus answered these prayers.

Materials

- glue
- paper
- shoebox
- crayons or markers

WORD SCRAMBLE

Preparation: Photocopy the Alphabet Puzzler on page 108, making one for each child.

Directions: Distribute Alphabet Puzzler to children. Children follow directions on page to write out the words of the memory verse.

Say: When we read this verse from the Bible, what are other words we could use? (*Children respond.*) What are some things we can ask Jesus to do? (*Children respond.*) We can ask Jesus for what we need and we can trust him to do even more than we expect! **God does more than we can imagine!**

Answer Key: *All glory to God who is able through his mighty power at work within us to accomplish infinitely more than we might ask or think. Ephesians 3:20*

Materials

- Alphabet Puzzler, page 108
- crayons or markers

ALPHABET PUZZLER

Each letter contains a word of the Bible verse. To put the words in order, work through the alphabet. The first one is done for you. Write the B word in the B blank and so on until you complete the verse!

ALL _____ _____ _____ _____ _____ _____ _____ _____
A   B   C   D   E   F   G   H

_____ _____ _____ _____ _____ _____ _____
I   J   K   L   M   N   O

_____ _____ _____ _____ _____ _____
P   Q   R   S   T   U

_____ _____ _____ _____ _____
V   W   X   Y   Z

22. JESUS IS LIVING WATER

JOHN 4; 7:37–38

The LORD [is] the fountain of living water.
Jeremiah 17:13

BIG IDEA

JOINING GOD'S FAMILY SATISFIES US

OVERVIEW

Say: (*Show a bottle of spring water.*) **What do you think is the difference between drinking water from a spring, like this water, and water that comes from a pond?** (*Children respond.*) **What do you think you would have to do with this water to drink it? Why?** (*Children respond.*) **What would you have to do to pond water so you could satisfy your thirst?** (*Children respond.*) **The Bible tells us that God is like a spring or fountain of living water. What do you think that means?** (*Children respond. Open with prayer requests, praises, and a time of prayer.*)

Materials
- bottle of spring water

BIBLE STORY

Say: We don't think about water much, until we are thirsty! But we all need water to live. For water to be good for us, it must be pure. Bacteria and other things that make us sick can live in water. We can't see those things. But they are harmful to us.

There are two kinds of water, groundwater and surface water. Living water is like groundwater. It is pure and safe to drink. It comes up from under the ground like a spring or fountain.

Surface water comes from the rain. Lakes, ponds, and streams are surface water. Surface water must be boiled or purified before drinking.

In the Old Testament, the prophet Jeremiah called God the "fountain of living water"(Jeremiah 17:13). God is the source of all we need. Later, Jesus said that he can give us living water, too. Listen to what he told a woman who had brought her jug to fill with water. (*Read John 4:7–11 aloud.*)

Do you think Jesus was talking about water to drink? (*Children respond.*) He was telling this woman that by believing in him, he would give her life that satisfied her. Life in Jesus is like having a cool drink of living water—fresh, safe, and pure—on a hot day!

Jesus told the woman at the well other things, too. (*Read John 4:25–26 aloud.*) Jesus told her that he is the Messiah, the one God promised to send. This was good news! The woman believed in Jesus.

The joy and excitement that bubbled up inside her really WAS like a fountain of living water! She couldn't keep it to herself. She went back into the town and brought others to meet Jesus. They believed in him, too!

Later on, Jesus said that the living water he gives us is his Holy Spirit! (*Read John 7:37–38 aloud.*) By believing in Jesus, we receive the Holy Spirit. Living in him is like being able to drink fountain water—pure and safe, good and satisfying. We can have all we want! **Joining God's family satisfies us!**

OPENING GAME
POM POM PICKUP

Preparation: Mark a start line with masking tape. Set bowl of pom poms at one side of playing area about 10 feet from start line. Place a roll of masking tape where each team will line up.

Alternate Idea: Use cotton balls instead of craft pom poms.

Directions: Children form even teams. Teams line up behind start line. First player must wrap masking tape around their hand to make a "sticky hand." Player runs to the bowl of pom poms and tries to pick up as many as possible with the "sticky hand." Player then runs back to tag the next player, who must also make a "sticky hand" before running. Play continues until all have run. Teams count the number of pom poms they have. Winners may repeat the memory verse or answer questions first.

Say: This relay has an extra step—you have to make a "sticky hand" in order to pick up pom poms from the bowl. Without sticky hands, it doesn't count!

Today we are talking about being satisfied. What if I told you AFTER this game, that to win, you each had to get ten pom poms on your hand? How would you feel? (*Children respond.*) Would you be satisfied with the number you got, or not satisfied? (*Children respond.*) Being satisfied is being happy or content with something. **Joining God's family satisfies us!**

Materials
- 2 rolls of masking tape
- large bowl
- craft pom poms

OBJECT LESSON
GLORIOUS GROUNDWATER

Say: We've talked about the two kinds of water—surface water and groundwater. Groundwater is like living water because it's safe and satisfying. Let's see how the groundwater system works!

Directions: Pour a layer of white sand into the bottom of the jar or glass. Add a little water, until it wets the sand. Point out how the water is stored in the sand.

Materials
- white play sand
- large clear glass or jar
- pitcher of water
- modeling clay
- clean gravel or small pebbles

Press clay into a flat circle large enough to cover at least half of the sand. Press clay to the glass so it sticks on one side. Pour a little more water onto the clay. Point out how this layer of clay holds the water for a while, until it trickles down around the edges.

Create some hills and valleys with the gravel. These represent the many other layers of Earth's surface. Pour water into this a little at a time, until your valleys are full. Point out how the rocks are porous and the little lakes that came from rainwater will eventually sink down through the rocks. The rainwater will fill the layers below. During that process, the layers will clean out the natural pollutants.

Alternate Idea: Instead of one large jar, use clear plastic cups to create a personal-sized version.

Say: We talked about how groundwater is safe and satisfying. In Bible times, this was true because there wasn't much to pollute the water. The only thing that polluted water was human and animal waste, and that usually was found only in surface water. Today, water treatment systems clean out many other kinds of pollutants. But some chemicals that pollute water are very hard to get rid of.

Groundwater, or living water, becomes chemically polluted when things like motor oil, fertilizer, or pesticide run into our gutters, off our lawns, from farm fields, and many other places. These chemicals are very hard to get rid of. And they can make us sick. So, we never pour chemicals into gutters or ditches or old wells. It is important that we use very little or none of these things. These chemical pollutants can't be cleaned out easily. We want our living water to stay pure and safe and satisfying. Like a drink of good water, **joining God's family satisfies us!**

OPTIONAL ACTIVITIES
MAKE A SPRING

Preparation: Cut cardboard to fit shoebox.
Cut small hole in center of cardboard.

Directions: Lay sponges in a layer on the bottom of the shoebox. Pour water into the shoebox so that it is absorbed by the sponges. Lay the cardboard on top of the sponges. Child volunteer presses down onto the board to see what happens. Water that comes up from around the edge is called a "seep." Water that comes up from the hole may be called a spring.

Say: We can't make a spring perfectly. It's much more amazing than this! But this helps us see how it works.

The layer of sponges in the bottom is like an aquifer. An aquifer is an underground layer of rock that holds water. Like the sponges, the aquifer releases water when pressure is added. In our model, we pressed down on the cardboard to make the water come up. In real life, pressure from inside Earth's crust pushes the water up and out of the aquifer layer.

Materials

- scissors
- cardboard
- several household sponges
- clear plastic shoebox
- water in a pitcher

Sometimes a spring just seeps out of the ground, as around the edges of our cardboard. And sometimes someone will dig a well, and the water has to be pumped out of the well. But if there is more pressure under the ground, the water will SPRING up! Spring water is considered the best water in the world. Like a drink of the best water, **joining God's family satisfies us!**

JOIN GOD'S FAMILY

Directions: Read John 3:16 aloud slowly. Then read it again, inviting each child to say their name in each of the following blanks: "For God so loved _____: He gave his one and only Son, so that _____ who believes in him, _____will not perish but have eternal life."

Explain to children who have not yet joined God's family, and would like to do this, that they can pray and tell Jesus they believe in him.

Alternate Idea: Write the verse on a whiteboard so all children can see.

Say: Like the woman with the water jug, you can ask God to forgive your sins. You can ask to be part of God's Kingdom and family forever—so simple, everyone can do it! Like drinking pure, clean water when we are thirsty, **joining God's family satisfies us!**

> ### Materials
> • Bible

NATURALLY CLEAN

Preparation: Photocopy the What Kind of Water? activity on page 113, making one copy for each child.

Say: We've seen some cool things about cool water today. Let's see what else we can learn about how God gives us pure, clean, and safe groundwater. God is our fountain of living water. He is all we need, because **joining God's family satisfies us!**

Directions: Distribute What Kind of Water? activity to children. Children add clouds and rain above the mountains.

Show pictures from your laptop or from books of geysers, hot springs, wells, and artesian wells.

> ### Materials
> • What Kind of Water? page 113
> • laptop or books with photos of kinds of springs
> • crayons or markers

WHAT KIND OF WATER?

The LORD [is] the fountain of living water.
Jeremiah 17:13

Jesus is living water! Living water is clear and fresh, just like groundwater. Color the picture to show how rain separates into surface water and groundwater. Add clouds and rain above the mountains.

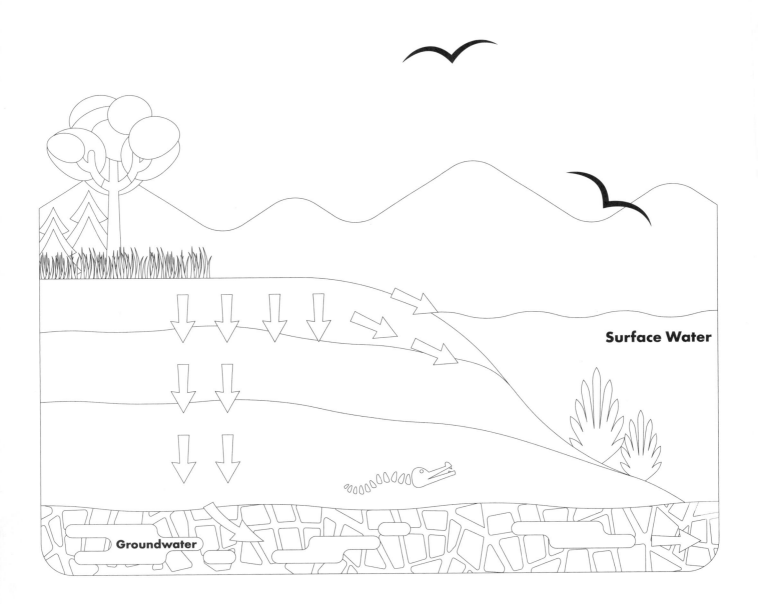

Surface Water

Groundwater

23. PAUL SHIPWRECKED

ACTS 27

The voice of the LORD echoes above the sea. . . .
The LORD thunders over the mighty sea.
Psalm 29:3

BIG IDEA
GOD IS MORE POWERFUL THAN ANYTHING

OVERVIEW

Say: Let's play an ocean trivia game! If you think you know the answer to a question, make a fish face!

- Is the ocean all one body of water? *Yes*

- What are some names we give to parts of the ocean?
  Arctic, Pacific, Atlantic, Indian, and Antarctic

- Does the ocean affect the weather? *Yes, the ocean currents affect air motion which changes air temperature. It also affects, fog formation, rain, and clouds.*

- What do you think can cause waves? *Ocean currents and wind*

Those are all a part of our story today. It's good to know that **God is more powerful than anything!** (*Open with prayer requests, praises, and a time of prayer.*)

BIBLE STORY

Say: The ocean is a powerful force of nature. What do you like best about the ocean? (*Children respond.*) What are some things that are scary about the ocean? (*Children respond.*) Psalm 29:3 tells us that God's voice is like thunder over the oceans. He is the one in charge of them, even when the waves are scary!

Today, we are going to learn about a follower of God named Paul. Paul told people everywhere about Jesus! Some people didn't like this. They got Paul arrested by the Roman government.

Paul decided to travel all the way to far-off Rome so that he could tell his side of the story to the Roman Emperor. Let's imagine we are on a sailing ship with Paul. We've traveled a long way from home and stopped to get supplies on an island. The winds became very strong.

Paul told our ship's captain not to leave this port, but listen to what happened! (*All rock back and forth as you read Acts 27:13–15.*) Wow! Paul's boat was tossed by the mighty wind and waves. Show me how you think the boat was rocking now. (*Children respond.*)

It was getting scary! (*Read Acts 27:18–20 aloud.*) This was a TERRIBLE storm! Everyone on the ship expected to die. There were no motors to power boats back then. If the boat filled with water or hit rocks, it went down!

God was watching over the ship. (*Read Acts 27:21–26 aloud.*) What good news! God sent an angel to tell Paul what would happen. TWO WEEKS later, they finally came close to an island and hit a sandbar. The boat began to break apart, so everyone grabbed anything that would float.

The passengers floated or swam to the beach. Just as God had promised, all the people on the boat were safe. **God is more powerful than anything!** We can always ask for his help, on the ocean or wherever we are!

OPENING GAME
PUZZLING RELAY

Tip: Use puzzles with the same number of pieces. Puzzles with ocean-related images will give children more to talk about!

Preparation: Mark a start line with masking tape for two relay teams. Lay one pile of puzzle pieces for each team at the other side of the playing area.

Directions: At your signal, children take turns to run to the puzzle pieces, grab a piece and then run back to tag the next player. Teams then work together to assemble their puzzles. First team to finish their puzzle repeats the memory verse.

Say: In this game, it doesn't matter who gets their puzzle pieces first. The team that can work together to put their puzzle together is successful.

What pictures are on your puzzles? (*Children respond.*) How long did it take you to guess what the picture might be? (*Children respond.*)

When Paul and his friends were on the ship in the storm, they had to work together, too. They were in a scary situation. But they had God's promise that they all would live. They were glad to know that **God is more powerful than anything!**

Materials

- 20- to 30-piece puzzle for each team
- masking tape

OBJECT LESSON
CREEPING WATER

Tip: Make more than one set up so that smaller groups of children may more easily see.

Directions: Cover area with newspaper or trash bags. Squeeze glue onto the paper plate to create a design of thick lines that intersect. Immediately pour salt over the lines, making sure to cover the glue completely. Shake any excess salt onto glue.

Saturate paintbrush with water so that it is very wet. Dip paintbrush in watercolor paint. Hold paintbrush at one place on a glue line. Watch to see how the salt absorbs the water in the paint, so that the color moves along the lines of glue. After color stops spreading, apply another color of paint at a different place.

Say: Let's see how the salt can pull the colored water along.

Water is made up of tiny bits called molecules. Think of the molecules all holding hands together. When the wet paintbrush touched the salt and glue, the water molecules moved in a line, coloring our salt and glue. Sometimes water is said to have "sticky" molecules. They will move to follow other water molecules.

We had to watch for a while to see how the water moved along as the salt absorbed it. Paul and his friends had to wait for two weeks until God's promise came true! But **God is more powerful than anything** and we can always trust his promises!

> ## Materials
> - newspaper or trash bags
> - glue
> - paper plate
> - salt
> - paintbrush
> - water
> - watercolor paint

OPTIONAL ACTIVITIES
WAVE ACTION

Directions: Use the funnel to fill the water bottle halfway with mineral oil. Add a few drops of food coloring to the bottle. Use the funnel again to fill the bottle the rest of the way with water. Replace cap and then wrap electrical tape tightly around the cap to seal it.

Say: Paul was tossed around by powerful waves, and in the end, the waves tore his ship apart. This bottle shows us how ocean waves work. These waves are easy to see because mineral oil floats on top of the water. God made the ocean waves. **God is more powerful than anything**!

> ## Materials
> - funnel
> - clear plastic water bottle with cap
> - mineral oil
> - blue food coloring
> - water
> - electrical tape

SALTY FLOATING

Preparation: Fill glass ¾ full of water. Cut carrot into a section short enough to float in the glass (or use a baby carrot).

Say: Do you float more easily in salt water than in fresh water? (*Children respond.*) **Let's find out!**

Directions: Drop the carrot into the water. A spoonful at a time, add salt. Keep on adding salt and notice what is happening. Add salt until the carrot has risen to float on the top of the water.

Say: Let's say this carrot is YOU.

- What happens when we drop the carrot into the water?
- What do you think we can do to make the carrot rise all the way to the top of the water?
- Do you think adding salt can make it float?
- Why do you think adding salt makes a difference?

Adding salt makes the water denser. That means that there are more tiny molecules in the water. Instead of just water molecules, now there is salt AND water molecules. The carrot then has more molecules to support it, so it moves higher in the glass.

Paul's ship was in danger of sinking down to the bottom of the ocean. God had a different plan. Like the salt that raised the carrot, God's power made Paul's ship float to safety.

In the same way, salt water in oceans is denser than fresh water. You can float more easily in the ocean than in a lake! And when we float in the ocean, we can remember that **God is more powerful than anything!**

> ## Materials
> - tall clear glass
> - water
> - carrot
> - knife
> - container of salt
> - spoon

MYSTERY IN WATER

Preparation: Photocopy the Ocean Code on page 118, making one copy for each child.

Say: Paul was in a very scary situation. His ship was tossed around by the wind and the waves. He was so confused, until the angel came to visit him. Today, we have a confusing message to complete. When we finish it, God's truth will be clear to us! We can remember that **God is more powerful than anything!**

Directions: Distribute Ocean Code to children. Children solve the code to discover the memory verse.

> ## Materials
> - Ocean Code, page 118
> - crayons or markers
> - books or websites that show the depths and configuration of the ocean floor

OCEAN CODE

Fill in the blanks according to the key at the bottom of the page.

"Th___ v___ ___ c___ ___f th___ L___RD

___ch___ ___s ___b___v___ th___

s___ ___ . . . Th___ L___RD th___nd___rs

___v___r th___ m___ghty s___ ___."

Ps___lm 29:3

A = 🐠 E = 🪸 I = 🐟(stingray) O = 🐚 U = 🐬

24. SUN STANDS STILL

JOSHUA 1:5–9; 10:1–15

Be strong and courageous. Do not be afraid; do not be discouraged.
For the LORD your God is with you wherever you go.
Joshua 1:9

BIG IDEA

GOD IS ALWAYS WITH US

OVERVIEW

Say: Let's see how many kinds of weather we can name! (*Children respond.*)

- What do you like best about a thunderstorm?
- What do you like about snow?
- How big was the biggest hailstone you ever saw?

Sometimes weather can be fun and sometimes, it can be scary. It's good to know that no matter what the weather is like, **God is always with us.** (*Open with prayer requests, praises, and a time of prayer.*)

BIBLE STORY

Say: Moses was the leader of God's people the Israelites. He led the people from slavery in Egypt into the desert. They were on a journey to a beautiful land God had promised them. But Moses disobeyed and God said he would not enter the Promised Land. So Moses told the people that his helper, Joshua, would lead them.

What a big job! Joshua may have wondered if he could handle it. Let's hear what God told Joshua. (*Read Joshua 1:5–9 aloud.*) God said he would be with Joshua and that he would never leave.

No matter what happened, no matter where Joshua went, God would be with him! How do you think God's words made Joshua feel? (*Children respond.*) God did many AMAZING things to help Joshua and the Israelites move into their new homeland! The people of a town called Gibeon could tell that God was with the Israelites, so they asked to be friends with them.

Not everyone was happy about this. (*Read Joshua 10:1–5 aloud.*) Gibeon was under attack by some of the nearby kings! The people of Gibeon called out to Joshua for help. Joshua knew he needed to help his friends.

He gathered up his troops and went into battle. God promised to be with Joshua and the Israelites. (*Read Joshua 10:8 aloud.*) The Israelites won the battle. As their enemies retreated, God sent a terrible hailstorm from the sky to stop the warriors!

Joshua saw that the sun was about to set, so he asked God for a special request. (*Read Joshua 10:12–13 aloud.*) God made the sun stay up until the battle was won. At dinnertime, the sun was still up. At bedtime, the sun was still up.

The sun stayed up for a WHOLE day! Never before or since has anything like this happened. God is more powerful than the forces of nature. He is always in control. Just like God was with Joshua and Israelites, **God is always with us!**

OPENING GAME
HAILSTONE TOSS

Materials
- aluminum foil

Preparation: Make several small balls from pieces of foil.

Directions: Children divide into two lines approximately three feet apart, and face each other. Hand a "hailstone" (foil ball) to the first player in one of the lines. Player tosses it to the player opposite them. Play continues, with the hailstone zigzagging between the lines. When the last player receives the hailstone, they move to the other end of their line and play continues. After a couple rounds, add additional balls.

Say: Boy, the hailstones were flying around in our game! But hailstorms aren't usually this much fun. They can cause a lot of damage. They killed the Israelites' enemies. When difficult times come in our lives, we can remember that **God is always with us!**

Alternate Idea: Instead of using foil balls, use a large foam or rubber ball. Children sit on the floor in a large circle and roll the ball across the circle to each other. As they roll the ball, each child says, **God is with [Drew]**, naming the child to whom they are rolling the ball.

OBJECT LESSON
TINY TORNADO

Materials
- 2 soda bottles, labels removed
- duct tape
- pencil
- pitcher of water
- glitter or bits of grass

Tip: Several setups can be made so small groups can experiment with the bottles more easily.

Say: What is a tornado? (*Children respond.*) A tornado makes the fastest wind on Earth! Near the center of it, called the vortex, the wind may blow at over 200 miles per hour! That's FAST. Let's see how a tornado behaves. It isn't just wind—it is wind in a particular pattern.

Directions: Lay a piece of tape firmly over the mouth of one bottle. Press it down around the bottle's neck.

Use the pencil to make a small hole in the tape that covers the bottle's mouth.

Fill the second bottle nearly full with water. Add some glitter or grass.

Turn the empty bottle upside down and then tightly tape it mouth-to-mouth to the bottle holding the water. Put more tape around the bottles' necks to secure and seal.

Turn the whole thing upside down. Move it around to start the water swirling. Watch to see how the shape of the vortex changes.

Say: Where does the glitter or grass go? (*Children respond.*) How is this like a real tornado? (*Children respond.*)

Tornadoes are related to thunderstorms, which sometimes contain hail like in our Bible story. When storm conditions are right, the wind in a thunderstorm may change directions. The wind gets stronger as it rises and that creates a rotating column of air. This column, or funnel, may not come down to the surface. But when it does, it looks very much like what is happening inside this bottle! No matter how scary the weather may be, **God is always with us!**

OPTIONAL ACTIVITIES
WEATHER MOVES

Say: Weather changes all the time. Let's play a game to see how quickly you can make the weather change!

Directions: With children, create a variety of motions, one for each kind of weather. For example:

- For rain, pat your thighs
- For wind, bend sideways and make loud whooshing sounds
- For a tornado, turn in a circle

Include motions for sunshine, hailstorm, fog, etc.

Call out a kind of weather. Children make the motions and sounds agreed upon until you call out the next kind of weather. To increase the challenge, change the kinds of weather more and more quickly.

Say: Weather can be a lot of fun! Sometimes it is scary. Joshua and the Israelites experienced some crazy weather when they fought their enemies. But no matter how scary the weather or anything else may be, **God is always with us!**

AIR PRESSURE ART

Preparation: Set out paint containers.

Directions: Children place a finger over the top of their straw, and then put their straw into paint. Over their papers, they remove their finger from the top of the straw. Paint will fall onto the paper. Children may then blow the paint as they desire before trying again with another color.

Say: Why does this work? (*Children respond.*) Air pressure! Air is pressing on the surface of the paint. When you put your finger over the end of the straw, you keep the air from pushing down on the paint. That keeps the paint in the straw. When you remove your finger, the air pushes down on the paint again, and it comes out. Air pressure is part of what makes our weather!

Joshua was under a lot of pressure to help his friends the Gibeonites. God told him not to be afraid because God was with him. God performed some miraculous weather signs to protect his people. Whatever the weather, we're glad **God is always with us!**

Materials

- tempera paint in containers
- straws
- paper

WEATHER WORDS

Preparation: Photocopy the Weather Words Puzzle on page 123, making one copy for each child.

Directions: Distribute Weather Words Puzzle to children. Children complete the word search puzzle.

Optional: Play weather sound effects as children work. Encourage them to guess what the sound is.

Say: God controls the weather. He made the sun stand still for Joshua and he sent hailstones on their enemies. There are many types of weather. It may be safe to think that everyone has seen a thunderstorm. But how many of you have ever been in a tornado? (*Children respond.*) **How many know someone who has?** (*Children respond.*) **How about a hurricane?** (*Children respond.*) **A hail storm?** (*Children respond.*) **In every kind of weather, God is always with us!**

Materials

- Weather Words Puzzle, page 123
- crayons or markers

Optional

- weather sound effects and player

```
O C D S D R I Z Z L E A B I S
L O B N V H J I U E V B Y T L
R I L O T E M P E R A T U R E
A G I W U T Y S T O R M Y T E
I A Z H Q H F A L L B S S W T
N O Z U E E W B O W Z P J V E
N B A R V R I H V K E R B P Q
N O R R D M N U E H W I H L Q
S K D I B O T M R A I N B O W
U K E C N M E I C I N G H D A
N X R A N E R D A L D F K L D
N F C N A T C L S D Y L C R Z
Y P Y E D E B N T H U N D E R
P D F S B R B T W T Q B A X Q
W E A T H E R S U M M E R Q R
```

WEATHER WORDS PUZZLE

Be strong and courageous. Do not be afraid; do not be discouraged.
For the LORD your God is with you wherever you go.
Joshua 1:9

BLIZZARD	RAIN	SUNNY
DRIZZLE	RAINBOW	TEMPERATURE
FALL	SLEET	THERMOMETER
HAIL	SNOW	THUNDER
HUMID	SPRING	WEATHER
HURRICANE	STORMY	WINDY
OVERCAST	SUMMER	WINTER

```
O C D S D R I Z Z L E A B I S
L O B N V H J I U E V B Y T L
R I L O T E M P E R A T U R E
A G I W U T Y S T O R M Y T E
I A Z H Q H F A L L B S S W T
N O Z U E E W B O W Z P J V E
N B A R V R I H V K E R B P Q
N O R R D M N U E H W I H L Q
S K D I B O T M R A I N B O W
U K E C N M E I C I N G H D A
N X R A N E R D A L D F K L D
N F C N A T C L S D Y L C R Z
Y P Y E D E B N T H U N D E R
P D F S B R B T W T Q B A X Q
W E A T H E R S U M M E R Q R
```

25. ELIJAH PRAYS FOR RAIN

1 KINGS 17:1–6; 18; JEREMIAH 10:12–13

Ask the Lord for rain in the spring, for he makes the storm clouds. And he will send showers of rain so every field becomes a lush pasture.
Zechariah 10:1

OVERVIEW

BIG IDEA

GOD PROVIDES FOR HIS FOLLOWERS

Say: Tell me about a time when you really wanted it to rain. (*Children respond.*) When was a time when you wanted the rain to stop? (*Children respond.*) Sometimes, we are VERY glad that the rain is falling. Without rain, no plants will grow. Without plants, there is no food! THAT can be a very big problem!

Sometimes, rain keeps us from doing things we want to do! Let's read our memory verse aloud. (*Children respond.*) Zechariah tells us that God is the one who sends thunderstorms and gives rain to everyone, so that everyone's plants will grow for food! **God provides for his followers!** (*Open with prayer requests, praises, and a time of prayer.*)

BIBLE STORY

Say: We know God made the world. Do you think God is interested in the world he made? (*Children respond.*) What makes you think that? (*Children respond.*) Listen to this! (*Read Jeremiah 10:12–13 aloud.*) What does this tell us about God? (*Children respond.*) He is ALWAYS paying attention to us.

Today, we are going to learn about the prophet Elijah. He lived during the time of King Ahab's reign. King Ahab was a very bad king. He worshiped the false god, Baal, and killed many prophets of God. This made God very angry.

God sent the prophet Elijah to King Ahab with a message. (*Read 1 Kings 17:1–6 aloud.*) Elijah had bad news for King Ahab. Israel would have NO rain until Elijah said so. Israel is a very hot place to live. Most people were farmers.

They raised plants for food. They raised animals for meat, milk, and other things. So, getting enough rain at the right times was VERY important to them. No rain meant that many people and animals could die.

God knew that King Ahab would be angry by the news. So God told Elijah to hide after he delivered the news. Elijah went to hide by a brook, but he was not alone! God sent ravens to bring him food.

King Ahab looked everywhere for Elijah, but he could not find him. For THREE YEARS there was no rain and the land dried up. King Ahab became desperate. He prayed to his god, Baal, but no rain came.

Then, Elijah arrived again with a challenge for King Ahab. (*Read 1 Kings 18:17–19 aloud.*) Elijah's challenge was to see whose god was real. Elijah and King Ahab's prophets built two altars—one to Baal and one to God. The prophets of Baal prayed all day long, asking Baal to light their altar on fire, but nothing happened.

In the evening, it was Elijah's turn. Elijah drenched the altar with twelve jars of water. Then, he prayed. (*Read 1 Kings 18:38–39 aloud.*) What did God do? (*Children respond.*)

God swallowed up the whole altar. He proved to the people that he was the one true God. Then, everyone believed. Elijah prayed to God for rain.

Elijah told his helper to go to the sea and look for rain clouds. The helper did not see any. Elijah prayed again and again. He sent his helper to the sea SEVEN times. Finally, his helper saw something. (*Read 1 Kings 18:44–45 aloud.*)

God is the one who sends the rain and thunder. He makes the clouds rise and the winds blow! **God provides for his followers.**

OPENING GAME
WET RELAY

Directions: Children line up in even teams. Give each child a paper cup. Fill cup of first player on each team about halfway with water. Child pours water into next child's cup; play continues as water is poured from cup to cup, going down the line and then all the way back to the first player. First team to finish tells three ways to be kind to an unkind person.

Say: We are talking about how God sends rain. God knows what we need. Let's see if we can pass some water down the line and back again, kindly. Being kind shows we are part of God's family, because **God provides for his followers** and we want to look like our Father!

Alternate Idea: Punch holes in the bottoms of the plastic cups. Children pass the "rainwater" down the line by placing their cup inside the cup next to them. The cups are stacked in a vertical fashion and passed down, each one catching the water from the cup above him or her! Last one in line has a cup with no holes.

OBJECT LESSON
MAKE IT RAIN

Say: Have you ever wanted to know how rain happens? (*Children respond.*) Let's try this experiment. It will show us something about how rain is made!

Directions: Fill the pie tin with ice. Wait for the tin to become very cold. Pour the hot water into the jar. Set the ice-filled pie tin on top of the jar of hot water. Watch to see what happens. When water drops form on the pie tin's bottom, tilt it so that the water falls into the jar.

Say: What do you think will happen when the hot water is poured into the jar and we set the ice on top of it? (*Children respond.*)

What do you see inside the jar now that we put the hot water in it and the ice on top? (*Children respond.*)

What happened on the bottom of the pie tin? (*Children respond.*) **Look! We made it rain!** The hot water in the jar gave off steam, or water vapor. We know heat rises. So, the warm vapor rose until it hit the cold layer—the pie tin. The cold turned the vapor back into liquid water. This is called condensation. When the water drops get too heavy, they fall!

On Earth, it works the same way. When the sun warms water, vapor rises. When that cloud of vapor rises to hit the layer of colder air, it condenses and falls as rain! This is called the water cycle. God made it work this way so that everyone could have rain. **God provides for his followers!**

> ### Materials
> - metal pie tin
> - ice cubes
> - large jar
> - thermal container of hot water

OPTIONAL ACTIVITIES
SOUNDS LIKE RAIN

Say: What does it sound like when it rains? (*Children respond.*) **What are ways we could make rain sounds?** (*Children respond.*) **What about thunder? What are some ways we could make thunder sounds?** (*Children respond.*)

When God sends the rain, our memory verse tells us he also sends the wind. What are some ways we could make wind sounds? (*Children respond.*) God knows that we need wind and rain for Earth to be happy. **God provides for his followers!**

Directions: Conduct children in a "rain symphony." They may tap fingers on desktops or slap thighs for rain sounds. They may stomp feet for thunder (or use a child's suggestion), and make mouth noises to indicate wind. After practicing the sounds together, lead the activity by calling out a part ("loud rain" or "gentle breeze," etc.). Children can follow your lead and create a series of sounds that seem like a rainstorm.

RAIN ART

Directions: Children draw with pastels as desired. Spray lightly with water to see the "rain" effect of the water.

Say: Have you ever left anything out in the rain? What happens to it? (*Children respond.*) It can get spots of water on it. Does that change the way it looks? (*Children respond.*) Let's try raining on our art to see what happens! God sends the rain so that we can live. **God provides for his followers!**

THE WONDERFUL WATER CYCLE

Preparation: Photocopy the God's Rainmaking on page 128, making one copy for each child.

Say: We know that God makes the rain. We've even seen the way God makes it happen! Let's see if we can color and label the parts of the water cycle. You probably know more about this than you think! God sends us rain. **God provides for his followers!**

Directions: Distribute God's Rainmaking to children. Children fill in the rain-cycle boxes with the words from the word box. Children color page.

Answer Key: A=Condensation; B=Rain; C=Evaporation

Materials

- watercolor pastels
- heavy paper
- spray bottles
- water

Materials

- God's Rainmaking, page 128
- crayons or markers

GOD'S RAINMAKING

Color the page. Fill in each box with the appropriate word from the word box.

Condensation (when water vapor hits the cold layer)

Rain

Evaporation (when the sun warms the water and vapor rises)

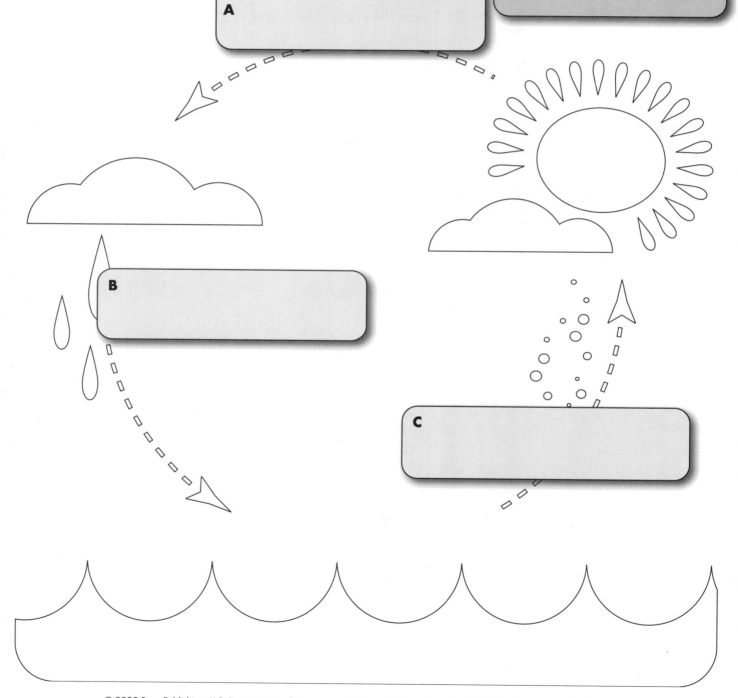

26. PHILIP AND THE ETHIOPIAN

ACTS 2:2;8:4–8,26–40

The wind blows wherever it wants. Just as you can hear the wind but can't tell where it comes from or where it is going, so you can't explain how people are born of the Spirit.
John 3:8

BIG IDEA

GOD'S POWER IS LIKE THE WIND

OVERVIEW

Say: Tell me about the biggest wind you have ever seen. (*Children respond.*) What are some things you know about the wind? (*Children respond.*) What are some ways wind helps us? (*Children respond.*) The wind has great power.

The wind dries out the wet earth. It moves seeds. It helps sailboats to move and carries birds along when they catch a wind current.

We can't tell where the wind started and we can't tell where it is going. Can you control the wind? (*Children respond.*) We can't control the wind, but we can see what it does. And if we know how it works, we can use it!

That is also how it is with God's power. **God's power is like the wind!** We can't always see it, but we know it's working. (*Open with prayer requests, praises, and a time of prayer.*)

BIBLE STORY

Say: What did it sound like when God's Spirit came to Jesus' friends in the book of Acts? (*Children respond.*) Let's find out. (*Read Acts 2:2 aloud.*) The Holy Spirit sounded like a windstorm!

Today we're going to learn about a man named Philip. He was not one of Jesus' disciples. But after God's Spirit came, he went out and told everyone about Jesus. This made the religious leaders ANGRY!

The religious leaders arrested people who spoke the truth about Jesus. Jesus' followers moved quickly to get away. (*Read Acts 8:4–8 aloud.*) When Philip went to Samaria, what happened? (*Children respond.*) That's right!

Philip preached the good news and did miracles in the name of Jesus. He did such a good job preaching that God

sent him an angel with a message. (*Read Acts 8:26–29 aloud.*) **Philip found an Ethiopian man reading God's word. But the man seemed confused.**

So Philip started jogging beside the chariot. "Do you understand what you're reading?" Philip panted.

The man looked up. He said, "How can I understand this unless someone explains it to me?"

Philip must have grinned. THIS was the reason he'd run down this dusty road! The Ethiopian invited Philip to sit with him and to explain what these words meant. The words were all about JESUS!

Philip told the Ethiopian all about Jesus and about God's Kingdom. The chariot continued to roll along. It passed some water. The Ethiopian said, "Look! Water! Is there any reason I can't be baptized RIGHT NOW?"

Philip must have laughed! Of course, GOD had sent him, and GOD had put water here at just the right place! They stopped and got out of the chariot. Philip baptized the Ethiopian—and suddenly, Philip was GONE! (*Read Acts 8:39 aloud.*)

God's Spirit had swept him away like the wind! The Ethiopian got back into his chariot, and went on his way, full of joy and praising God!

What happened to Philip? (*Read Acts 8:40 aloud.*) **He was suddenly in the city of Azotus, and he just kept on telling people about Jesus! God had done amazing things. God's power is like the wind!**

OPENING GAME
WIND RELAY

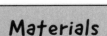

Alternate Idea: Children can blow the balloons with their mouths if they like.

Preparation: Use masking tape to make a start line. At the opposite side of playing area, lay a 10-foot square of masking tape. Where each team will line up, set a paper plate and a balloon.

Directions: Children form two or more even teams. Each team lines up beside its balloon and plate.

First child in line takes the paper plate and fans the balloon into the masking-tape square. Child picks up the balloon and runs back to the line to give materials to the next child in line.

Play continues until one team finishes. Play several rounds.

Say: What makes the balloon move, even though we cannot see it? (*Children respond.*) Yes, we can't see the moving air, but we can FEEL it. And we can SEE what it does! The power of the wind moved your balloons into the square.

> ### Materials
> - masking tape
> - paper plates
> - inflated balloons

God's power is like the wind! God's power moved Philip from one city to another so that he could preach the good news. Let's be like Philip and tell others about Jesus, too.

OBJECT LESSON
CARRIED ON THE WIND

Tip: Ahead of time, find other kinds of seeds that are wind-borne. Bring those examples for children to look at and try.

Preparation: Cut paper into strips about 1-inch x 6-inch.

Say: Philip was an enthusiastic preacher of God's word. He was so good that God literally took him on the wind to a new place to preach. Other things, like seeds, travel on the wind, too. They are carried by the wind to new places, so that the baby plants have space to grow. Today let's make a model of one kind of seed that is carried on the wind!

> ### Materials
> - scissors
> - paper
> - rulers
> - crayons or markers
> - paper clips

Directions: Give each child at least one strip of paper. Children do the following steps themselves: Measure and draw a line about two inches long down the center of the strip. Cut along the line. Fold either resulting piece in an opposite direction. Fold the corners of the uncut end into a point. Slide paper clip onto the uncut end. Toss model seed up into the air to see how it flies!

Say: These models are like maple tree seeds. They move a little bit like a helicopter does. This motion helps the seed to move out away from the tree. Other seeds are designed to glide like a bird or flutter like a butterfly. When we see how God designed these kinds of seeds to be carried on the wind, it reminds us that God designed US to be carried by his power! **God's power is like the wind!**

OPTIONAL ACTIVITIES
SEEDY ART

Preparation: Go outdoors and gather as many kinds of seeds as you can find, looking especially for flying seeds.

Directions: Children use scissors to trim plant materials. Children glue them on paper in any way they like.

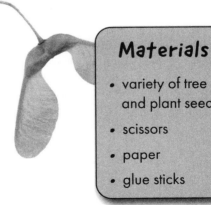

> ### Materials
> - variety of tree and plant seeds
> - scissors
> - paper
> - glue sticks

Say: Look at all the kinds of seeds God made. God had a plan for every kind of seed. He didn't forget about any one of them. In the same way God designed every seed, God designed us to be carried along by his power. He wants us to be his witnesses! **God's power is like the wind!**

FLY A KITE

Directions: Child follows these instructions to make a very simple kite.

1. Fold paper down the center width-ways (hamburger style).

2. Decorate it if you like!

3. Bend the front corner of the paper back to touch the fold. Staple or tape this. This is your first wing.

4. Repeat the process for the other side. This is your second wing.

5. Place tape near the front of the kite to reinforce the spot where you will punch your hole.

6. Use a hole punch to make a hole near the front of the crease.

7. Thread string through the hole and tie.

8. Take your kite to a breezy place and try it out!

Say: So many things use the wind to move—sailboats and sailboards, gliders and kites. We're going to try to make very simple kite so you can see how it flies. Just like the kite moves on the wind's power, God designed us to "go" on his power. **God's power is like the wind!**

Materials

- paper (8.5x14-inches)
- stapler or tape
- hole punch
- string

TUMBLING ON THE WIND

Preparation: Photocopy Moved by God's Power on page 133, making one copy for each child.

Directions: Distribute Moved by God's Power to children. Children draw "seeds of faith" on the tumbleweed. Beside each seed, children write words or draw symbols that remind them of Jesus. Show children videos about tumbleweeds on your laptop.

Say: Philip traveled to many places declaring the good news about Jesus. As he traveled, the number of believers grew. Think of the spread of the gospel like a tumbleweed. The tumbleweed rolls along the ground, scattering seeds.

Wherever the wind blows, that's where the weed goes. Has anyone seen one before? (*Children respond.*) Tumbleweeds are amazing. A single plant may produce 250,000 seeds. When the plant dries up, the wind picks it up. **God's power is like the wind!**

Materials

- Moved by God's Power, page 133
- laptop
- crayons or markers

MOVED BY GOD'S POWER

The wind blows wherever it wants. Just as you can hear the wind but can't tell where it comes from or where it is going, so you can't explain how people are born of the Spirit.
John 3:8

Draw "seeds of faith" on the tumbleweed. Beside each seed, write words or draw symbols that remind you of Jesus.

 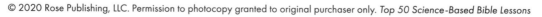

27. RED SEA SPLITS

EXODUS 14

Let all that I am wait quietly before God, for my hope is in him.
Psalm 62:5

BIG IDEA

WHEN WE WORRY, GOD GIVES US REST

OVERVIEW

Say: Look around. What things do you see that are at rest? (*Children respond.*) "At rest" means that the item is not moving. Another word for it is inert. Inertia is the state of being at rest. What would it take for (this book) to move? (*Children respond.*)

It takes an outside force to move something that is at rest. What are times that people rest? (*Children respond.*) What makes us move? (*Children respond.*) When our moms call us to get up, we can move on our own! God says that even when we are getting up or running or working we don't have to keep our minds busy with worry. **When we worry, God gives us rest**! (*Open with prayer requests, praises, and a time of prayer.*)

BIBLE STORY

Say: Since we are talking about rest and inertia today, let me ask you a question. Do you think it's easier to DO something when you are worried, or to rest and wait? (*Children respond.*) Many times, when we are worried or afraid, we start to think of things to do instead of stopping and asking GOD what to do!

Let me tell you about a time when God's people were in trouble. They were slaves in Egypt. They wanted to DO something—they wanted to RUN AWAY! God sent Moses to free them, but soon they were stuck! They were stuck between the Red Sea and the Egyptian army who wanted to attack them. (*Read Exodus 14:9–11 aloud.*) They cried out to God, but they didn't stop to listen for his answer!

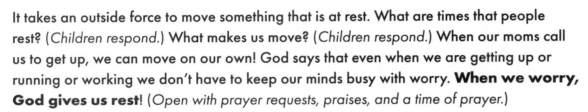

The Israelites complained to Moses. Listen to what Moses told them. (*Read Exodus 14:13–14 aloud.*) They didn't NEED to do ANYTHING! Moses told them to stand still and GOD would take care of them. God would fight.

How do you think God did that? (*Children respond.*) **Let's find out.** (*Read Exodus 14:15–16 aloud.*) NOW it was time for them to move—because God said so! God's directions were for them to do something IMPOSSIBLE. (*Read Exodus 14:21–22 aloud.*)

God sent a strong wind to blast the water aside. God's people moved out, walking RIGHT THROUGH the sea on dry ground! What a miracle.

They rested their minds and hearts on God. Then they could wait until God told them what to do. And then, they moved when God told them to move.

The Egyptian army came right after the Israelites! God was prepared for them. He jammed the wheels of their chariots. He made them confused! They began to realize that they were fighting against God.

God told Moses to hold up his staff again. (*Read Exodus 14:27–28 aloud.*) WOW. The water covered the WHOLE Egyptian army. The Israelites were safe on the far side of the sea—and God had fought that battle FOR them. They didn't need to worry; they only needed to obey God! **When we worry, God gives us rest**!

OPENING GAME
INERTIA TAG

Optional Preparation: Use masking tape to mark the boundaries of the playing area, if needed.

Directions: Play a game like freeze tag. Choose one child to be the "inertia tagger." Other children move around the playing area, trying to avoid being tagged and becoming inert (at rest). Round ends when all children are at rest; last child to be tagged becomes the new "inertia tagger."

Optional Materials

- masking tape

Say: It's fun to be chased in this game. Is it easy or hard to not move when you are tagged? (*Children respond.*) Sometimes we really want to move when we must STOP! What are times when it can be scary to be chased? (*Children respond.*) At those times, we might need to run away or find a safe place. But even in those situations, we can pray to God and ask him to take care of us. We can listen for him to tell us what to do. We don't have to worry. **When we worry, God gives us rest**!

> **Tip:** Choose a second child to be the "motion tagger." This player touches those who have been made inert and is the outside force that makes them move.

OBJECT LESSON
INERTIA ZINGERS

Preparation: Cut each soda bottle in half. Tape the top ends of two soda bottles together so that the mouths are at opposite ends to make a "zinger." Thread a paper clip on the yarn. Drop the paper clip through one bottle's mouth. The paper clip will act as a weight to pull the yarn through the mouth of the opposite bottle (image a). Ensure that the lengths of yarn are even, then cut the yarn at the paper-clip location. Remove paper clip (image b).

Tip: It would be best to make a setup like this for every four children. Also, since the bottles can hurt hands when they collide, have children wear gloves while playing with the zinger.

Say: We know that this soda-bottle zinger is at rest. It's just lying here. What will it take for it to move? (*Children respond.*) Let's find a way to make it go fast!

Directions: Stand with a partner so that the strings are parallel to the floor. Each partner holds the two strings at their end in each hand. Partners take turns to snap the ends of the strings apart. Instruct children to observe what happens to the zinger. It will move rapidly along the strings to the opposite side.

a.

b.

Materials

- plastic soda bottles (two for each zinger)
- scissors
- masking tape
- 16-foot lengths of yarn
- paper clip
- gloves (one pair for each completed zinger)

Say: What happens when one of you snaps the strings apart? (*Children respond.*) The law of inertia says that that zinger won't move unless an outside force makes it move. When you snap the strings apart, you create that outside force! The force pushes the zinger in the opposite direction. Sometimes things make us move, too! What are times you need to move quickly? (*Children respond.*) But even in those times, we can pray to God and ask his help. We can trust him to help us. **When we worry, God gives us rest!**

OPTIONAL ACTIVITIES
RAMP IT UP

Directions:

1. Cut down along the corners of the box. Go down about halfway.
2. Cut away the sides of the box above the cut.
3. Turn the cut-down box on its side.

Materials

- large cardboard box
- scissors
- wide tape
- small cars

4. Cut the leftover pieces of cardboard into strips wider than your cars.

5. Tape the strips where you want to make ramps inside the box.

6. Tip the box back a little. Slide extra cardboard under the front edge to keep it tipped.

7. Use the cars to demonstrate the way rest and inertia work.

Say: These cars are stopped unless there is something moving them. When they go downhill, what force is moving them? (*Children respond.*) Inertia! What might make us want to run fast? (*Children respond.*) Even when we are running, we can be praying. The Israelites were running away from the Egyptian army. They were scared, but they trusted God to help. **When we worry, God gives us rest!**

CHAIN OF MOVEMENT

Directions: Set three checkers in a row. While holding the center checker still, flick a side checker into the center checker with some force. Notice what happens to the checker on the other side. Add more checkers to see what happens.

Say: The moving checker has been moved by a force— you! That's called kinetic energy. That energy is transferred through the still checker into the checker on the other side of the still checker. That center checker remains at rest, but energy is going through it to move something else.

That's kind of like us. Even when we feel frozen with fear, we can ask God to help us. The Israelites were frozen with fear. They were stuck between the Egyptian army and the Red Sea. God saved them. In the same way, he can send us his energy and help! **When we worry, God gives us rest!**

Materials
- checkers
- tabletop

WHY SEAT BELTS?

Preparation: Photocopy Seatbelt Safety on page 138, making one copy for each child.

Say: How many of you have NEVER ridden in a car? (*Children respond.*) Most of us ride in a car every day! But did you know that the thing we talked about today—inertia—is the reason we have seat belts in cars? We'll find out on our sheet why even a car accident is less dangerous if we are wearing a seat belt!

Directions: Distribute Seatbelt Safety to children. Children answer the questions. Talk about resting our minds and hearts in God through prayer.

Say: Being in a car accident can be scary and dangerous. But we can talk to God even when we are in danger! **When we worry, God gives us rest!**

Materials
- Seatbelt Safety, page 138
- pencils
- crayons or markers

SEATBELT SAFETY

Let all that I am wait quietly before God, for my hope is in him.
Psalm 62:5

One law of inertia is that once something is set in motion—once it is moving, it keeps on moving until something stops it, or until it runs out of energy. It's easy to understand inertia when you think about riding in a car. Answer the questions below to discover if you are a super safe passenger.

When you are riding in the car and there is a sudden stop, what happens?

_____

If you are in the back seat and the car stops, what will stop your forward motion?

_____

If you're in the front seat, what will stop your forward motion?

_____

Do you wear a seatbelt every time you are in a car?

_____

When you wear a seatbelt, is it over your lap AND chest?

_____

Do you always ride in the backseat?

_____

Do you wear a seatbelt even if others don't buckle up?

_____

28. Proverbs Speaks of Wisdom

PROVERBS 8; JAMES 1:5

You set the boundaries of the earth, and you made both summer and winter.
Psalm 74:17

OVERVIEW

Say: If I drop my pen, what happens to it? (*Children respond.*) If I drop it, it doesn't float up into the air sometimes. It falls to the floor. It doesn't fly sideways. It always falls right to the floor. That's one of the laws of nature that God made. It's called the law of gravity. What are some other things we can count on to happen? (*Children respond.*) God made our world wisely. We can count on day and night, on the seasons, on the way water flows, and more. **Creation shows us God's wisdom!** (*Open with prayer requests, praises, and a time of prayer.*)

BIG IDEA

CREATION SHOWS US GOD'S WISDOM

BIBLE STORY

Say: What are some wise ideas? (*Children respond.*) It's wise to brush your teeth. It's wise to stop and look before you run into the street. It is wise to jump in the water feet first, the first time. Wisdom—knowing what is best to do—is part of who God is.

Today, let's listen to what Proverbs 8 says about wisdom. In this chapter, Wisdom is speaking like a person. (*Read Proverbs 8:1, 6–8 aloud.*) Wisdom has good advice. She wants people to do what is right and wholesome.

Then, Wisdom tells about being with God when God created the world. (*Read Proverbs 8:22–25 aloud.*) Wisdom says she was the first thing created, even before the oceans. Are the sea levels of the oceans always in the same place? (*Children respond. Read Proverbs 8:29 aloud.*)

Wisdom was there when the boundaries of the oceans were set. These boundaries change slightly during the day because of the tides. The water comes in farther onto the shore at high tide. It moves farther into the water at low tide. This happens every day!

Every six hours, it is either high or low tide, all around the world. God made those

boundaries between the water and the land. Did you know that the moon affects the ocean tides? The gravitational force of the moon and the sun pulls the water of Earth's oceans toward the moon. The spinning of the Earth is also part of this amazing tidal flow.

God made these things work together to make the ocean tides something we can trust. God's wise ways are truly amazing! Let's find out how Wisdom felt about being God's helper at creation. (*Read Proverbs 8:30–31 aloud.*)

If we want to be happy, we will listen to God's wisdom. **Creation shows us God's wisdom**! Creation shows us how thoughtful God is. It shows us that he cares deeply for us. We know we can ask God for wisdom. (*Read James 1:5 aloud.*) We can trust him to guide us to what is best to do!

OPENING GAME
TIDE JUMP

Preparation: Use masking tape to make two lines about four to eight feet apart (depending on the ages and sizes of your class members). These are the high and low tide lines.

Say: In this game, we have two clear boundaries, a high tide line and a low tide line. Besides that, this game has one law: no one can be called out. If you make a mistake, keep going!

Directions: Children all stand on one line. Designate that as the "high tide" line. Give various commands such as:

- Jump to the low tide line!
- Stomp in the water between the tide lines.
- Step out of the water on the high tide side.
- Slide your feet from the high tide line to the low tide line.
- Use your left foot to step outside the water.

Continue with various commands, speaking faster or making them more complicated. Don't call anyone out.

Say: This was fun! Did anyone make a mistake? (*Children respond.*) Did it matter? (*Children respond.*) No, because we had a law or rule about not being called out. Everyone was included! In the same way, everyone is included in God's world. God makes wise boundaries and makes wise rules. He made this world good and made it so that we can feel secure and at home in it. **Creation shows us God's wisdom!**

Materials
• masking tape

OBJECT LESSON
MAGNETIC FIELDS

Say: Another wise way God made the world is the consistent force called the magnetic field. It is all around the planet. The magnetic field on our planet can't be seen, but it is strong! It is also stable. That means it stays the same. When we use a compass, it works because of the magnetic field. Playing with these magnets will show us how it works. **Creation shows us God's wisdom**!

Directions: Lay one or two magnets on a table. Point out the N and S on the ends of the magnet. Lay a sheet of paper over the magnets. Scatter some iron filings or some paper clips over the paper. Invite children to move the metal bits and see what happens.

Try this experiment with other kinds of magnets. Watch the patterns the metal makes, and invite children to tell why they think it happens.

Say: What happens to the filings or paper clips when we place them on the paper? (*Children respond.*) When you move them, what do they do? (*Children respond.*) Why do you think this happens? (*Children respond.*)

There is a north pole and a south pole marking on the magnets. That is because the magnetic field pulls north and south. When we line up a compass needle with the big letter N, we are lining up the compass with the north end of the magnetic field!

One thing Earth's magnetic field does is to protect us from some kinds of solar radiation! God's wisdom protects us even when we can't see the magnetic field forces or the radiation!

Bonus Idea: Explore solar magnetic fields; bring a laptop and show a short video about the subject.

Say: Did you know that there are magnetic fields on the sun, too? They are not as stable as the magnetic fields on earth. They go through a cycle of change about every eleven years! Scientists don't understand how the magnetic fields change on the sun. They do know that sun spots and solar winds are two of the results of the changes in the sun's magnetic fields.

Materials

- magnets (bar magnets best show north and south poles)
- iron filings or paper clips
- sheets of white paper

OPTIONAL ACTIVITIES

LAWS OF FLOTATION

Directions: Let children do a series of simple sink and float experiments—predicting whether they think an item will float, and then testing it. After items have been tested, invite interested children to use rubber bands to attach corks to some items.

Say: God created some things to float and other things to sink. How can you predict which things will float? (*Children respond.*) What happens when we attach a cork to something that normally sinks? Why? (*Children respond.*) **The cork makes things float that would normally sink. What are ways that we can be wise when we are near water?** (*Children respond.*) **Creation shows us God's wisdom!**

Materials

- dish pan or large plastic bowl
- water
- small items (some that float and some that sink)
- corks
- rubber bands

GRAVITY GAMES

Directions: Invite children to sit in chairs. Tell them to sit all the way back in their seats, and then to cross their arms over their chests. Tell them to stand up without leaning forward or using their hands. Allow children to struggle for a few moments before telling them it's impossible.

Instruct them to bend forward, grab ahold of their toes and then to jump forward without letting go of their toes. Again, they won't be able to.

Say: Why weren't you able to stand (or jump)? What was stopping you? (*Children respond.*) **You weren't able to stand (or jump) because of gravity. Basically, when you restrict your center of gravity, it holds you down! We don't often think about things like the law of gravity. But without it, we'd go floating off into space! God sure knew what he was doing when he created the world. Creation shows us God's wisdom!**

Materials

- chairs

MAP A WORLD

Preparation: Photocopy Map It on page 143, making one copy for each child.

Say: Because God made the world in wise ways, we can count on some things. We know water flows downhill. We know hills are higher than valleys. Let's use what we already know to make a map. **Creation shows us God's wisdom!**

Directions: Distribute Map It to children. Children use the symbols shown on page 143 to draw a map of a land they create, and then color their maps as desired. Children fill in key with their own colors for sea, shore, forest, and ground.

Materials

- Map It, page 143
- crayons or markers

MAP IT

Create your own land! Use the symbols shown below to draw a map of your land. Fill in the boxes in the key with your own colors for sea, shore, forest, and ground. Color your maps.

⏜ roads
--- paths
⬭ buildings
∿ rivers
● stops
^^^ hills
☐ sea
☐ shore
☐ forest
☐ ground

29. JESUS DIED AND ROSE AGAIN

MATTHEW 27:45–46,50–51; MARK 15:16–17

Anyone who belongs to Christ has become a new person.
The old life is gone; a new life has begun!
2 Corinthians 5:17

BIG IDEA

JESUS' LOVE CHANGES US

OVERVIEW

Say: If I said you could have a brand new video game system, or one that has been around for about ten or fifteen years, which one would you choose? (*Children respond.*) The NEW one! Of course, we like new things. They're usually a huge improvement over what came before.

Today, we're going to talk about transformation—when something is added or changed to a thing, creating something totally different. Did you know what God transforms us? Today's verse tells us that when we decide to follow Jesus and become a member of God's family, we become a whole new person! **Jesus' love changes us!** (*Open with prayer requests, praises, and a time of prayer.*)

BIBLE STORY

Say: Today's story is the most important story in the Bible. In fact, it's the most important story in the world. Can you guess what story it is? (*Children respond.*) Today's story is about the time when Jesus died.

Jesus paid the price for our sins by dying on a cross. Jesus suffered a great deal before and during the time he was on the cross. But he did it willingly, because he loves us and knew we need him to be our Savior. Let's read about what happened. (*Read Mark 15:16–20 aloud.*)

What a terrible thing! Jesus was mocked and forced to wear a crown of thorns. Even though Jesus had done nothing wrong, he suffered a terrible punishment—our punishment for the wrong things we do. Let's read more about what happened. (*Read Matthew 27:45–46,50–51 aloud.*)

Jesus felt completely alone and abandoned on the cross. When he finally died, Earth felt it. It shook and rocks split apart, but that's not the end of the story! Three days after Jesus died, he rose from the tomb!

Death could not stop Jesus or his love. Jesus is alive! And everyone who accepts Jesus' forgiveness for their sin knows that **Jesus' love changes us!**

OPENING GAME
LETTER TOSS

Tip: Post the memory verse in a place where kids can easily see it.

Preparation: Print each letter in the sentence "Jesus' love can change us!" on a paper plate. Make two sets of plates, using different colors of marker for each team. Scatter all the plates throughout the playing area. Use masking tape to make a start line.

Directions: Children divide into two teams and line up behind the start line. Assign a color to each team. On your signal, the first player on each team searches for the first letter in the Big Idea sentence on a paper plate, written in their team color. When the correct letter is found, player returns to the team and tags the next player to take a turn. Play continues until both teams have spelled out the Big Idea. The first team to finish recites the memory verse.

Say: Today's Bible story was the amazing story of just how much Jesus loves us. Because of his love, he was willing to die and take the penalty for our sin. Once we accept Jesus' gift of salvation and forgiveness of sin, we become members of God's family—a whole new person! **Jesus' love changes us!**

> ### Materials
> - paper plates
> - crayons or markers
> - masking tape

OBJECT LESSON
LOVE LAYERS

Preparation: Pour some corn syrup into one glass, add red food coloring, and stir to make syrup red. In another glass, pour a couple inches of water, add blue food coloring, and stir to make a very dark blue. Place corn syrup glass, water glass, baby oil, and remaining empty glass where you will lead the activity.

Say: (*Pour some baby oil into the remaining empty glass.*) **The oil in this glass represents God. Before he created the world, there was only God. Then God created the world and everything in it, including people.** (*Hold up glass with red corn syrup.*) **This red fluid represents Adam and Eve, the first people.** (*Carefully pour the syrup into the glass with baby oil. The corn syrup will pool under the oil. Hold up glass so children can see the layers.*) **God and Adam and Eve were so close! This is the way God wants things to be with us. Nothing is separating God from people.**

> ### Materials
> - 3 clear glasses
> - light corn syrup
> - red and blue food coloring
> - spoon
> - water
> - baby oil
> - bleach

But things changed. Something came between God's relationship with Adam and Eve. (*Carefully pour the blue water into the layered glass. The blue water will slip between the oil and syrup to form a middle layer. Hold up glass so children can see the layers.*) **Can anyone tell me what happened? What does the blue water represent?** (*Children respond.*) **Adam and Eve sinned! The blue water represents sin, and that sin separates us from God.**

Ever since, everyone has been separated from God because we all sin. But God loves us so much, he made a way for us to be forgiven for our sin and be close to him again. Jesus died on a cross to pay the penalty for our sin. He came to life again and can forgive us! (*Carefully pour the bleach into the layered glass. The bleach will react with the blue water, transforming it clear again. Hold up glass so children can see the layers.*) **This bleach is like Jesus' forgiveness. It removes the sin from our lives so that we can be close to God—we become members of God's family! Jesus' love changes us!**

OPTIONAL ACTIVITIES
LIKE A LAVA LAMP

Directions: Children fill glasses ¾ full with water and add a few drops of food coloring. Children use spoons to stir food coloring into the glasses. Children pour an inch or so of baby oil on top of the water. Because the oil is less dense than the water, the oil will float on top of the water. Hold up the antacid tablets, and ask children what they think will happen if the antacid is added to the glasses. After children have responded, break tablets in half and give each child half to add to their glasses.

Say: When the antacid tablets mix with the water, they release a gas called carbon dioxide. The gas bubbles capture some of the colored water and then rise up through the oil, and finally burst when they reach the surface. A transformation takes place when something is added to something that already exists, changing it into something new. In the same way, **Jesus' love changes us!**

> ### Materials
> - clear plastic glasses
> - water
> - food coloring
> - plastic spoons
> - baby oil
> - fizzing antacid tablets

PRETZEL CROSSES

Directions: Children place pretzel sticks in cheese cubes to form crosses. They place crosses on paper plates and then eat them.

Say: We've been talking about transformation today. If someone asked you what a transformation was, how would you answer? (*Children respond.*) A transformation means a thing has changed because of something new being added to it. The Bible tells us that when we become followers of Jesus, we become new people. **Jesus' love changes us!**

Materials

- pretzel sticks
- cheese cubes
- paper plates

MIXED UP LETTERS

Preparation: Photocopy the Dot-to-Dot Scramble on page 148, making one copy for each child.

Directions: Distribute Dot-to-Dot Scramble to children. Children unscramble the words and complete the dot-to-dot.

Say: Jesus paid the ultimate price to save us from sin. Today, the sign of the cross is the reminder of his sacrifice. Post your dot-to-dot somewhere you will see it often. Keep it as a reminder that **Jesus' love changes us**.

Answer Key: Jesus' love changes us.

Materials

- Dot-to-Dot Scramble, page 148
- crayons or markers

DOT-TO-DOT SCRAMBLE

Anyone who belongs to Christ has become a new person. The old life is gone; a new life has begun!
2 Corinthians 5:17

Complete the dot-to-dot. Unscramble the words at the bottom and write the message on the blank line.

1
13

2

11

12

3

4

10

9

6

5

8

7

sjesu' leov ghceans su!

_____

30. PENTECOST

MATTHEW 3:11; JOHN 14:16–17; ACTS 2:1–41

When the Father sends . . . the Holy Spirit—he will teach you everything and will remind you of everything I have told you.
John 14:26

BIG IDEA

THE HOLY SPIRIT IS HERE TO HELP US

OVERVIEW

Say: How would our world be different if we didn't know how to make fire? (*Children respond.*) It would ALL be completely different! What are some of the things fire does for us? (*Children respond.*) Besides keeping us warm, all the processes we need to make metal things like cars are based on fire.

It takes a lot of heat to make metal from the rocks in the ground. Fire helps us do more things than we can even count. The Holy Spirit is like fire. The Holy Spirit does so many things to help us, we can't even imagine them! But it's good to know that **the Holy Spirit is here to help us!** (*Open with prayer requests, praises, and a time of prayer.*)

BIBLE STORY

Say: We talked about fire and how the Holy Spirit is even more important than fire! Today, we are going to learn about the Holy Spirit. First let's hear what Jesus' cousin, John the Baptist, had to say about the Holy Spirit. (*Read Matthew 3:11 aloud.*)

John the Baptist baptized many people in water, but he told people that someone more important was coming with a different kind of baptism. Jesus would baptize people in the Holy Spirit and fire.

Later, after Jesus had died and resurrected, he told his disciples that they would not be alone. He promised them that the Holy Spirit would be with them. (*Read John 14:16–17 aloud.*) The Holy Spirit would help the disciples in so many ways! He said the Holy Spirit would remind them of all the things Jesus taught them. Jesus told them that the Holy Spirit would help them spread the gospel news and do many other things.

Jesus' friends wondered when the Holy Spirit would come! (*Read Acts 2:1–4 aloud.*) Jesus' friends waited in Jerusalem until one day, there was a sound like a BIG

WIND. But there was no wind! Then, what looked like little flames came and sat over the head of each person in the room—Jesus' friends, men and women, young and old!

They began to talk in languages they did not know. (*Read Acts 2:5–8 aloud.*) A crowd gathered—people from many countries—because they had heard that wind sound. Each of the people in the crowd heard Jesus' friends speaking in a language they understood! Soon Peter talked to everyone and told them that it was the Holy Spirit that gave them the languages they needed and the power to tell about Jesus.

(*Read Acts 2:38–41 aloud.*) Peter told these people all about Jesus and what had happened. The people wanted to join God's family, right then and there! Over 3,000 people joined God's family that day! THAT is because God's Holy Spirit helped them in so many ways! It is still the same for people who belong to God's family. **The Holy Spirit is here to help us**!

OPENING GAME
HERE TO HELP

Preparation: Mark the boundaries of the playing area if needed. Lay the sheet or towel where teams line up.

Directions: Children form teams of at least four. Each group of four holds the corners of a sheet or beach towel. Toss a beach ball into the center of each sheet and invite the teams to work together to make the ball bounce but not bounce off the sheet. (This takes practice!)

Once teams have successfully bounced the ball ten times, they run while bouncing the ball on the sheet, to the finish line and back. First team to complete the challenge repeats the memory verse. Play several rounds.

Say: What would happen if one person dropped their corner of the sheet? (*Children respond.*) This game only works if people help each other. They need to pay attention to each other and respond to each other. That's the way the Holy Spirit is with us. He is always with us. **The Holy Spirit is here to help us!**

Materials

- large sheet or beach towel (one per team of four players)
- masking tape
- beach balls

OBJECT LESSON
HEAT POWER

Preparation: Use tape to bundle three matches together. Tape the penny to the bottom of the bundle so that the bundle can stand with tips upward.

Directions: Wearing protective eyewear, place the quarter in the pie plate to one side. Add a few drops of food coloring to the water. Pour the water into the pie plate just enough to cover the quarter.

Say: We can see that the quarter is covered with water. But what can I do if I want my quarter back, and don't want to get my hands wet? How do you think we could get the water out of this plate? (*Children respond.*) I am going to show you one way to move this water. We'll try it several times, if you like.

Directions: First, stand the bundle of matches in the center of the pie plate. As soon as you light the match bundle, set the glass upside down over the burning matches.

Say: What happened when I placed the glass over the burning matches? (*Children respond.*) As the matches burned, they took the oxygen out of the glass. This created a vacuum. The vacuum pulled the water into the glass.

When the water pulls up into the glass, we can slide the dry quarter out of the pie plate! The fire created something that we could not have done without it! The Holy Spirit is like that. It gave Jesus' followers the power to speak different languages.

This allowed them to spread the gospel to many different people. The Holy Spirit is still with us today. **The Holy Spirit is here to help us**!

> ### Materials
> - wooden matches
> - tape
> - penny
> - protective eyewear
> - quarter
> - glass pie plate
> - food coloring
> - ½ cup water
> - glass cup

OPTIONAL ACTIVITIES
MAKE A FIRE

Directions: Children draw a picture of the three elements that make up fire—fuel, heat, and air.

Say: Fire helps us in more ways than we can count. When we make fire, there are several things that must happen. What three things do we need to make fire? (*Children respond.*) Fuel (or wood), heat, and air. Like fire, God's Spirit can do things we can't do on our own. And more than fire, **the Holy Spirit is here to help us!**

> ### Materials
> - paper
> - crayons or markers

FROM LIGHT TO FIRE

Preparation: Lay newspaper or leaves in the pan.

Directions: Children take turns to use the magnifying glasses to focus the light on some of the dry material. As soon as material smokes, congratulate the child and pour water on the material.

Say: When you are in the woods and need to make a fire, this is one way you can do it. We can't build fires indoors, but knowing this can save your life outdoors. Fire helps us in many ways. The Holy Spirit descended on Jesus' followers like fire. It gave them a passion to spread the gospel to many people. The Holy Spirit gives us the strength to do things we couldn't do before. **The Holy Spirit is here to help us!**

Materials

- newspaper or dry leaves
- large flat pan
- magnifying glasses
- study lamp
- cups of water

FLASH THE FLAMES

Preparation: Photocopy Tongues of Fire Maze on page 153, making one copy for each child.

Say: God sent the Holy Spirit as tongues of fire! Trace your way through this Tongues of Fire Maze to help it reach the believers who were present at Pentecost.

Directions: Distribute Tongues of Fire Maze to children. Children trace through the maze. Collect the words from the memory verse along the way and write them on the lines provided.

Say: Remember how the Holy Spirit came on each person like a fire? Every one of those people was different. But the Holy Spirit did not ignore anyone. He came to young, old, male, female, Jews, and non-Jews. The Holy Spirit does not care who you are or what you look like. He only cares that you believe in God. **The Holy Spirit is here to help us!**

Materials

- Tongues of Fire Maze, page 153
- crayons or markers

TONGUES OF FIRE MAZE

When the Father sends . . . the Holy Spirit—he will teach you everything and will remind you of everything I have told you.

John 14:26

Find your way through the maze. Collect the words from the memory verse along the way and write them on the lines below.

_____

_____

_____

_____

_____

_____

_____

_____

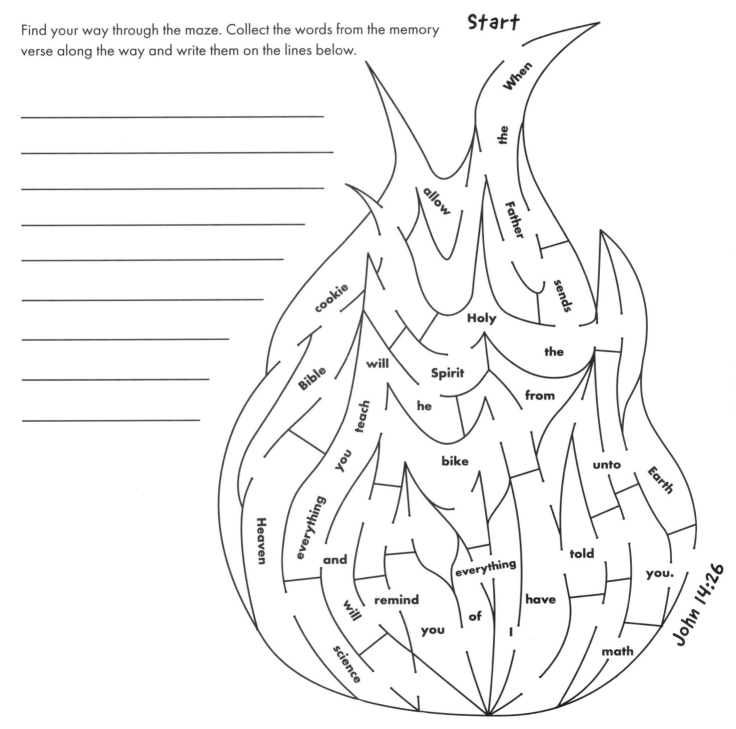

31. THE GREATEST COMMANDMENT

EXODUS 20:1–17; MARK 12:28–34

I am the LORD, and I do not change.
Malachi 3:6

BIG IDEA

LOVE GOD BY OBEYING HIM

OVERVIEW

Say: What are some laws you know? (*Children respond.*) There are all kinds of laws. One law might be, "speed limit thirty miles an hour." Another might be, "don't steal" or "don't lie." What happens to us if we disobey these rules? (*Children respond.*) Even if they are not rules that came from God, like the speed limit, those laws have consequences!

Those laws also help us live in the best way. If someone drove eighty miles an hour through your neighborhood and you were playing in the street, what might happen? (*Children respond.*) That law is made to keep us safe. We know it would be too hard to stop if we drove eighty miles an hour on your street. So even obeying the speed limit is a way to show love for other people. **Love God by obeying him!** (*Open with prayer requests, praises, and a time of prayer.*)

BIBLE STORY

Say: When the Israelites were wandering in the desert, God gave Moses the Ten Commandments. Who can tell me what the Ten Commandments are? (*Children respond. Read Exodus 20:1–17 aloud.*) These are laws for God's people to follow. In some ways, these laws are like the law of gravity.

When I drop a ball from my hand, which direction does it move? (*Children respond.*) Why is that? (*Children respond.*) We can rely on the law of gravity. It's the reason we turn the ketchup bottle upside down! We know gravity will pull on the ketchup so it comes out.

God's laws are like that, too. God tells us that if we do things another way—for instance, if we lie instead of telling the truth, we will have trouble. So he tells us not to lie!

When Jesus was on Earth, the religious leaders asked him questions about the Ten Commandments. They were

hoping that they could get Jesus to say something they thought was wrong. But of course, Jesus just kept giving them good answers—after all, he IS the Word of God!

Finally, one religious teacher had a BIG question. Let's read it. (*Read Mark 12:28 aloud.*) This man wasn't trying to trip Jesus up. He had a good question! You see, in the Old Testament, there were many laws. Besides the Ten Commandments, the religious leaders had made MANY MORE laws.

The people around Jesus were used to doing MANY things a certain way so they didn't break the rules. Which law do you think Jesus said was most important? (*Children respond.*) Let's read it. (*Read Mark 12:29–31 aloud.*)

What were the two laws Jesus said were the most important? (*Children respond.*) Love God and love your neighbor as yourself. When we love God with everything we have, then we will show it by the way we treat other people. If we treat other people like they don't matter, we are NOT loving our neighbor as ourselves.

Jesus did NOT mean "neighbor" like the person who lives next door. He meant any person who needs our help—even people who have been mean to us. EVERY person is our neighbor, no matter if they look like us or live like we do.

When we LOVE God with all our hearts, then we're glad to do what he asks! It is easy to love other people—because God will even help us to do that if we ask him! **Love God by obeying him!**

OPENING GAME
HELPING OUT

Preparation: Cut paper-towel tubes in half lengthwise to make troughs. You will need one for each player. Gather marbles or round rocks (which move slower, so easier for younger children).

Directions: Children form two equal team and teams stand in a line. Give each child a tube trough. Give a marble or rock to the first player in each line. First player sets the marble in the trough and then tips it to pass the marble to the next person in line. First team to successfully pass the marble down the line and back to the first person recites the memory verse or says one of the Ten Commandments. Play several rounds and try using different objects to pass.

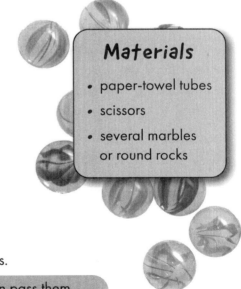

Materials
- paper-towel tubes
- scissors
- several marbles or round rocks

Tip: If you have only two or three troughs for each team, players may then pass them to the next person who will need it—increasing the speed and the challenge of the game!

Say: What was hard about this game? (*Children respond.*) **What was easy?** (*Children respond.*) We had to figure out just how much to tip the troughs, because gravity was pulling on our marbles. We live inside the law of gravity and we understand it, even though we don't think about it! That's the way we want to live in God, too.

When we learn God's commands, they stay with us. If we see a bank robbery, we don't have to sit there and think, "is this right or wrong?" We know it's wrong because we know God's commands. **Love God by obeying him**!

OBJECT LESSON
GRAVITY FUN

Preparation: Set the metal ruler across two stacks of blocks or books about a foot high, like a bridge. In several places, set a magnet under the ruler. (Or experiment with setting a magnet either on top or under the metal ruler). Cut string into 12-inch sections, making one for each child.

Tip: If you have a large group, make several of these setups.

Say: Today, we are talking about gravity. Because we live inside the earth's gravitational pull, we often forget that it is there! There are some things that would be different if gravity were not pulling everything toward the center of the earth. What do you think would change? (*Children respond.*)

Materials

- metal ruler
- blocks or books
- small magnets (strong ones, like rare earth magnets)
- steel paper clips (one per child)
- crayons or markers
- string
- scissors

MANY things would be different! For instance, we would not be able to set a glass of milk on the table. It would float up to the ceiling! We would have to hold onto it to drink it. It would also need a top and a straw to keep the milk from floating out of the cup! The milk would come UP the straw at us, so we would have to stop it! Let's look at how gravity always pulls, and how we can break the pull of gravity!

Directions: Give each child a paper clip, crayons or markers, and a string. Child ties the string to the paper clip and to the crayon or marker. Child experiments with holding the crayon or marker at different angles to prove that no matter what angle the string begins, the paper clip is always pulled straight toward the earth.

Children then observe as you take one of the paper clips on a string and lay the crayon or marker beneath the magnet apparatus. The paper clip will rise toward the magnet. Children experiment with their own paper clips and the magnets on the rulers.

GRAVITY LAB

I am the LORD, and I do not change.
Malachi 3:6

Roll the ball to a partner. What do you notice about gravity?

_____

Bounce the ball to a partner. What do you notice?

_____

Which takes more pushing, rolling the ball or bouncing it?

_____

Why do you think this works differently?

_____

With a partner, each drop a ball at the same time. Which lands first? Why do you think this happens?

_____

Do you think this always happens? Why or why not?

_____

How does God's law relate to the law of gravity?

_____

What are God's two most important commands?

_____

How can you love others today?

_____

32. TRUTH SETS YOU FREE

JOHN 8:26–34

*You are truly my disciples if you remain faithful to my teachings.
And you will know the truth, and the truth will set you free.
John 8:31–32*

BIG IDEA

TRUTH AND LIES NEVER MIX

OVERVIEW

Say: Would you believe me if I said you won a million dollars? (*Children respond.*) Why don't you believe me? (*Children respond.*) What if I told you that if you drink from my water bottle, you'll grow to be six feet tall? (*Children respond.*) What? Why don't you believe me? (*Children respond.*)

We don't believe those statements because we know some things that ARE true. We know that people don't win a million dollars when they don't enter any contest with a million-dollar prize! People don't grow to be six feet tall by drinking from someone's water bottle. Because we know things that ARE true, we can decide what is NOT true. **Truth and lies never mix**! Today, we will learn the law of immiscibility—when two liquids are so different that they do not mix. (*Open with prayer requests, praises, and a time of prayer.*)

BIBLE STORY

Say: When it came to telling the truth, Jesus was very good at it! But often, Jesus said things that the religious leaders did not like. So they tried to argue with Jesus and tried to make Jesus look bad.

One day, Jesus was teaching in the Temple in Jerusalem. (*Read John 8:26–29 aloud.*) Jesus was talking about the fact that God his Father had sent him to Earth. Jesus only said the things God told him to say. When Jesus talked about "lifting up the Son of Man," he was talking about his crucifixion. He knew that these same people wanted to see him die on a cross. Those who were listening didn't understand what Jesus was talking about.

Still, some people DID believe in Jesus. He told them the words of our Bible verse. Let's read it aloud. (*Read John 8:31–32 aloud.*) What do you think Jesus meant by truth setting people free? (*Children respond.*)

We are free when we tell the truth because then we don't have to remember any lies! Our minds are clear. We don't have to wonder how to make that lie match what we told someone else! That is being free—not afraid, not trying to fool people. Because when we sin, we are not free. Listen to what Jesus said about sin. (*Read John 8:34 aloud.*)

As long as we do wrong, we are slaves to that wrong. Even when it isn't a wrong that others can't see, it doesn't feel right. If we want to be free people, then we learn to be people of truth. Let Jesus teach us more truth. **Truth and lies never mix!**

OPENING GAME
TRUE OR FALSE

Directions: Mark a line of masking tape down the center of the room. Designate one side as the "true side" and the opposite side as the "false side."

All children begin standing on the masking-tape line. Ask children questions. Children decide whether the statement is true or false and move to the appropriate side of the room. Once everyone has voted, children move back to the center line.

Say: Today we learned that the truth will set you free. I'm about to ask you some questions, and you get to decide if they are true or false. If you think the answer is true move to this side of the room. (*Indicate true side.*) If you think it's false, move to this side of the room. (*Indicate false side.*)

- You are fifteen.
- You know your address.
- You just won a million dollars.
- You have braces.
- You know what John 3:16 says (*test them!*)
- You have a giraffe in your bathroom.
- You are wearing jeans.
- You've ridden a horse.

(*Continue, making up other true or false statements, or invite children to add one.*)

This was a funny game! But lies are never funny. They hurt us, they hurt others and they break God's law. **Truth and lies never mix!**

OBJECT LESSON
IMMISCIBLE ICE

Preparation: To make colored ice cubes for this experiment, add food coloring to the water before freezing it in ice cube trays. Fill plastic cups halfway with vegetable oil.

Tip: Make several setups, or one for each child.

> **Materials**
> - masking tape

> **Materials**
> - food coloring
> - ice cubes
> - ice cube tray
> - clear plastic cups
> - vegetable oil
> - coffee stirrers

Say: Today we are going to learn about immiscibility. That's a big word that means two liquids will not mix. They are enemies no matter what. Who can tell me if this is true: oil and water don't mix. (*Children respond.*) Why do you think that is so? (*Children respond.*) Oil and water do not mix. But did you know that ICE will float on top of oil? Let's see what happens when we try to mix these things together!

Directions: Gently place an ice cube into the cup of oil. Notice whether it sinks or floats. Observe what happens when blowing warm breath on the ice cube, or hold the cup in warm hands. Observe how the melted ice (now water) moves below the oil. After the ice melts into water, stir the cup vigorously. Watch to see what happens.

Say: The ice floats on top because frozen water is less dense than oil. This means that the little molecules that make up ice are spread farther apart. Think of all the little molecules inside of ice holding hands with their arms stretched out. This makes ice lighter than oil.

Think of the oil molecules as holding hands, but standing shoulder to shoulder. There is less space between them when compared to ice. Ice is also less dense than liquid water. But when the ice melts, it becomes denser than the oil. Think of the little molecules moving closer together.

Water also has very different molecular bonds than oil. The water molecules hold hands or "bond" in a different pattern than the oil molecules. Those very different bonds keep these two from ever mixing.

Even when we tried to mix them up, what happened? (*Children respond.*) It's like truth and lies. **Truth and lies never mix!** Jesus said that we will be slaves to sin, but the truth will set us free. Let's always strive to be truthful and free.

OPTIONAL ACTIVITIES
FORCES THAT REPEL

Say: Magnets have positive and negative charges. They are attracted to opposite charges. If I have a negative-charged magnet, what type of magnet will it attract? (*Children respond.*) A positive magnet!

Let's look at the magnets we have here. Remember that they will attract the opposite, but they will push away a similar charge. (*Try to press together two similarly charged magnets.*) These magnets can never come together when we hold this side against that side. You can try as hard as you want, but a negative will never attract a negative.

That is like truth and lies. We can push, and hold, and try, but they don't come together. **Truth and lies never mix!** Let's see how the magnets react to other metal objects.

> ## Materials
> - magnets (any shape)
> - metal objects (paper clips, etc.)

Directions: Children experiment with magnets and how they repel each other from a particular side. Observe how repelling forces keep the magnets apart.

TEN TRUE THINGS

Directions: Children try to write down nine true things and one false thing in a short time. Read aloud the answers and invite children to guess what is true and what is false.

Say: What are some things you know are true? (*Children respond.*) Today, we're going to have a contest to see who can tell what's true and what's false!

You know some good things that are true. Remember, the best way to know what is a lie is to know what is true. God's word is always true. **Truth and lies never mix!**

Materials

- paper
- crayons or markers
- timekeeping device

FINDING TRUTH

Preparation: Photocopy True Words on page 164, making one copy for each child.

Say: We are going to see if we can find some words related to truth and to things that are not true. If you have a hard time, work with a partner or with one of our helpers. It's good to know what is true and what is not. Truth sets us free. **Truth and lies never mix**!

Directions: Distribute True Words to children. Children search for words related to truth and lies and categorize them in the boxes under the word search.

Materials

- True Words, page 164
- crayons or markers

Answer Key: Truths: BIBLE, HONEST, JESUS, JUST. Lies: AVOID, BULLY, CHEAT, GOSSIP, LIE, MEAN, STEAL.

```
V U J G F M V J D V I T L D F
G S C U V M V Q H E N P W R L
J E K H S V T E H L Q U L R Q
L M N T E T P F O H I G R Z Z
V D A L V A B F N G Z E K V N
G H B V F H T I E J S T E A L
H I Z F O G O S S I P V B B K
B L W F F I O M T B B R L U O
M B I P K N D M G I I M S L U
U U C T X I B N W I I Z R L S
W N V J W Q G H L Z O K M Y F
U G G E H K U M E A N U Z A A
U D E S A E R P S L W F V Y Q
X Q G U K I X M C W Y X Q J T
A Z P S E Z M L B Z C L A E Q
```

TRUE WORDS

Circle the listed words in the word search. Then, write each word related to truth in the "Truths" box, and each word related to lies in the "Lies" box.

V	U	J	G	F	M	V	J	D	V	I	T	L	D	F
G	S	C	U	V	M	V	Q	H	E	N	P	W	R	L
J	E	K	H	S	V	T	E	H	L	Q	U	L	R	Q
L	M	N	T	E	T	P	F	O	H	I	G	R	Z	Z
V	D	A	L	V	A	B	F	N	G	Z	E	K	V	N
G	H	B	V	F	H	T	I	E	J	S	T	E	A	L
H	I	Z	F	O	G	O	S	S	I	P	V	B	B	K
B	L	W	F	F	I	O	M	T	B	B	R	L	U	O
M	B	I	P	K	N	D	M	G	I	I	M	S	L	U
U	U	C	T	X	I	B	N	W	I	I	Z	R	L	S
W	N	V	J	W	Q	G	H	L	Z	O	K	M	Y	F
U	G	G	E	H	K	U	M	E	A	N	U	Z	A	A
U	D	E	S	A	E	R	P	S	L	W	F	V	Y	Q
X	Q	G	U	K	I	X	M	C	W	Y	X	Q	J	T
A	Z	P	S	E	Z	M	L	B	Z	C	L	A	E	Q

AVOID

BIBLE

BULLY

CHEAT

GOSSIP

HONEST

JESUS

JUST

LIE

MEAN

STEAL

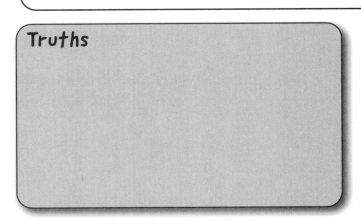

Truths

Lies

33. RUTH

RUTH 1–4

Give all your worries and cares to God, for he cares about you.
1 Peter 5:7

BIG IDEA

GOD CARES FOR US IN SURPRISING WAYS

OVERVIEW

Say: What are some big worries you have heard people talk about? (*Children respond.*) Which of these big worries do you think is the biggest? (*Children respond.*) You did a good job of rating those worries! What do you think the word "anxiety" means? (*Children respond.*) When we are anxious, it means we feel worried or nervous. Often, it is because we have a problem and we can't do anything about it. But can God do something about our problem? (*Children respond.*) We can get rid of our anxiety and worries because the Bible tells us God cares about us. God cares for us in surprising ways! (*Open with prayer requests, praises, and a time of prayer.*)

BIBLE STORY

Say: One big worry that all people have is having enough food. What happens if you don't have food to eat? (*Children respond.*) The ladies in our Bible story had some BIG worries. (*Read Ruth 1:1–2 aloud.*)

What do you think a famine is? (*Children respond.*) A famine is when there is no rain, so plants die. Food doesn't grow. Animals starve. Then people starve. What would you do if our country had a famine? (*Children respond.*)

Elimelek took his wife Naomi and his sons to another country where there was food. God provided for them. Then, Elimelek died. Naomi had her sons to take care of her. In those days, women did not have jobs outside of the home. If their men died, they might starve.

Naomi's sons married girls from Moab, named Ruth and Orpah. Then, both of Naomi's SONS died, too! This was a BIG problem. Now, Naomi had two daughters-in-law to care for. Without a husband or sons, there were THREE women with no food and no help! But God provided in a surprising way! (*Read Ruth 1:6 aloud.*)

Naomi's homeland was thriving with food! Naomi started to pack, but she didn't want to take

these women with her. They would not be accepted in Bethlehem, her old town. (*Read Ruth 1:8–9 aloud.*) Naomi told them to go back to their parents' homes. She cried. The women cried.

Orpah left for her parents' home, but Ruth clung to Naomi. (*Read Ruth 1:16–17 aloud.*) Ruth refused to leave. So they set out for Bethlehem, where Naomi was born.

When Ruth and Naomi got to Bethlehem, it was time for the barley harvest. Barley is a type of grain. Ruth wasn't going to let her mother-in-law starve! So she volunteered to pick up any leftover barley in any field.

Now, Naomi's dead husband had a relative named Boaz. Guess whose barley field Ruth was picking up the leftovers from? (*Children respond.*) Boaz's field! God had provided again in a surprising way!

Ruth was a beautiful woman and a hard worker. Boaz found out that Ruth was a relative of Naomi. He had heard about Ruth's loyalty to Naomi and her kindness. Listen to what Boaz said to her. (*Read Ruth 2:8 aloud.*) Boaz allowed Ruth to stay in his field and take as much barley as she wanted.

Boaz gave Ruth extra food, too. He even told his workers to leave PLENTY of grain for Ruth to pick up! Soon, Naomi realized that Boaz cared for Ruth. She told Ruth just what to do to show Boaz she cared for him, too!

Soon Ruth married Boaz, and they had a baby. Now, Naomi had a home and a family! That baby became the grandfather of King David! God had provided in a surprising way again. He put this foreigner into Israel's royal family! When we are worried, we can always give our worries to God. **God cares for us in surprising ways!**

OPENING GAME
GLEANING

Preparation: Cut the colored construction paper into 1-inch-wide strips. The strips will be your barley. Make enough so that there will be plenty for the children to gather (ten per child). Scatter these, with colors mixed together, across the floor.

Directions: Children form three teams. Each team gleans only one color of "barley" and tries to pick up all the pieces in their color first. First team to place all their barley in the bucket, recites the memory verse. That team gets to re-scatter the "barley" for the next round. Play several rounds. Challenge children to see if they can improve their time.

Say: When have you picked up something to eat off the ground? (*Children respond.*) Some of us have probably never done that. But what are other ways you have gotten food? (*Children respond.*) What were some surprising or unusual ways? (*Children respond.*) God always has a way to take care of us. He cared for Naomi and Ruth when they were widows. We can trust him to care for us, too. **God cares for us in surprising ways!**

> ## Materials
> - construction paper in 3 colors
> - scissors
> - 3 buckets or boxes
> - timer

OBJECT LESSON
GRINDING GRAIN

Tip: If you have children with allergies, modify the grains available.

Say: Where does our bread come from? (*Children respond.*) Who here has ever made bread? (*Children respond.*) Is our bread fluffy or flat? (*Children respond.*) In ancient times, people ground grain with a rock to make flour for bread. Let's try this and see if we can make flour out of our grain.

Directions: Children form trios and take turns to place grain in the tin. Children use the stone to grind the grain into flour. Children describe what the process is like.

Say: What was easy about this? (*Children respond.*) What was hard? (*Children respond.*) Our lives are easy compared to the lives of people in earlier times. Ruth had to gather the grain in the harsh sunlight. Then, she had to ground it for hours before baking it. We can buy flour already ground and bread already made! What are other ways God cares for us that are unusual? (*Children respond.*) **God cares for us in surprising ways!**

Optional: You should have at least 2½ cups of flour after the barley is ground. If there is not enough, supplement with commercial flour. After children have dumped their flour into the mixing bowl, children add sugar and yeast. Let sit for five minutes until yeast is dissolved. Add water, oil, and some salt. Mix to make a dough. Add commercial flour if needed. Children take turns to make a ball of dough, flatten it, and then cook their flatbread in the electric skillet.

Materials

- barley or other soft grain (rice, oats, etc.)
- disposable pie tins
- clean fist-sized stones
- mixing bowl
- spoon

Optional

- commercial flour
- 1 cup of water
- 1 tablespoon oil
- 1 teaspoon salt
- electric skillet
- 1 teaspoon sugar
- 2 teaspoons instant yeast

OPTIONAL ACTIVITIES
PLANTS FOR FOOD

Directions: Children brainstorm names of plant-based foods, which an adult writes on the whiteboard.

Say: Let's see how many kinds of food we can name that come from plants. (*Children respond.*) Let's make our list even bigger. What about meat? (*Children respond.*) What do cows or chickens eat? (*Children respond.*)

Materials

- whiteboard
- dry-erase marker

So it turns out that everything we eat is plant-based if we go back far enough! Ruth got her food from the ground, too. She worked very hard to care for Naomi and get her enough food. Her hard work paid off. Not only did she have enough food, but God also gave her a husband! **God cares for us in surprising ways!**

FOOD QUILT

Preparation: Cut paper into 8 x 8-inch squares, one for each child.

Directions: Children draw a picture of their favorite food on their quilt square. Make a central quilt square that says, "Thank You God for Plants!" Children color and decorate their squares, and then help you to tape them into a quilt. Hang quilt on the wall for parents to view.

Say: There are so MANY wonderful foods to eat. There are fruits, veggies, hamburgers, and chips. We have so many choices today. In Bible times, Ruth did not have many choices. She was a widowed foreigner in a new land. She needed food to care for Naomi. God was looking after Ruth and Naomi. **God cares for us in surprising ways!**

Materials

- paper
- scissors
- ruler
- crayons or markers
- packing tape or duct tape

ANXIOUS TOSS

Directions: Distribute Throw Away Worries to children. Children draw or write in each square something that makes them anxious, fearful, or worried. Children cut squares apart.

Pass the wastebasket around. Children crumple up their worries and toss them in the wastebasket in the following order:

- Round 1: my smallest worry
- Round 2: things my family worries about
- Round 3: my future worries
- Round 4: my biggest worry

If your group is large, children crumple and toss in two worries at a time.

Say: Naomi and Ruth had a lot to worry about. What are some things that they worried about? (*Children respond.*) They worried about protection, food, and the future. The Bible says we can throw all our worries to God, because he cares about us! **God cares for us in surprising ways!**

Materials

- Throw Away Worries, page 169
- crayons or markers
- scissors
- wastebasket

THROW AWAY WORRIES

Give all your worries and cares to God, for he cares about you.
1 Peter 5:7

Write or draw your answers in each section. Then cut the sections apart.

My Biggest Worry	My Future Worry
Things My Family Worries About	**My Smallest Worry**

34. NEHEMIAH REBUILDS JERUSALEM

NEHEMIAH 1—4

[Jesus said,] "I am the vine, you are the branches. Those who remain in me, and I in them, will produce much fruit. For apart from me you can do nothing."
John 15:5

BIG IDEA

STAY CONNECTED TO GOD

OVERVIEW

Say: Today, we're going to meet someone who did BIG things because he stayed connected to God! Nehemiah lived far from his home in Israel. Most of his family had been forced to move to a different country. Even far from home, Nehemiah stayed connected to God. He never forgot that he could talk to God anytime. When his relatives brought him sad news about Jerusalem, his home city, Nehemiah knew what to do—because he **stayed connected to God.** (*Open with prayer requests, praises, and a time of prayer.*)

BIBLE STORY

The Israelites had been forced into exile in a country called Babylon. Nehemiah was living in Babylon when his relative came to see him. Nehemiah asked about Jerusalem, the city he loved, and about his relatives who were still there. Let's read what the relative said (*Read Nehemiah 1:3 aloud.*) This was TERRIBLE news! There was no wall or gates for protection.

Even though Jerusalem was far away, the city and the people were important to Nehemiah. He was very sad. What do you think he did? (*Read Nehemiah 1:4–6 and 11 aloud.*) Nehemiah fasted. That means he didn't eat food. He spent the time he would have been eating in prayer!

Nehemiah's prayer is longer than what we read, but you can see that he was asking God to forgive the sins of the Israelites. He really wanted God to help his people! Of course, God had already been planning something for a long time—guess who was part of that plan? (*Children respond.*) Nehemiah!

Nehemiah knew that God had given him an important job for a reason. He was the king's cupbearer. He tasted the drink in the cup before the king to make sure it was not poisoned! It was an important job, and it meant that he saw the king very often!

One day, Nehemiah was very sad. He had been fasting and praying and weeping for Jerusalem. Then, the king wanted something to drink. Nehemiah brought a cup to the king, but he still looked sad.

The king looked at Nehemiah. He had never seen him sad. What do you think the king said? (*Children respond. Read Nehemiah 2:2–5 aloud.*) Nehemiah wanted to rebuild Jerusalem.

Did you notice what Nehemiah did when the king asked him what he wanted? (*Children respond.*) He PRAYED! Then, he answered! The king and queen were happy to help Nehemiah. They gave him the people and materials he needed. They made sure he had the right connections with all sorts of people along the way.

There were many hard times along the way to rebuilding Jerusalem—but God helped Nehemiah through them all! Nehemiah **stayed connected to God**. He prayed to God, he listened to God, and he trusted God. God made the way for him to go back and help his people do something they thought would NEVER happen!

OPENING GAME
CONNECTION TAG

Directions: This game works well indoors or out. (See tip.) Designate play area boundaries; all players spread out around the playing area.

To start the game, two players volunteer to "connect." These two hold hands and work together to chase and catch other players. As each player is tagged, that player joins the connection chain.

Play continues until all players are connected! The game continues until the last player is connected to one of the groups.

Tip: If playing with a large group outdoors, add this rule: When the group reaches six players, group splits and each trio goes on to tag three more members before splitting again.

Say: There were so many connections in this game. As the chain of people got longer, was it easier or harder to tag people? Why? (*Children respond.*)

Connections are important. Today, we are going to learn about Nehemiah. He stayed connected to God during a very sad time in history. The more he prayed and fasted, the closer he felt to God. We should always remember to **stay connected to God.**

OBJECT LESSON
COLOR UP EXPERIMENT

Preparation: One day ahead, fill several glasses halfway with water. Add several squirts of food coloring to each cup. Cut celery from its root and stand a stalk in each cup of water. Leave one stalk out of water as a control.

Before class, lay out paper and crayons or markers near the experiment. Use a black sharpie to mark on the celery the level at which the color has risen.

Directions: As children enter the classroom, invite them to look at the stalks. Children write on the paper what they think is happening and why. Don't offer information; allow them to observe and comment.

After the opening game, invite children to gather around the experiment.

Say: What did we think was happening here? (*Children respond. Read aloud the written observations.*) **These are all good observations. Observation—looking carefully and thinking—is the basis for all science.**

(*Point to the marks on stalks you made earlier.*) **I made this mark (half an hour) ago. The color had risen that high. Has it risen more? Why do you think this is happening?** (*Children respond.*) **This is the same thing that happens when a plant is connected to its roots.** (*Show the stalk of celery that has been cut off and not put into water.*) **When a plant is not connected, what happens?** (*Children respond.*) **The plant dries up!**

Let's look at our memory verse. (*Read John 5:15 aloud.*) **Jesus said that for us to grow the fruit of the Holy Spirit, we must stay connected to him. He is the vine and we are the branches. What does that mean? How are we like branches?** (*Children respond.*) **That's right, branches are connected to vines. Branches that stay firmly connected produce good and yummy fruit.**

How do we separate ourselves from God? (*Children respond.*) Sin separates us. Sin cuts us off from the vine. When we are separated, our lives start to look like this stalk of dried-up celery! When we spend time with God, we soak up all his blessings—the same way the celery soaks up the food coloring.

What are ways to stay connected to Jesus? (*Children respond.*) When we spend time with Jesus by reading God's Word, by listening to what God says through songs or stories, by praying, by talking to him all the time throughout our day, we are staying connected! Let's **stay connected to God.**

Materials

- Bible
- 4 clear glasses
- water
- food coloring
- celery
- sharp knife (adult use only)
- paper
- crayons or markers
- black sharpie

OPTIONAL ACTIVITIES

PLAY WITH YOUR FOOD

Directions: Provide a variety of vegetables for children to eat and explore. Include some roots (carrots, beets, jicama, etc.), stems (pineapple, celery, etc.), leaves (spinach, kale, etc.) and fruiting bodies (broccoli, peppers, squash, etc.)

Use the paring knife to cut apart the various items. Children observe common plant structures—root, stem, leaf or fruit—and discuss the function of each one. Children may arrange food items they select on a paper plate to create patterns, people, or animals and then eat them!

Say: God made many tasty foods for us. What are your favorite fruits or veggies? (*Children respond.*) What happens to these plants when they are cut off from the roots? (*Children respond.*) It's important for plants to stay connected to the earth when they are growing. When they are mature, we can dig them up or pick them and eat them.

Nehemiah stayed rooted to God through prayer. When Jerusalem was destroyed, he prayed for the king's favor. God answered Nehemiah's prayer. Let's **stay connected to God**, like Nehemiah.

Optional: Bring ranch dressing for dipping vegetables.

Materials

- washed vegetables
- paper plate (one per child)
- paring knife

Optional

- ranch dressing
- bowl
- spoon

HUMAN KNOT

Tip: Game works best in groups of 6–10 players. For some extra fun, set a timer. See how long it takes children to get untangled!

Directions: Children stand in a circle facing each other. Children reach their right arm towards the center and grab a hand—but not the hand of a person next to them. Children reach with their left arm to grab someone else's hand. Again, make sure it's not the person right next to them.

Children work together to stay connected while they untangle themselves. The goal is to untangle the human knot without letting go of any hands. Children can carefully go over or under each other's arms, or through legs if needed! Encourage them to do whatever they want, as long as they don't break the connection.

Say: We got all tangled up today. Was it hard or easy to stay connected? (*Children respond.*) Sometimes, in life, we get all tangled up by focusing on things that are not important. What are some things that can distract us from God? (*Children respond.*)

What did Nehemiah do to stay connected to God? (*Children respond.*) He prayed no matter how sad he was. What are ways that help you stay connected to God? (*Children respond.*) Let's **stay connected to God**, like Nehemiah.

CRAZY COLOR CODE

Preparation: Photocopy the Foody Frenzy on page 175, making one for each child.

Directions: Distribute Foody Frenzy to children. Children color the picture according to the number guide.

Say: There are many ways to **stay connected to God**. Can you name some ways? (*Children respond.*) Prayer, reading the Bible, listening to God's rules—these are great ideas. What happens when we stay connected to God? (*Children respond.*) We bear good fruit. In today's activity, let's follow the color code to discover what fruits and veggies are hidden in the picture.

FOODY FRENZY

Color the picture according to the number guide.

light green — 2
pink — 4
yellow — 6
purple — 8
green — 1
red — 3
orange — 5
blue — 7

35. FAITH LIKE A TREE

PSALM 1:1-3

Let your roots grow down into [Jesus], and let your lives be built on him. Then your faith will grow strong.
Colossians 2:7

BIG IDEA

BE ROOTED IN GOD'S GOODNESS

OVERVIEW

Say: Plants make food for themselves and for us, too! But what products do plants and trees make for us that are NOT food? (*Children respond.*) They make:

- cotton for clothes
- wood for houses and fireplaces
- papyrus leaves for paper

Did you know that plants also make oxygen? It's another amazing system God has set up to help us live! When we rake a lot of dead leaves, we can be thankful for the oxygen every single leaf made for us to breathe! God has given us many good things to be thankful for. We can **be rooted in God's goodness!** (*Open with prayer requests, praises, and a time of prayer.*)

BIBLE STORY

Say: What do you know about trees? (*Children respond.*) Did you know that the Bible compares us to trees? (*Read Psalm 1:1 aloud.*) **What are the things that this person does NOT do?** (*Children respond.*)

- follow the advice of the wicked
- stand around with sinners
- join mockers

What is a mocker? (*Children respond.*) Mocking is making fun of other people, saying bad things about them to each other. It is something that a lot of people do. But THAT is just as wrong as hanging out with people who steal or lie or beat people up!

Now, remember that we are all sinners. We all do wrong. We are not comparing good and bad people. We are comparing good and bad behavior. Psalm 1 talks about people who LIKE to do wrong. Those are people we don't want to stay around.

It's wise to avoid people who don't do right. Now, let's find out what we should do to be rooted in God's goodness does this. (*Read Psalm 1:2–3 aloud.*) **What are ways to delight in God's law, or the things God says?** (*Children respond.*)

- listen to people talk about God
- read the Bible
- pray

What does this Psalm say we will be like if we obey God? (*Children respond.*) **Yes! Trees that are planted by the water never worry about being thirsty. They give fruit, shade, and grow tall, because they have the good things they need.**

When we avoid doing wrong, and spend time listening to God, we grow our roots deeper into God's love and goodness. Like our Bible verse says, we can get stronger and stronger. We can be rooted in God's goodness!

OPENING GAME
TALL TREES

Preparation: Lay a long strip of masking tape on each side of the room. It should extend the length of the playing area. Place the same number of beanbags behind each line.

Directions: Children form even teams, and then each team lines up behind one of the sidelines. The object of the game is for each child to quickly run behind the other team's line and pick up one of the beanbags. Child puts the beanbag on their head, and walks like a tall tree back to their team's side before dropping the beanbag. If the beanbag falls off their head, the child must start over.

Call time after about three minutes. Team with the most beanbags on their side recites the memory verse.

Say: **What is easy about this game?** (*Children respond.*) **What is hard?** (*Children respond.*) **When we carry a beanbag on our heads, what do we have to do?** (*Children respond.*) **If we were really trees, we could not walk. We would be rooted. What are ways to get rooted into God's love and goodness?** (*Children respond.*) **Praying or reading the Bible are great ideas! We can be rooted in God's goodness!**

Materials
- masking tape
- beanbags
- timer

OBJECT LESSON
BREATHING TREES

Preparation: Several hours ahead of time, drop a clear plastic bag over the plant so that it covers the plant entirely. Secure the bag around the base of the plant with twist ties. Bag should be snug at the base.

Directions: Children observe the plant inside the bag and tell why they think there is moisture inside the bag.

Say: Earlier today, I covered this plant with a clear bag. Now what do you see? (*Children respond.*) **Why do you think there is moisture collecting in the bag?** (*Children respond.*) It could be that the plant is melting. Maybe it is sweating. But did you know that plants BREATHE?

This is one of the most important things plants and trees do for us. You might have heard people worry about bad gas called carbon dioxide. There is a lot of it in our air. When we breathe out, carbon dioxide comes out of our mouths. Carbon dioxide also comes from volcanos and burning fuels for power.

Guess what? Plants absorb carbon dioxide! They breathe it into their cells. Then, they convert the carbon dioxide into oxygen. They breathe in carbon dioxide and then BREATHE OUT oxygen. That is the amazing way God made plants to help us!

So when we plant a tree, we are helping to get rid of too much carbon dioxide in the air. We are helping to make more oxygen—every day for the rest of that tree's life!

Now, let's take the plastic bag off so that our plant can breathe freely again and put oxygen into the air for us! (*Take the bag off the plant.*) **When our plant is rooted and healthy, it makes something important. When we are rooted in God's goodness and growing in him, we give off good things too! We can be rooted in God's goodness!**

OPTIONAL ACTIVITIES
TREE OF LIFE

Directions: Children draw the cross section of a tree, one ring for each year they have been alive. This is their tree of life. Children draw or write between their tree rings times that they felt God's love, ways they can grow in God, etc.

Say: We know that trees live a long time. The oldest trees are thought to be thousands of years old! Every season, a tree adds a layer of growth. When the tree is cut down, we see those layers

of growth. We call them tree rings. (*Show photos.*) **When we grow, there are things we can do to help us be rooted in God's love and goodness. As you make your tree rings, write words or draw pictures of ways you can be rooted and grow strong in God. We can be rooted in God's goodness!**

TREE ID

Directions: Children attempt to identify pictures of trees.

Alternate Idea: Children accompany adults on a nature walk to name and learn about the trees nearest their building. Take note of the kinds of root systems different trees have and other characteristics. Invite children to breathe deeply near the trees, remembering that the trees are breathing out oxygen.

Materials

- book or laptop with pictures of trees

Say: Each of these trees is part of God's way to provide oxygen for us. Each tree is different. Each tree has different kinds of leaves. Yet, each one is rooted and growing. **We can be rooted in God's goodness!**

LUNGS AND TREES

Preparation: Photocopy Like a Tree on page 180, making one copy for each child.

Directions: Distribute Like a Tree to children. Children compare the tree shape with the lung shape. Children press fingers on stamp pads and make fingerprints to create leaves on the tree illustration.

Materials

- Like a Tree, page 180
- stamp pads in various colors
- wipes
- crayons or markers

Say: What do our lungs look like? (*Children respond.*) **Tree roots! This reminds us that trees are rooted and give off life-giving oxygen. When we are rooted and growing, we are like a tree. We can help others know life in Jesus. We can be rooted in God's goodness!**

LIKE A TREE

Look at and compare the tree shape with the lung shape. What looks the same? What looks different? Press your fingers in stamp pads to make fingerprint leaves on the tree. Then, write some of the good gifts from God that give us life.

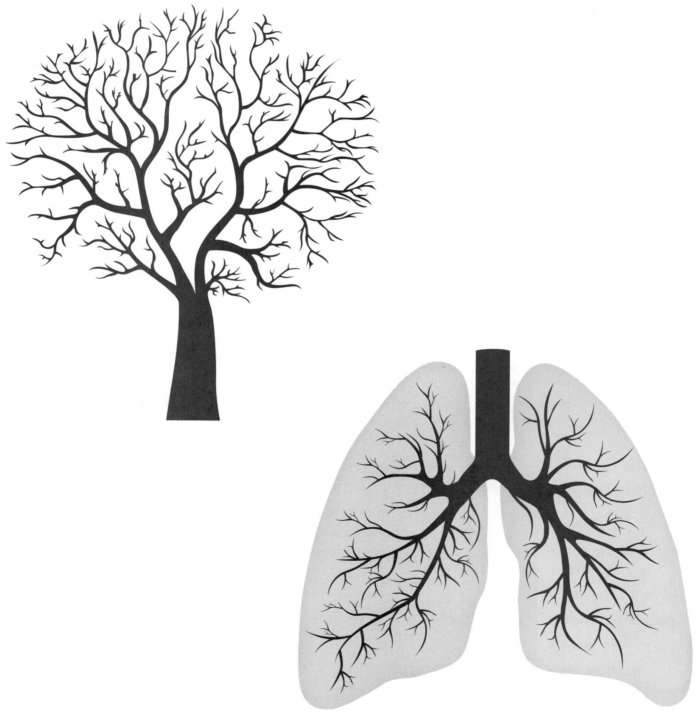

36. GOD IS MY SHEPHERD

PSALM 23

The LORD is my shepherd. I have all that I need. He lets me rest in green meadows; he leads me beside peaceful streams.
Psalm 23:1–2

BIG IDEA

GOD GIVES US WHAT WE NEED

OVERVIEW

Say: (*Hold up plant images.*) How many things can you count that are green? (*Children respond.*) Great work! Now, how many shades of green can you count? (*Children respond.*) Why do you think plants are green? (*Children respond.*) It turns out that if there were no sunlight, there would be no green! When plants are not exposed to light, they stop being green! So God created a system that included sunlight, air, soil, and water to make plants grow—and to give us food to eat! **God gives us what we need!** (*Open with prayer requests, praises, and a time of prayer.*)

Materials
- images of green plants

Tip: If the weather permits, do this activity outside.

BIBLE STORY

Say: What do you know about sheep? (*Children respond.*) Sheep aren't always the smartest animals. They will eat the grass they need, right down to the roots. That kills the plants! So, sheep need to keep moving. They need to be led to places where they can eat green plants, but not destroy them. Today, let's read a poem where God is a shepherd and we are his sheep.

(*Read Psalm 23:1–3 aloud.*) God is a very good shepherd. He knows his sheep need green pastures and clean water. This poem was written by King David. He was a shepherd when he was young. He led sheep to good pasture and clean water. He knew how to take care of everything a sheep needed!

When the sheep needed to go through a scary place, they were safe. (*Read Psalm 23:4 aloud.*) The shepherd could use his big strong stick, the rod, as a weapon. If a wild animal came, he could fight it off with his rod. His staff was a stick for leading the sheep and pulling a sheep out of a dangerous place.

(*Read Psalm 23:5 aloud.*) Why do you think a shepherd would pour oil over his sheep's head? (*Children respond.*) There are flies that try to lay their eggs on the sheep's nose. The eggs become worm-like larvae. These little worms go up into the sheep's nose and head.

It bothers the sheep so much that the sheep rubs and bangs its head. The sheep can kill itself by hitting its head! So the shepherd pours oil over the sheep's nose and head to protect it from the flies.

Like the shepherd, God takes care of us by giving us what we need, too. We need fresh food and safe water, protection, and healing from things that try to hurt us. God does this for us. He cares for us in all the best ways. **God gives us what we need!**

OPENING GAME
GATHER THE SHEEP

Preparation: Mark a start and finish line with masking tape. At the finish line, pour the 100 cotton balls into a bowl or basket. Set a roll of masking tape where each team will line up.

Directions: Children form even teams and line up beside a roll of masking tape. First child wraps masking tape, sticky side out, around their hand, and then runs to the finish line. At the finish line, child tries to gather as many cotton balls or "sheep" as possible using only the masking-tape hand. First child runs back to tag the next player.

Children keep masking tape on their hands. When all children on a team have run, call time. Children count to see how many "sheep" each team has gathered. Play several rounds.

Say: It's a lot of work to be a shepherd and gather up the sheep. What are some things that shepherds have to do? (*Children respond.*) Sheep need a lot of things. They need green grass and water. They need medicine and protection. We need those things, too. **God gives us what we need!**

> ### Materials (one per team)
> - masking tape
> - bag of 100 cotton balls
> - large bowl or basket

OBJECT LESSON
GREEN POWER

Say: How do plants make food? It's an amazing system. Let's see if we can find the food factories inside our plants!

Directions: Give children the following instructions:

1. Lay newspaper in front of you.
2. Lay a section of white fabric onto the newspaper.

> ### Materials
> - newspaper
> - sections of old white fabric (bed sheets)
> - green leaves, flowers, and stems from a variety of plants
> - rubber mallets or blocks

3. Lay some plant parts on the white fabric.
4. Lay another piece of white fabric over the plants.
5. Lay newspaper over that.
6. Pound the plant with the mallet or blocks until everything is very flat.
7. Peel back the newspaper and then the top piece of fabric.
8. Peel off any bits of plant.
9. Children observe the green substance left after the pounding. They should try this several times.

Tip: If white fabric is not readily available, use paper that is mildly absorbent—such as white construction paper.

Say: The green you see is called is chlorophyll. When the sun shines on the leaves, chlorophyll captures the sun's energy. It converts that energy into food for the plant. It combines the sun energy with carbon dioxide (a gas from the air), water, and minerals from the roots. This is called photosynthesis. Plants are green only because of the sun. Just like God gives every plant what it needs, **God gives us what we need!**

OPTIONAL ACTIVITIES
WHERE'S MY PIZZA?

Preparation: Tape mural paper to the walls or floor.

Directions: Children answer questions about how to make pizza. Teacher writes out the steps on mural paper. Children draw the steps from growing green plants to eating a pizza. Children add prayers of thanks to God for food and plants.

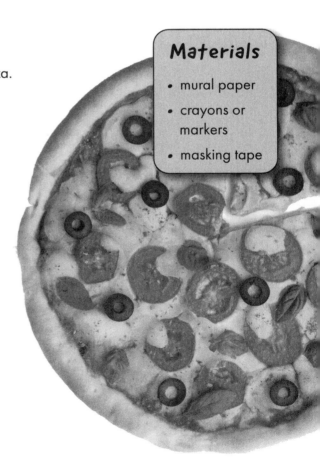

Materials
- mural paper
- crayons or markers
- masking tape

Say: Let's list the steps it takes for us to get a piece of pizza. Ask children the following questions:

Where is pizza made? (*Children respond.*) **At a pizza place.**

What kind of ingredients do you need? (*Children respond.*)

Where does the pizza place get the ingredients? (*Children respond.*) **Farmers grow all sorts of food.**

Where do the farmers get it? (*Children respond.*) **From the earth! Perfect.**

How does the earth grow the food? (*Children respond.*) **Photosynthesis.**

Just like God gives the plants what they need to grow, God gives us what we need!

BAG BIOME

Directions: Each child moistens a paper towel and places it in the bottom of the bag. Child selects some beans or peas and drops them into their bags. Do not use broken beans as they may not germinate. Child seals the bag and sets it in a sunny place at home to see what happens.

Say: Every seed that is not damaged has life inside it. Even seeds that have been found in the pyramids of Egypt have sprouted and grown—and those seeds are thousands of years old! These will need to be planted into soil to become full-grown plants. God gives seeds water, soil, and air so that they can grow. **God gives us what we need!**

Materials

- paper towels
- water
- resealable sandwich-sized plastic bags (one per child)
- variety of beans or peas

FIND THE GREEN

Preparation: Photocopy the Green Bingo on page 185, making one for each child.

Directions: Distribute Green Bingo to children. Children flip through books with pictures of plants for items mentioned on the bingo board. Children illustrate or write the name of each item that is found.

Say: God takes care of us like a shepherd cares for his sheep. He gives us water and food. He protects us when we are somewhere scary. God made so many wonderful plants for us. **God gives us what we need!**

Alternate Idea: Children take Bingo sheet outdoors and look for the items mentioned on the sheet.

Materials

- Green Bingo, page 185
- books or magazines with pictures of plants
- crayons or markers

GREEN BINGO

Look through books or magazines to find examples of the plants (or parts of plants) listed on the board below. Draw a picture of what they look like or list the name of the plant you found. When you get five in a row, call out "Bingo!"

BUD	DESERT PLANT	MOSS	FRUIT	BLOSSOM
BARK	TINY PLANT	BIG PLANT	PLANT BIRDS MIGHT EAT	PLANT THAT MAKES SHADE
STICKY LEAVES	PLANT WITH NO LEAVES	**FREE SPACE**	HOUSE PLANT	POISONOUS
ROOT	STEM	BUSH	SMOOTH LEAVES	PLANT THAT ISN'T GREEN
FUZZY LEAVES	TREE	VEGETABLE	GRASS	UNDERWATER PLANT

37. FRUITS OF THE SPIRIT

MATTHEW 7:1–2,6–20; GALATIANS 5:19–23

Wisdom from above is first of all pure. It is also peace loving, gentle at all times, and willing to yield to others. It is full of mercy and the fruit of good deeds.
James 3:17

BIG IDEA

WHEN WE ARE ROOTED IN GOD, WE GROW GOOD FRUIT

OVERVIEW

Say: (*Show pictures of several kinds of fruit trees on them.*) How can you tell what kind of tree this is? (*Children respond.*) Yes! We can tell this is an (apple tree) because we see the (apples) on it! If these trees and plants were not healthy, what do you think their fruit would look like? (*Children respond.*)

What kind of fruit would you rather eat, fruit from a healthy tree, or from a sick tree? (*Children respond.*) Why? What is the difference? (*Children respond.*) There are many kinds of trees, and many kinds of good fruit. Only a healthy tree bears good fruit.

It is the same with God's family. Our memory verse tells us that wisdom from God is full of mercy and good fruit. What kind of good fruit do you think that might be? (*Children respond.*) Love, kindness, peace, patience—those are a few good fruits that come from God. **When we are rooted in God, we grow good fruit!** (*Open with prayer requests, praises, and a time of prayer.*)

Materials

- pictures of fruit trees

BIBLE STORY

Say: Jesus was once talking to a large crowd of people. Listen to the first thing he said. (*Read Matthew 7:1 aloud.*) Jesus said that they should not judge other people. What is judging? (*Children respond.*) Judging is deciding we know what that person is thinking or feeling.

It is thinking we are so smart, we can know what people are like on the inside. We can't know what people are thinking or feeling! So when we think something bad about another person, we judge them. Jesus said this only makes trouble for us.

The only way to know what someone is thinking or feeling is to watch their honest actions. Honest actions are what people do when no one is looking. So Jesus told the people how to know if their teachers were telling the truth. (*Read Matthew 7:15–18 aloud.*)

When people listened to these false teachers, they needed to look at their "fruit." No, not their snacks! Look at the things they said and did when they were not teaching. How can you notice bad fruit if you don't know what good fruit is? (*Children respond.*)

What are some things that are considered bad fruit? (*Children respond. Read Galatians 5:19–21 aloud.*) Those are some big words. Let's simplify them: breaking the law because we are selfish, worshiping anyone besides God, being mean, speaking hateful words, starting fights, hurting others, those kinds of fruit tell us, "UH OH—that tree isn't a healthy, good tree."

What are some things that are considered good fruit? (*Children respond. Read Galatians 5:22–23 aloud.*) Love, joy, peace, patience, kindness, are easy to understand. When we say goodness, we mean being the same through and through, like pure chocolate! Faithfulness means we stick with what we're doing, even when it gets hard. Self-control means we can say "no" to what we want because we want what God wants.

Those are the kinds of fruit that show our roots are deep in God and that we are growing in healthy ways! **When we are rooted in God, we grow good fruit!**

OPENING GAME
APPLES AND ORANGES

Preparation: Inflate and tie balloons (equal numbers of red and orange). Set wastebaskets at either end of the playing area.

Directions: Play a game like soccer, using multiple balloons. Place all balloons on the floor in the middle of playing area.

Children form two teams; children remove shoes. Assign each team a color of balloon. Teams line up at opposite ends of the playing area. Choose one child to be scorer (like goalie). Scorer stands behind opposing team, but in front of wastebasket.

At your signal, all children run to the middle of the playing area and try to kick balloons of their team's color to their scorer. Scorer grabs their team's balloons and puts them into the wastebasket. Play continues until one team has all balloons of their color in their basket.

If play takes too long, call time and have scorers count the number of balloons in their team's basket. Team with the most balloons recites the memory verse. Play several rounds.

Tip: To increase the challenge, tell children to use only their left feet to kick the balloons.

Materials

- red and orange balloons (at least one per child)
- 2 large wastebaskets

Say: These balloons don't really look much like apples or oranges, do they? The colors are alike, but would these taste like fruit, just because they're the same color? (*Children respond.*) That's right. Good fruit—real fruit—tastes good! People who are following Jesus show their good fruit, too. Kind words, sharing with others, telling the truth, doing what is right—those are good "people fruit." **When we are rooted in God, we grow good fruit!**

OBJECT LESSON
LEMON VOLCANOS

Preparation: Slice the bottom off the lemons so they sit flat. Flip over and slice out the cores of the lemons. Place lemons in a tray or shallow pan.

Say: Who here has seen a volcano? (*Children respond.*) What do you know about volcanos? (*Children respond.*) When the hot magma builds up so much pressure under a mountain, it blows the top off the mountain. The hot magma flies and flows. Do you think we can make a volcano out of FRUIT? (*Show lemons.*) These lemons contain something that will unleash a volcano—but not of magma!

Directions:

1. Children use craft sticks to press into the center of the lemons. Try to get the most juice out of the lemon pulp. Be sure to keep the juice in the lemon.

2. Squirt food coloring deep into each lemon's hole.

3. Squeeze a bit of dish soap into the same hole.

4. Place a spoonful of baking soda in each hole.

5. As it starts to bubble, stir it to release more lemon juice.

6. If you need to, pour extra lemon juice into the center of your volcano, add more baking soda and dish soap. All will help to keep the reaction going.

> ## Materials
>
> - 2 lemons
> - paring knife (for adult)
> - tray or shallow pan
> - craft sticks
> - food coloring (several colors)
> - dish soap
> - baking soda
> - extra lemon juice
> - spoon

Say: Why does this experiment work with lemons? (*Children respond.*) Lemons contain acid in their juice. When acid mixes with baking soda, which is a base, then gases erupt! The food coloring and dish soap were to make it pretty and to make the bubbles larger.

Would this experiment have worked if we had lemons from a sick tree? (*Children respond.*) No. We would have had to pour lots more extra lemon juice on them. But the healthy lemons are true to their nature and make a great volcano!

When we show we love and follow Jesus, we show we are rooted in God and growing in healthy ways on the inside. What are some of the fruits of the Spirit? (*Children respond.*) Love, joy, peace, patience, kindness, goodness, faithfulness, gentleness, and self-control. **When we are rooted in God, we grow good fruit!**

OPTIONAL ACTIVITIES

WHO AM I?

Directions: Show one of the objects. Ask children to tell what they might learn about a person who uses that object often. For example, a wrench might indicate a car mechanic, a plumber, or a machine fitter. Invite children to tell what other things they can judge from just the item.

Alternate Idea: A volunteer closes their eyes, feels an object, and tries to guess what it is. Then, answers questions about occupations that require that object.

Say: We can judge people by how they look on the outside. But we can look at the things they say and do to tell what they are like on the inside. What are ways people who follow Jesus might show that they belong to Jesus? (*Children respond.*) The Bible calls that good fruit! **When we are rooted in God, we grow good fruit!**

> ## Materials
>
> a variety of items related to various kinds of jobs (hammer, pen, gardening glove, wrench, basketball, paintbrush, etc.)

SEED AND FRUIT

Preparation: Ahead of time, cut up the fruit for children to taste. For each fruit, save the seeds in a resealable plastic bag. Set the fruit on a tray or plate.

Directions: Children wipe their hands and taste the fruit. Children try to match the seed to the fruit.

Say: Not every kind of fruit has the same kind of seed. Yet, healthy fruit always makes seeds. This is the way plants continue to have babies and keep their species growing. The only plant not like this is the navel orange. Navel oranges don't have seeds. Each one is a clone of the first navel orange tree. But every tree that is rooted and healthy bears fruit and seed. We are like that too. **When we are rooted in God, we grow good fruit!**

> ## Materials
>
> - a variety of fruits
> - knife (for adult)
> - resealable plastic bag
> - tray or plate
> - wipes

ROOTED IN GOD

Preparation: Photocopy the What Kind of Fruit? on page 191, making one copy for each child.

Directions: Distribute What Kind of Fruit? to children. Children fill out the chart and color the fruit.

Say: Just like there are many kinds of fruits and veggies, there are many kinds of roots, too. Roots are important. Roots pick up the water and minerals in the soil. They keep the plant firm so it won't be destroyed by bad weather. **When we are rooted in God, we grow good fruit**! What are ways to be rooted in God? (*Children respond.*) What are the fruits of the Spirit? (*Children respond.*)

WHAT KIND OF FRUIT?

For each fruit of the Spirit, write a way you can demonstrate that fruit. For example, you might express love by hugging a friend or writing a card. Then color the fruit.

How I Can Practice This Fruit?

LOVE

JOY

PEACE

PATIENCE

KINDNESS

GOODNESS

FAITHFULNESS

GENTLENESS

SELF-CONTROL

38. MANNA AND QUAIL

EXODUS 16:1–31

The eyes of all look to you in hope, you give them their food as they need it.
Psalm 145:15

BIG IDEA

GOD SHOWS LOVE THROUGH FOOD AND WATER

OVERVIEW

Say: Think of your favorite food. It makes you smile just thinking of it. Today, we're going to focus on how God gives us food and water. We'll also talk about how much we like to taste and eat food! What's something you eat every day? (*Children respond.*) What's something you NEVER eat? (*Children respond.*)

Let's see if we can list a different food for each letter of the alphabet. (*Children call out names of food as you write them down on the whiteboard.*) **God shows love through food and water!** (*Open with prayer requests, praises, and a time of prayer.*)

Tip: Save the list for the Opening Game on page 193.

Materials

- whiteboard
- dry-erase marker

BIBLE STORY

Say: The Israelites had been enslaved in Egypt for 400 years. God sent Moses to free them. He was to lead them to the Promised Land. First, they had to cross a desert.

There were MANY people who left Egypt all at once, with their animals, too. Of course, that meant that they all needed food and water. Even if it had been a short trip, they could not have gathered enough food and water to keep them going.

When people get hungry and thirsty, how do they act? (*Children respond.*) Hungry people tend to feel grumpy and do a lot of complaining! Listen to what the Israelites told Moses. (*Read Exodus 16:2–3 aloud.*)

What did they eat in Egypt? (*Children respond.*) Meat and bread. What did they say Moses had done?

(*Children respond.*) He lead them to starve in the desert. They were very grouchy! Listen to what God told Moses about the people! (*Read Exodus 16:11–12 aloud.*)

GOD would feed these people in a special way. It would SHOW them that the food was from God. God wanted them to understand that he loved them. He was with them through everything.

What would you have asked God to send for food? (*Children respond.*) Those all sound pretty good! Let's find out what God sent them. (*Read Exodus 16:13–15 aloud.*) As evening came, small birds called quail COVERED the camp. They were everywhere! So they became dinner.

In the morning, it looked like there was some kind of frosted flakes on the ground—but when the sun got warm, they disappeared! They called it *manna* because that was their word for "What is it?"

Even though the Israelites complained, God loved them. They missed the meat and bread from Egypt. So God sent them meat and bread from heaven. He brought food to them in a special way!

God wanted his people to know he would take care of them. He was not going to leave them to starve. He sent them what they needed! **God shows love through food and water!**

OPENING GAME
TASTY CORNERS

Directions: Children stand in the middle of the playing area. A volunteer reads aloud the first four foods listed on the alphabetical list of foods made during the Overview time. Indicate which food is represented by each corner. Children move to the corner of which food they like best. Play more rounds until the list is finished, or make up more ideas as children show interest!

Say: There are lots of kinds of food. Some foods we like to taste more than others. Do you know what the four main tastes are? (*Children respond.*) Sweet, sour, salty, and bitter.

Our tongues are covered with about 10,000 taste buds. Those taste buds send signals to our brains about what we are eating! Because when food tastes bad, that bad taste signals our bodies that something is wrong with the food. It's something we should not eat, so that we don't get sick. Food and water should taste good to us! **God shows love through food and water!**

> **Materials**
> - list of foods from Overview time

OBJECT LESSON
TESTING TASTES

Say: When you eat, what are some things that happen inside your mouth? (*Children respond.*) Today we're going to have a tasty time finding the quickest way to dissolve candy in our mouths.

Directions:

1. Children number their paper 1–3.

2. Start timer. Children put candy in their mouth without chewing or wiggling their tongue against it. Use the stopwatch to see how long it takes for the candy to dissolve. When it is dissolved, children raise their hands to indicate an empty mouth. Children record time for method number one.

3. Start timer. Children put candy in their mouth. Children move the candy around with their tongue, but don't chew. When it is dissolved, children raise their hands to indicate an empty mouth. Children record time for method number two.

4. Start timer. Children put candy in their mouth. Children both chew it and use their tongue to move it around inside their mouth. When it is dissolved, children raise their hands to indicate an empty mouth. Children record time for method number three.

Say: Which way did the candy dissolve fastest? (*Children respond.*) **Why do you think that is?** (*Children respond.*) **Did the third candy taste different? Why?** (*Children respond.*)

Our mouths constantly make saliva or spit. Saliva dissolves the candy into a solution we can swallow! When more surfaces of the candy touch saliva, it breaks down faster.

Your mouth is the door to your digestive tract. So when you pop a piece of candy into your mouth, your tongue helps push it around while you chew. When you're ready to swallow, the tongue pushes that mushed-up food toward the back of your throat and into the opening of your esophagus. This is the second part of the digestive tract.

God gave us all kinds of food to make our taste buds and our bodies happy and healthy! He showed the Israelites that he cared for them by sending manna and quail. He cares for you, too. **God shows love through food and water!**

Tip: If you have the opportunity, bring in a cow's tongue for children to examine. Available at most butcher departments.

Materials
- Wrapped, soft candy (three pieces per child)
- timer
- paper
- crayons or markers

OPTIONAL ACTIVITIES

TASTE AND SMELL

Directions: Children close their eyes and then pinch their noses closed. Place a small piece of food in their hands for them to sample. Children taste, chew, and swallow the food while keeping their noses pinched shut. Give them another piece of the same food, which they eat without pinching their noses closed. Talk about the difference it makes in the taste of food when we can also smell the food.

Tip: Ask about food allergies beforehand.

Say: Have you ever been sick, and felt like your food didn't taste good? (*Children respond.*) That's because your nose was clogged. Did you know that our taste buds and scent collectors work together to give us taste? Scents from food go into our noses and affect the way the food tastes. God made our bodies in special ways. **God shows love through food and water!**

> **Materials**
> • several common foods (dry cereal, apple slices, etc.)

DOWN YOUR GULLET

Preparation: Find and cue up an age-appropriate video from the Internet about the digestive tract and how it works.

Directions: Children watch the video. Children talk about what things they thought were interesting about digesting food.

Say: It's amazing how God created our digestive system. Our bodies get energy, vitamins and minerals, water, and other needed things from our food. God is so good to us! **God shows love through food and water!**

> **Materials**
> • laptop

DIGESTIVE SYSTEM

Preparation: Photocopy the Digestible Doings on page 196, making one copy for each child.

Directions: Distribute Digestible Doings to children. Children color the digestive tract by following the instructions on the paper. In the empty box, children draw their favorite food.

Say: God provided for the Israelites when they were hungry in the desert. Let's look at the series of tubes that make up our digestive tract! When we eat a bit of food, so many things happen. Saliva breaks down the food in our mouths. Our stomach adds acids to break it down more. Then our intestines suck out the nutrients from the food bits. Tiny intestinal blood vessels transfer the energy and other good things all over our body. Our large intestines take the leftovers! **God shows love through food and water!**

> **Materials**
> • Digestible Doings, page 196
> • crayons or markers

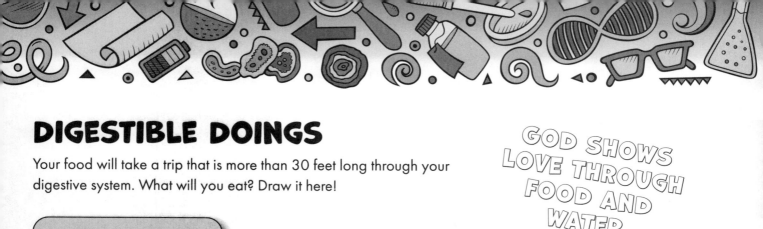

DIGESTIBLE DOINGS

Your food will take a trip that is more than 30 feet long through your digestive system. What will you eat? Draw it here!

GOD SHOWS LOVE THROUGH FOOD AND WATER

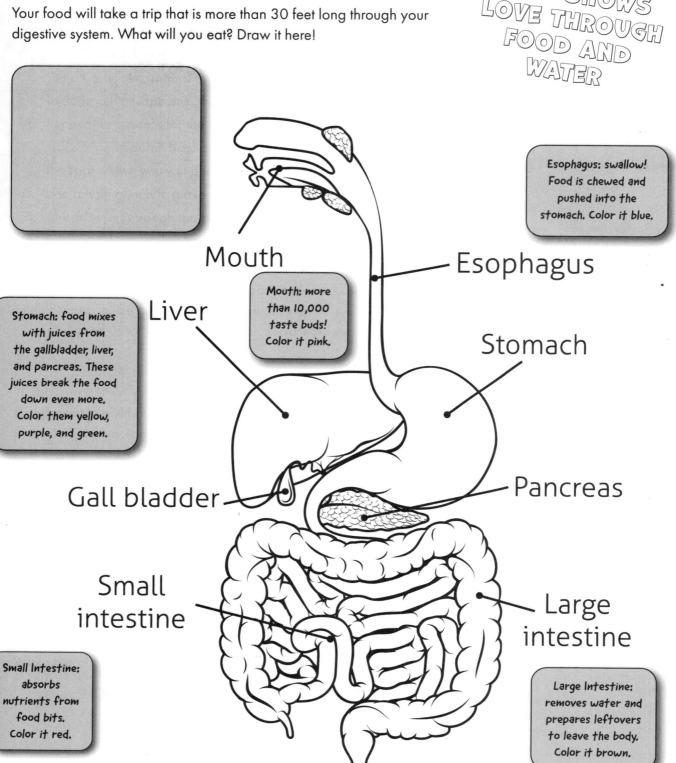

Esophagus: swallow! Food is chewed and pushed into the stomach. Color it blue.

Mouth

Liver

Mouth: more than 10,000 taste buds! Color it pink.

Esophagus

Stomach

Stomach: food mixes with juices from the gallbladder, liver, and pancreas. These juices break the food down even more. Color them yellow, purple, and green.

Gall bladder

Pancreas

Small intestine

Large intestine

Small Intestine: absorbs nutrients from food bits. Color it red.

Large Intestine: removes water and prepares leftovers to leave the body. Color it brown.

39. SAMUEL ANOINTS KING DAVID

1 SAMUEL 16:1–13; PSALM 139:1–4,13–14,16

Thank you for making me so wonderfully complex!
Your workmanship is marvelous.
Psalm 139:14

OVERVIEW

Have you ever felt different from others? (*Children respond.*)
Sometimes, we feel like we don't fit in. We feel like it's bad to be
different from everyone else. We might even want our parents to
buy us a certain kind of shoes or a popular toy because we want to be like
other people. Did you know that God made you to BE different? He wants you to
be the UNIQUE person he made—a person who is not like anyone else! So it's OK to be
different! **God made you unique!** (*Open with prayer requests, praises, and a time of prayer.*)

BIG IDEA

GOD MADE YOU UNIQUE

BIBLE STORY

Say: God's people had never had a king. They had been ruled by judges for many years. God chose these
judges to give wisdom to the Israelites. This was a unique way to govern. All the surrounding countries were
ruled by kings. Eventually, the Israelites did not like being different. They wanted to be like the other countries
and have a king. God did not like the idea, but because the Israelites complained so much, he gave in.

Samuel was the judge at the time. He anointed Saul to be king. He was a good king
at first, but then he turned away from God. This made God very angry so he called
Samuel to anoint a new king. (*Read 1 Samuel 16:1 aloud.*)

Samuel followed God's directions and went to Bethlehem. He met a man
named Jesse who had eight sons. Samuel met the oldest son first. He was
tall and handsome! (*Read 1 Samuel 16:6–7 aloud.*) Samuel was surprised
when God told him not to judge people by their outward appearance.
Samuel was thinking like a human, but God doesn't think like a human.
God is not distracted by handsomeness. God looks at who we are inside.

God said that NONE of those sons were good enough to be king. Samuel asked Jesse if he had any more sons. Jesse told Samuel that his youngest son, David, was out taking care of the sheep. They had to go find him and bring him back!

David arrived and Samuel knew this was the next king of Israel. God saw David's heart. God saw a man who loved him. So God chose him to be king. David was different from his brothers!

Listen to what David wrote. (*Read Psalm 139:1–4 aloud.*) **God knows all about us. What are some things David said God knows about us?** (*Children respond.*) **God knows how we move. He knows what we think. He knows where we're going and what we're going to say before we even say it! And he loves us! He doesn't stop loving us when we do something wrong.**

Do you think God loves us and knows us only when we're older? (*Children respond.*) **Do you think God loves babies, too?** (*Children respond.*) **Listen to what else David said.** (*Read Psalm 139:13–14 and 16 aloud.*) **God knew each of you BEFORE you were even a baby! He knew you when you were still inside your mother! God has always loved you. He has always had good plans for you. He has never forgotten you. God made you unique!**

OPENING GAME
WONDERFULLY MADE

Preparation: Write out a set of cards containing the words of the Bible verse, writing one word on each card. Make a second identical set. Use masking tape to mark start and finish lines for the relay. Mix up the order of cards in each set and place cards at the finish line.

Directions: Children form two teams and play a relay game. First player runs to the cards, picks up a card and then returns to the start line, tagging the next runner. Play continues until all cards are picked up and each team has arranged the cards in verse order. Play several rounds.

> **Materials**
> - index cards
> - marker
> - masking tape

Tip: If you have more than ten children, make more sets of cards. Create more teams, so that teams are about five people.

Say: What does our verse say about each one of you? (*Children respond.*) You are made in amazing ways! There is no one on earth who is just like you—even if you are an identical twin! **God made you unique!**

Alternate Idea: To challenge older children, lay Bibles open to Psalm 139 at the finish line. Highlight the memory verse in each. Instead of picking up a card, child reads and remembers three words of the verse and then returns to tag next player. At the end, children try to say the verse in order using the three-word phrases they remember.

OBJECT LESSON
AS UNIQUE AS YOUR FINGERPRINTS

Say: What are some things about you that are not like anyone else? (*Children respond.*) There are two things about you that show you are unique—like no one else. One is your voice. Scientists can now make "voice prints." Those prints are unique—it only sounds like one person. Today, we're going to explore another part of you that is unique. No one else has the same fingerprints as you do!

Directions: Children make fingerprints on white paper, either by covering fingertips with graphite pencil or by pressing onto an ink pad. Children use magnifying glasses to compare their fingerprints with others. Children use markers to turn fingerprints into animals, trees, or other shapes if desired.

Tip: Because children will get graphite or ink on their fingertips, provide several containers of wipes where everyone has easy access.

Say: Every fingerprint is different. No one else has the exact fingerprint pattern you have. That is the reason that we use fingerprints on official documents and for background checks. A person might change their name or their hair color, but fingerprints are unique! Let's use our other unique feature—our voices—to sing a song of praise to God! **God made you unique!**

Materials

- ink pads or soft graphite pencils
- white paper
- magnifying glasses
- fine-tipped markers
- wipes

OPTIONAL ACTIVITIES
GUESS ME

Preparation: Cut paper into strips wide enough for children to write on.

Directions: Children write something about themselves that others don't know. Collect paper strips. Read the statements aloud and children guess whose is whose.

Materials

- paper
- scissors
- crayons or markers

Say: These are things about each of us that make us different from everyone else. God made us each to be unique—that is, not like anyone else! If we were all the same, life would be so boring. Remember that God doesn't care what we look like on the outside. He wants us to be good people on the inside. What can we do to show that we are good on this inside? (*Children respond.*) We can be kind to others, pray, and many other things. Remember, **God made you unique!**

EDIBLE DNA

Preparation: Set up laptop or books to show pictures of DNA models.

Directions: Children slide three marshmallows onto each toothpick. Children insert either end of the toothpick into a licorice piece. Repeat until there is a "ladder" of marshmallow-filled toothpicks inserted into the licorice. Show pictures of DNA strands.

Children look at pictures and twist their "DNA models" as they are shown in the pictures. Children eat their creations!

Tip: A lower-sugar version could include tender celery, grapes or melon balls, and skewers.

Say: Each person in the world has unique DNA. It's like a map that tells your body how to make different cells. Nose cells look different from bone cells, which look different from eye cells. Even though you may look physically the same as your family, there is only one special you. Remember that God doesn't look at the outward appearance, he looks at the heart. **God made you unique!**

Materials

- laptop or books with pictures of DNA models
- toothpicks
- mini marshmallows
- red licorice

YOU ARE SPECIAL

Preparation: Photocopy Unique Bingo on page 201, making one copy for each child.

Directions: Distribute Unique Bingo to children. Children move around to find others who can sign their squares based on the descriptions. Call time when you see that most children have finished. Child with the most signed boxes repeats the memory verse.

Materials

- Unique Bingo, page 201
- crayons or markers

Say: When Samuel was looking for the new king of Israel, he thought he knew what to look for. How would you expect a mighty king to look? (*Children respond.*) Because kings are in powerful positions, we expect them to be handsome, strong, and have loud voices. But God has different standards. What does God look at? (*Children respond.*) God looks at the inside. God chose David to be king because he was different from all of his brothers. He loved God the most. That made him unique. **God made you unique**, too!

Tip: For an extra challenge, children can only sign each person's paper once!

UNIQUE BINGO

Move around the room and talk to people. If one of the descriptions below applies to them, have them sign that box. Talk to at least three different people!

I like to play basketball.	I have at least one sister.	I am the oldest child.	I love pizza!
My favorite color is blue.	I have a birthday in July.	I know words in Spanish.	I have a pet dog.
I have been to another country.	I like math.	I have moved houses.	I like to sing.
I am an only child.	I'm homeschooled.	I've been to a zoo.	I can swim.

40. KING JEHOSHAPHAT

2 CHRONICLES 20:1–26

*Don't be afraid, for I am with you. Don't be discouraged, for
I am your God. I will strengthen you and help you.*
Isaiah 41:10

BIG IDEA

GOD BALANCES OUR FEARS

OVERVIEW

Say: Think of a time you saw someone upset. Without telling any names,
what made that person upset? (*Children respond.*) There are many reasons people
get upset. It is normal to be upset when something happens we don't like. But after we
have been upset for a while, we can feel as if life will always be bad. That is not true.

In our Bible verse, God speaks to Israel through Isaiah his prophet. He reminds them that he chose
them to be his people. God wanted them to know that they did not need to be upset or discouraged.
God promised them strength. He promised he would balance and hold them steady. It is the same
today. **God balances our fears!** (*Open with prayer requests, praises, and a time of prayer.*)

BIBLE STORY

Say: What do you think is the worst thing that could happen to a
kid your age? (*Children respond.*) What if your country was about
to invaded by other countries? What if enemy soldiers wanted to kill
your people? That rates pretty high on the scale of scariness!

This is exactly what was happening in Judah during King Jehoshaphat's
reign. King Jehoshaphat loved God. But he got some very UPSETTING news.
(*Read 2 Chronicles 20:2 aloud.*) Wow! Enemies were about to attack.

What would YOU do if you heard such scary news? (*Children respond.*)
King Jehoshaphat was UPSET! (*Read 2 Chronicles 20:3–4 aloud.*) First, he
talked to God. He ordered everyone to come together—not to celebrate
like they usually did in Jerusalem, but to put away food and pray.

Everyone came, even the little kids. (*Read 2 Chronicles 20:12–13
aloud.*) King Jehoshaphat prayed, and everyone prayed with him!
Notice that he said they didn't know what to do, but he looked to God
for help. That means they were not going to try to figure this out. They
were waiting for God to tell them what to do. And God did!

First, God gave his answer to one of the priests. (*Read 2 Chronicles 20:15–18 aloud.*) Wow! God promised that he would win the battle for them. The people bowed down in thankfulness. They felt much better. They got ready to watch GOD fight this battle for them!

The next morning, King Jehoshaphat called together the people. He told the singers to march in front of the army! They sang and praised God! (*Read 2 Chronicles 20:22–23 aloud.*) GOD took care of all the enemy soldiers. They fought with each other!

King Jehoshaphat's army looked out over the valley full of enemy soldiers. NO ONE WAS MOVING. Not one soldier was coming after them! GOD had won the battle for them! They called that place the "Valley of Blessing" because of what God did for them there.

God has not changed. When we are scared or angry, he wants us to come to him first! God balances our fears!

OPENING GAME
FIND YOUR CENTER

Directions: Pair up children of similar height. Children sit back-to-back on the floor. Children reach back to lock elbows with child behind. Pairs work to slowly stand, balancing against each other as they do so.

Invite children to try this several times with the same partner. Then try it with other partners, even those of a different height. Talk about what happens and why.

Say: What happened when you tried this exercise with someone who is a different height? (*Children respond.*) It makes a difference when the person you rely on for balance is not the same size as you. Everyone has what is called a "center of gravity." It's where your weight is the most evenly dispersed. It's usually where your body is heaviest.

Your center of gravity can change as you take on different positions. When you do this with a person of the same height, it is much easier. Your center of gravity is in the same place!

What did you have to do so that you could keep your balance and stand? (*Children respond.*) You had to rely on each other! We can rely on God in the same way. When we feel like we've lost our balance, when things are unsteady or out of control, we can rely on God. **God balances our fears!**

OBJECT LESSON
STAYING STEADY

Preparation: Use masking tape to make a line down the center of your playing area.

Tip: If setting up this activity outdoors, use chalk to mark a twenty-foot line or use a painted line that is already there.

Directions: Mark a ten-foot line with masking tape. Children practice the following:

- balance on one foot
- balance on one foot with their eyes closed
- walk on a line

Say: Which was the easiest task to do? (*Children respond.*) Which was the hardest? (*Children respond.*) Balancing without your eyes makes it much harder to balance, doesn't it? We need our sight to help us balance. When our eyes are closed, our brains don't have all the information they need to keep our bodies in balance.

When you walked the line, what made it easier to do? (*Children respond.*) Yes! You have to use your eyes again! If you look at the end of the line, instead of looking down, your eyes and your body focus on where you are going. That is what helps you to keep your balance.

When we are off-balance or in trouble, we should LOOK to God in prayer. King Jehoshaphat knew that prayer was the only way to defeat his enemies. He was right. It's like opening our eyes and looking at the end of the line to get ourselves back into balance. **God balances our fears**!

Materials
- masking tape or chalk
- timer

OPTIONAL ACTIVITIES
BALANCED STATIONS

Directions: Set up each activity as a station. Split children into three teams. Teams will rotate between each station together.

Jump Across

Cut yarn into 4-foot lengths. Lay out lines of yarn, at least 2–3 feet apart. This is your "stream." The goal is to jump over the "stream" without getting their feet wet, landing on both feet at the same time. Children may:

- Take a few running steps toward the line.
- Stand still, swing their arms backwards then forwards, and then jump.

Materials
- masking tape
- scissors
- blue yarn
- beanbags
- large inflated balloon

To increase the challenge, make the "stream" wider. Children may:

- Jump without running up or swinging their arms.
- Try landing with feet about shoulder-width apart.
- Raise their arms up and out (like a gymnast) to balance at the end.

Balance Beans

Begin to walk the masking-tape line while a volunteer lays a beanbag on child's head or shoulder. Children may:

- Carry the beanbag to the end of the line without dropping it.
- Try carrying more than one beanbag. Talk about how it feels to walk in balance.

Flamingo Flap

Try standing on one foot while a volunteer bats a balloon to you. Children may:

- Try to bat the balloon back.
- Try to get a volley going.
- Talk about what makes it harder or easier.

Say: These activities give us more ways to think about balancing! Some things can really upset us. They can make us feel like we're falling down, down, down into a hole! But God is always ready to help. We can pray to him anytime, even when we are upset! **God balances our fears!**

BALANCE BALL

Directions: Children experiment with balancing on the balls. Talk about how it feels to be balanced on the ball.

Say: What upsets your balance when you were on the ball? (*Children respond.*) It's easy to lose our balance on these balls if we are not noticing what we are doing. That is why people sit on these balls. It is supposed to help them sit straight and balanced. But when we lose our balance, we panic! That's the time to talk to God. **God balances our fears!**

Materials

- yoga balls or large playground balls

OUT OF BALANCE?

Preparation: Photocopy Balanced Life on page 207, making one copy for each child.

Directions: Distribute Balanced Life to children. Children circle pictures that make life balanced. Children cross out pictures that make life unbalanced.

Say: Some things in life help us stay balanced, but some things might take us out of balance. These activities give us more ways to think about balancing! Some things can really upset us. They can make us feel like we're falling!

Remember King Jehoshaphat? He was overwhelmed with fear because his enemies were invading. But he knew that prayer and fasting would balance him. God is always ready to help. We can pray to him anytime, even when we are upset! **God balances our fears**!

Materials

- Balanced Life, page 207
- crayons or markers

BALANCED LIFE

Circle pictures that help make life balanced. Cross out pictures that can make life unbalanced. Next to each one, explain why you think it will or won't help balance your life.

41. JESUS HEALS A LEPER

MATTHEW 8:2–4,16–17

The LORD is merciful and compassionate, slow to get angry and filled with unfailing love.
Psalm 145:8

BIG IDEA

JESUS IS FULL OF LOVE AND COMPASSION

OVERVIEW

Say: Let's take ten seconds to think about what you can physically feel right now. Raise your hand if you can feel the chair under you. (*Children respond.*) Raise your hand if one of your feet is uncomfortable. (*Children respond.*) Raise your hand if you can feel any itching or hurting on your skin. (*Children respond.*) Those feelings all come through our sense of touch!

Each of us has a huge network of nerves that control our sense of touch. If we could look at our nervous systems, it would look like a tree. Think of your spine as the trunk of the tree. From those spinal nerves, the nerves branch out more and more, becoming smaller and smaller.

When the nerve endings reach our skin, they send signals to our brains about the sensations we feel— cold, hot, smooth, rough, pressure, tickle, itch, pain, and more. Jesus gave us these amazing bodies. **Jesus is full of love and compassion!** (*Open with prayer requests, praises, and a time of prayer.*)

BIBLE STORY

Say: What things might be hard to do if your hands could not feel anything? (*Children respond.*) How would you feel if no one could touch you because you had a disease? (*Children respond.*) When Jesus lived on Earth, leprosy was a very contagious disease. People stayed FAR away from anyone with leprosy. It was against the law to be close to a leper!

Lepers lose the ability to feel in their hands and feet. They have pain, but their nerves are damaged by the leprosy. Some people with leprosy get badly hurt and they can't tell—because their pain nerves are damaged.

But we know that Jesus is full of love and compassion! (*Read Matthew 8:2 aloud.*) The leper begged Jesus to heal him. What do you think Jesus might do? (*Children respond.*) No one was supposed to touch this man! Let's find out if you're correct! (*Read Matthew 8:3 aloud.*)

Let's stop here for a minute. Why do you think Jesus touched the man? (*Children respond.*) Jesus did not have to touch this man! He could have simply said, "Be healed." Right? But Jesus put his hand out on purpose! Maybe he touched the man because Jesus is full of love and compassion. Touching another person in kindness expresses love.

Once JESUS touched the man, he didn't have leprosy anymore! So now ANYONE could touch him! He could go home to his family! He did not have to be alone anymore! After the man was healed, Jesus told the man to do two things. (*Read Matthew 8:4 aloud.*)

In Bible times, a person proved they were cured of leprosy by showing themselves to the priest. They also had to offer a gift of thanks to God. But Jesus did not want the man to tell everyone. He didn't need to get fame or credit for healing the man. (*Read Matthew 8:16–17 aloud.*) Jesus was glad to heal people because **Jesus is full of love and compassion!**

OPENING GAME
FIND MY PALMS

Directions: Children form pairs of roughly even height and do the following:

1. Stand facing each other.
2. Hold out their hands at shoulder height, and touch their palms together.
3. Close their eyes and bend their elbows to pull their palms straight back at shoulder height.
4. Spin around one time with eyes still closed.
5. Try to touch their partner's palms again with eyes still closed.

Talk about how hard or easy it was and why. Repeat the process, increasing the challenge by increasing the number of spins each time.

Tip: If children seem frustrated, invite them to try the activity with a different partner. Let younger children practice this several times with eyes open before closing eyes and spinning.

Say: People who have leprosy often have eye problems. Sometimes, they lose their sight as well as their ability to feel. What things could you not do if you could not see or feel with your hands? (*Children respond.*)

What is hard about finding your partner's palms again? (*Children respond.*) **What is easy?** (*Children respond.*) **What would make it easier?** (*Children respond.*)

How do you think your ears might also be involved in this process? (*Children respond.*) There are special organs inside your ears that help you to stay balanced. All these systems work together so that we can understand where we are in relation to other things. Jesus made our bodies so amazing! **Jesus is full of love and compassion!**

OBJECT LESSON
PENNY TRICK

Directions: Children pair up.

1. On a flat surface, pairs lay out their five pennies in a line.
2. First child closes eyes and tells other child to choose one penny from the line.
3. First child tells second child to hold the penny tightly.
4. Second child chooses a penny and holds it tightly while both count slowly to ten.
5. Keeping eyes closed, first child tells second child to replace the penny in line.
6. First child opens eyes and places fingers close to each penny to feel which penny is warmest.
7. First child chooses warmest penny and then asks if it is the correct penny.
8. Children then switch assignments and practice several times.

Tip: If penny is not warm enough, invite children to count together slowly to thirty before replacing the penny.

Say: Pennies are made of copper—a metal that conducts heat well. When your partner held the penny, it heated up quickly. How did your sense of touch help you find the correct penny? (*Children respond.*) When you hold your fingers near the pennies, you can tell which one has been warmed. Jesus is so kind to give us a good sense of touch! **Jesus is full of love and compassion!**

> ### Materials
> - pennies (five per pair)

OPTIONAL ACTIVITIES
SOCK HANDS

Directions: Children take turns to put one sock on their dominant hand. Children go around the room, trying simple actions that they normally do (open a cupboard, pick up a small item, etc.). Children may also put socks on both hands at once.

Say: People with leprosy have a hard time using their hands—partly because their nerves are damaged, and partly because their hands often are damaged. Have you ever wondered what it would be like to not use your hands well? (*Children respond.*) Let's explore that together. I'm glad Jesus heals people who have diseases. **Jesus is full of love and compassion!**

> ### Materials
> - pairs of heavy socks (one pair for several children)
> - small items (toys, building blocks, erasers, etc.)

FEATHER TOUCH

Directions: Children form pairs. One child is blindfolded. Other child touches first child gently on the arm with one of the items provided. Blindfolded child then guesses what item was touching them. Children switch roles and continue the exploration.

Tip: If children object to being blindfolded, invite them to simply close their eyes.

Say: How can we tell the difference between a (feather) touching us and a (penny) touching us? (*Children respond.*) What makes them feel different? (*Children respond.*) Isn't it amazing that we can have such an ability! We can also tell the difference between a playful tap and a mean punch. Touch can have many meanings, but Jesus' touch is always gentle. **Jesus is full of love and compassion!**

Materials

- a variety of items (feathers, soft cloth, scouring pad, penny, etc.)
- blindfolds

SENSE OF TOUCH

Preparation: Photocopy Touch Telling on page 212, making one copy for each child.

Directions: Distribute to children. Child outlines their hands. Child tries to unscramble the words, writing the unscrambled words inside the hand outline.

Say: Look at all the things we can tell just by our sense of touch. Thankfully, leprosy is not as common as it used to be in Jesus' time. Still, Jesus reached out to touch a sick man and heal him. This does not mean that we should touch sick people. Only Jesus can do that and not get sick. But we can still be loving to people who do not feel well, whether physically, emotionally, or spiritually. Jesus is so good to us. **Jesus is full of love and compassion!**

Materials

- Touch Telling, page 212
- crayons or markers

Answer Key:

odlc = cold
letick = tickle
ssreurep = pressure
toh = hot
chit = itch
inap = pain
thooms = smooth
oghur = rough

TOUCH TELLING

The LORD is merciful and compassionate, slow to get angry and filled with unfailing love.
Psalm 145:8

Outline your hand here! When you've unscrambled the words, write them inside your hand outline.

letick

odlc

ssreurep

oghur

toh

thooms

chit

inap

42. GO LAST, NOT FIRST

MARK 9:33-37;10:42-45

The Son of Man came not to be served but to serve others and to give his life as a ransom for many.
Mark 10:45

BIG IDEA

BEING GREAT IN GOD'S KINGDOM COMES FROM BEING LAST, NOT FIRST

OVERVIEW

Say: Who would you say is the greatest (baseball player, gymnast, soccer player, president, etc.)? (*Children respond.*) What do you think makes a person great? (*Children respond.*)

We often think that a very smart person, a very rich person, or a very skilled person, is greater than others. It is true that person may have more money or ability than another person. But what makes them great? Jesus said that in God's Kingdom, things are just the opposite! So if that is true, who do you think is the greatest person in God's Kingdom? (*Children respond.*) We never have to be rich or famous or the best athlete to be great in God's Kingdom. **Being great in God's Kingdom comes from being last, not first!** (*Open with prayer requests, praises, and a time of prayer.*)

BIBLE STORY

Say: We already talked about what people usually say will make a person great. But today we're going to hear what Jesus said makes a great person in God's Kingdom.

One time, Jesus and his friends were walking together to Capernaum. BUT his friends were hanging back behind Jesus, because they were arguing! What do you think Jesus' friends might argue about? (*Children respond.*) Let's find out! (*Read Mark 9:33-34 aloud.*)

They didn't want to tell Jesus that they were arguing—or that they were fighting about who was the greatest. The Bible doesn't tell us what they thought made them great. But it DOES tell us what Jesus said would make them great! (*Read Mark 9:35-37 aloud.*)

Wait a minute! What's great about being LAST? What's great about being everyone else's SERVANT? (*Children respond.*) What is great about a little kid? (*Children respond.*)

Little kids really can't do much but be themselves! They can love and trust. But JESUS said that when we welcome a little child, we are welcoming him—and God who sent him! That's a really good reason to be kind to our little brothers and sisters!

By the world's way of looking at things, being last, being a servant, or a little kid, are NOT great. But Jesus also said that he came to turn things upside down—to make the first one last and the last one first! Jesus looks at our HEARTS and MINDS. He knows that if we put others first, we become more like him.

Listen to what Jesus said another time two of his friends thought they should be the greatest in his kingdom. (*Read Mark 10:42–45 aloud.*) Jesus IS the GREATEST. But what did Jesus say about himself when he called himself the Son of Man? (*Children respond.*)

Jesus did not come to be the boss. He did not come to get people to serve him. He came to serve others—and to die in their place so that they could be brought back to God! Jesus was willing to serve even if it meant he had to DIE! So if we are part of God's Kingdom, Jesus tells us to be last, to be servants, to be like little kids—loving him, trusting him, and obeying him! **Being great in God's Kingdom comes from being last, not first!**

OPENING GAME
SERVING UP RELAY

Preparation: Mark start and finish lines with masking tape. At the start line, set one plate and four cups.

Directions: Children form even teams and line up behind start line. Children set the four cups on top of the plate like a serving tray. First child picks up the "tray" with cups. Child must hold it like a server, carrying tray of cups to the finish line and back before giving tray to next player. If cups fall off, child must replace them before continuing.

Team which finishes LAST, not first, is applauded by you!

Tip: Heavier paper plates will work better as trays.

Say: This team finished first. But I'm declaring the team that finished LAST to be the greatest! What do you think about that? (*Children respond.*) In our world, we're used to trying to be first! But that is not the way Jesus said to live. Jesus looks at our HEARTS and MINDS. He wants us to THINK of others before ourselves.

What would be hard about being a servant? (*Children respond.*) Do you think it would be fun or not fun? (*Children respond.*) Jesus tells us that we should not seek to be first, to be the boss, or the greatest, but to serve others. Even Jesus came to serve others. Being a servant means we let others be first. We help others be better. **Being great in God's Kingdom comes from being last, not first!**

Materials

- masking tape
- paper plates (one per team)
- paper cups (four per team)

OBJECT LESSON
GETTING LOW

Say: We are usually looking for the strongest person, the tallest person, the biggest person. But did you know that sometimes being the SHORTEST person can be the most important? Today, we're going to talk about what we call our "center of gravity." This is the place where most of our weight is concentrated. A shorter person has a lower center of gravity than a taller person. This is the reason why it is easier for a shorter person to throw a taller person in activities like judo.

Directions: Children form trios and stand in a line beside each other. Center person bends their arms and makes fists close to their shoulders. Other two try to lift the center person by grabbing their elbows and lifting. Trios trade positions and try again, so everyone has a turn.

One person sits in the chair, with back pressed against the chair back. Another child presses a finger on sitter's forehead to keep them from moving forward. Sitter tries to rise. All take turns sitting and trying to rise.

Say: What makes it easier or harder to do these tasks? (*Children respond.*) When our elbows are close to our center of gravity, our friends lifted us more easily. When we could not move forward to shift our center of gravity to be over our legs, we couldn't get out of the chair. Today, we found out that to be great, we don't have to be the tallest, strongest, or biggest. God cares about our hearts and minds. **Being great in God's Kingdom comes from being last, not first!**

> ## Materials
> - chair (one for every three children)

OPTIONAL ACTIVITIES
BOSS OR SERVANT?

Directions: Children take turns to role-play being the boss and saying commanding words such as "Do this" or "What I say goes." After each boss statement, invite a volunteer to play the servant role. Servant finds a way to state that same idea but in a different way. Include body language, too!

Say: We're used to hearing things like, "Like a BOSS!" or "He's in charge!" But Jesus thinks differently than humans. Jesus cares about our hearts and minds. Our actions and words show others what is in our hearts and minds. When Jesus' disciples were arguing about who was greatest, they were not thinking like Jesus. **Being great in God's Kingdom comes from being last, not first!**

RUN TO LAST PLACE

Preparation: Set two chairs to mark the edges of the playing area.

Directions: At your signal, children move in the way you suggest (tiptoe, hop, slide, etc.), starting behind one chair and moving around the other chair to return to the start. The goal is to end up in the last place in line. But no one can move until the last child arrives, and then everyone has ten seconds to try to take the last place in line.

Say: We're always trying to be first. But Jesus said it is even BETTER to be the last one. He wants to teach our hearts and minds to think like HIM. **Being great in God's Kingdom comes from being last, not first!**

Materials
- 2 chairs

PRAISE WITH MY WORDS

Preparation: Photocopy the Praise Poem on page 217, making one copy for each child.

Directions: Distribute to children. Children may circle, write, or dictate their ideas to fill in the blanks. The goal is to fill in the blanks with the antonyms of the words in parentheses. For example, in the first line, children can thank God that they are weak because he is strong. Children draw a picture of themselves serving.

Say: God knows everything about us. He knows our hearts and minds. He doesn't want our minds to think like regular humans. Regular humans are selfish and want to be the first at everything. **Being great in God's Kingdom comes from being last, not first!**

Materials
- Praise Poem, page 217
- crayons or markers

PRAISE POEM

The Son of Man came not to be served but to serve others and to give his life as a ransom for many.
Mark 10:45

Write a poem to God by filling in the blanks. You can choose words from the suggestions or use your own ideas. Try to say the opposite of what people might expect!

Dear God, I thank you that I am (strong, tall, handsome, bold) _____.

Sometimes I feel (brave, excited, proud, sad) _____
when I think of how much you love me.

I thank you that when I feel (wise, full, happy, perfect) _____,
you love me no matter what.

I'm glad you made (strong, same, rich, smart, famous) _____**people.**
Every person matters to you.

Thank you for helping me learn to be a (boss, buddy, leader, winner) _____ **to others.**

I want to be (least, biggest, strongest, richest) _____**in your Kingdom!**

Draw a picture of a way you might serve another person.

43. JESUS HEALS ON THE SABBATH

LUKE 14:1–6

Wherever your treasure is, there the desires of your heart will also be.
Matthew 6:21

BIG IDEA

JESUS HEALS PROBLEMS WE CAN'T SEE

OVERVIEW

Say: Can you all point to where your heart is? (*Children respond.*) How can you tell where your heart is? (*Children respond.*) We can feel it thumping. Let's all make a fist. (*Children respond.*) Our hearts are muscles that are about the same size as our fists.

The heart muscle is the strongest muscle in our body. When people have a sickness in their hearts, can we see it? (*Children respond.*) But Jesus knows everything about us—even the parts of us no one can see. I'm so glad that Jesus loves us and wants to help us! **Jesus can heal problems we can't see.** (*Open with prayer requests, praises, and a time of prayer.*)

BIBLE STORY

Say: We talk a lot about people's hearts. Sometimes we say, "That person has a good heart." What do you think we mean by that? (*Children respond.*) We don't mean the person's heart muscle is strong. When we talk about hearts, we sometimes mean the deepest part of who we are. That's our spiritual heart.

The other kind is the muscle that pumps our blood and keeps us alive! That is our physical heart. Both kinds of hearts matter to Jesus!

In today's Bible story, we're going to meet people with BOTH kinds of heart problems. (*Read Luke 14:1 aloud.*) Jesus had been invited to dinner with some religious leaders—on the Sabbath day.

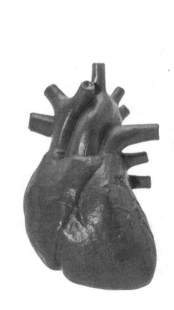

What do you know about the Sabbath day? (*Children respond.*) The Sabbath was a day of rest. In Jesus' day, the religious leaders had many rules about NOT working on the Sabbath day. These leaders wanted everyone to follow THEIR rules as well as God's rules! These leaders had invited Jesus to catch him breaking one of their rules! Do you think they had a heart problem with their physical hearts, or their spiritual hearts? (*Children respond.*) Their spiritual hearts were not right. They were too focused on their rules!

Let's find out what Jesus did. (*Read Luke 14:2 aloud.*) The religious leaders had brought this man into the house so Jesus would see him. This man had a problem with his PHYSICAL heart. His body's heart wasn't working well, so his body swelled up with fluid.

Jesus cared about this man's physical heart. He wanted to heal his heart problem. But first, Jesus asked a question of the men who had the OTHER kind of heart problem.

(*Read Luke 14:3–4 aloud.*) Jesus wanted the religious leaders to understand that a person's life is more important than the rules they had made. Of course, the leaders didn't say anything—they were waiting for Jesus to do something they could complain about! But Jesus showed he cared about the sick man. He healed him and the man left.

Then, Jesus asked these leaders a question. (*Read Luke 14:5–6 aloud.*) NOW the religious leaders didn't say anything because THEY were embarrassed! They knew that if they found their valuable cow in a pit, they would help their animal out of the pit RIGHT THEN—even if it was the Sabbath day!

Jesus showed the leaders that people (and even animals) are more important than rules. He showed them that their SPIRITUAL hearts were not honest. Jesus loved these men, too. He wanted to help them and heal their spiritual heart problems! **Jesus can heal problems we can't see.**

OPENING GAME
STRONG HEART ACTIONS

Preparation: On nine index cards, write one of each of the following: ten jumping jacks, five deep knee bends, thirty-second jog in place, ten toe touches, five pushups, ten sit-ups, ten elbow to knee, five side stretches, ten arm windmills. Tape cards in a large grid pattern. Mark a line about five feet from the grid with masking tape. Children will stand to toss the beanbag on the line.

Directions: Children stand with an arm's distance between them. Children take turns to toss beanbag onto or near one of the index cards on the grid. Lead children in that activity.

Say: It is good for our physical hearts to get exercise. Which exercise is your favorite? (*Children respond.*) Which of these do you do at home? At school? (*Children respond.*) Even though we can't see our physical hearts OR our spiritual hearts, there are ways to tell they are there! Sometimes either kind of heart can have a problem. But the good news is that **Jesus can heal problems we can't see.**

> ## Materials
> - 9 index cards
> - marker
> - masking tape
> - beanbag

OBJECT LESSON
RUN AND REST

Say: We all have felt our pulse. We know that we have physical hearts, even though we cannot see them. How many times do you think your heart beats every minute? (*Children respond.*) **There are many ways to count our heartbeats. But today, let's try looking at the vibrations!**

Directions: Children do the following:

1. Make a pea-sized ball of clay.
2. Insert the end of the match into the ball.
3. Flatten the ball against a table top.
4. Lay your arm flat on a table, palm up.
5. Place the clay ball on the thumb side of your wrist.
6. Move the ball around until you see the match begin to wiggle.
7. Watch the vibrations for one minute. Remember how many there are.
8. Run in place for one minute.
9. Count the heartbeat vibrations again.

Say: Which number was higher, the first or the second? (*Children respond.*) Why do you think that is? (*Children respond.*) **We can see by the vibrations in our wrists that there is a river of blood pumping through our bodies! Because the blood vessels in your wrist are close to the skin, it is easier to count the beats of your heart there.**

What happened when you exercised? (*Children respond.*) **Why does that happen?** (*Children respond.*) **No matter what we do, the body keeps the blood moving to our cells so that we have the oxygen we need! And if our hearts are weak, we can ask Jesus for help. Jesus can heal problems we can't see.**

OPTIONAL ACTIVITIES
BLOOD MODEL

Say: Our heart pumps blood all over our bodies. Blood looks like red liquid. But there are many parts to blood—it is very complex! Let's make a model of some of the main parts.

Directions: Fill the container about half full with corn syrup. Add a small handful of lima beans. Add a heaping handful of cinnamon candies. Add a handful of lentils.

> ## Materials
> - modeling clay
> - paper match (from a matchbook) (one per child)
> - timer

> ## Materials
> - clear glass jar
> - light corn syrup
> - lima beans
> - cinnamon candies
> - lentils

Say: If we could magnify our blood and see the parts of that red liquid, we would see something that looks like this! The lima beans stand for our white cells that fight infection. The red dots stand for red cells that carry oxygen. The lentils stand for platelets, which help to stop the bleeding when we cut ourselves. We can't usually see our blood. But even when our blood gets sick, Jesus can help us. **Jesus can heal problems we can't see.**

FIVE FINGER PRAYER

Directions: Children trace their hand on the paper. Children think of people who are sick—physically or spiritually. Children write those names in their fingers outlines as a reminder to pray for them this week.

Say: Our hearts pump blood all the way to our fingertips and toes and back again. They are like rivers that take oxygen and food to every cell. We don't often think about whether our blood is delivering food and oxygen—unless we have a problem with those unseen parts. But Jesus loves and helps every part of us—the parts we see and the parts we can't see, because **Jesus can heal problems we can't see.**

SHOW LOVE THROUGH PRAYER

Preparation: Photocopy the Prayer Doctor on page 222, making one copy for each child.

Directions: Distribute Prayer Doctor to children. Children write or draw prayers on the heart. Children color in the heart. Children can take the hearts home with them as reminders to pray, or post them together on a wall.

Say: Doctors use stethoscopes so they can listen to the sounds our hearts make. The pattern of our heart beat helps them know if something is wrong. Jesus listens to our hearts, too, but in a different way. We can pray to him and tell him any problem we have.

Sometimes, our spiritual hearts have a problem, and sometimes our physical hearts can have a problem. But either way, **Jesus can heal problems we can't see.**

> ### Materials
> - paper
> - crayons or markers

> ### Materials
> - Prayer Doctor, page 222
> - crayons or markers

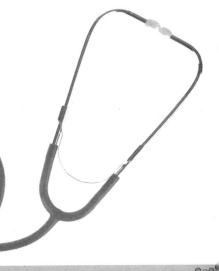

PRAYER DOCTOR

Wherever your treasure is, there the desires of your heart will also be.
Matthew 6:21

Write or draw prayers on the heart. Use it as a reminder to bring your problems to God. Remember, Jesus can heal problems we can't see.

44. JESUS HEALS A BLIND MAN

JOHN 9:1-41

Faith shows the reality of what we hope for; it is the evidence of things we cannot see.
Hebrews 11:1

BIG IDEA

BY FAITH, GOD SHOWS US THINGS BEYOND WHAT WE CAN SEE

OVERVIEW

Say: What is something you cannot see but you know it exists? (*Children respond.*)

- Electricity is something we rely on all the time, yet we do not see it.
- Wind is another good example. We don't see the wind, but we can see what it does. We even build sailboats to catch the wind we can't see.
- The Internet is invisible. We can't see the Internet, but we are sure it exists because it sends all kinds of data to our devices.

So faith is knowing something is real, even if we can't see it. Those simple faith examples are only the beginning. When we trust in God, he shows us things that we would never have even thought of otherwise. **By faith, God shows us things beyond what we can see!** (*Open with prayer requests, praises, and a time of prayer.*)

BIBLE STORY

Say: If you were blind, what things would you have to have faith about? (*Children respond.*) You would have to trust other people to help you. You would have to trust that cars wouldn't hit you when they saw you crossing the street.

One day, Jesus and his friends were leaving the Temple in Jerusalem. They passed a blind man who was begging others for money. He had been born blind. Listen to what Jesus' friends asked Jesus. (*Read John 9:2-3 aloud.*)

Jesus' friends thought that the man or his parents had done something wrong. They thought the man was being punished with blindness. But Jesus said no. This man was blind so that God could show his greatness through him.

Jesus bent down and picked up some dirt from the ground. He spit in it to make a muddy paste. Then he dabbed that mud on the blind man's eyes. He didn't even ask the blind man what he thought! Jesus told the man to go to the Pool of Siloam and wash the mud off his eyes.

The blind man must have been so surprised! But he was used to having a lot of faith in other people, because he could not see. So he went to the pool. He got down and splashed water on his eyes. Then he wiped his eyes—and HE COULD SEE! He could see everything!

Of course, he excitedly went back home! He told his neighbors that Jesus had done this! His neighbors were SO amazed. They didn't know what to think. So they took him back to the Temple.

At the Temple, the leaders didn't believe the man. They said he had never been blind! So they called the man's parents to come! His parents didn't know how it was that he could see. They were afraid of the leaders, and said they should ask their son again.

Listen to what the healed man told the leaders. (*Read John 9:31–33 aloud.*) The healed man believed that Jesus was God! Wow! **The healed man really made the leaders mad! So they threw him out of the Temple and told him never to come back.**

Jesus knew what had happened, and he found the man. Jesus introduced himself and the man bowed and worshiped Jesus! Jesus had given him something no one else believed he would ever have—his sight! **By faith, God shows us things beyond what we can see!**

OPENING GAME
CLAP AROUND

Directions: Children stand in a circle with their hands out to the sides. First person begins by clapping their hand onto the next person's hand. Child then claps their own hand "transferring" the clap to the other hand before clapping the nearest hand of the child beside them. Play this several times, challenging children to move faster each time. Next, invite children to close their eyes and see if they can pass the clap with their eyes closed.

Say: Do you think we can do the same game without our sight? (*Children respond.*) Close your eyes and we will try it a few times! Even when we could not see, we could touch and hear. That helped us to play the game without seeing. **By faith, God shows us things beyond what we can see!**

OBJECT LESSON
WALK-THROUGH PAPER

Say: Look at this piece of paper. Do you think I could fit my whole body through this piece of paper? (*Children respond.*) That LOOKS impossible! But could this thing that looks impossible BE possible? Let's see if we can practice having faith.

Preparation: Practice directions several times so that it is easy to do when you are presenting.

Directions:

1. Fold the paper lengthwise.
2. Make a cut, starting at the folded edge and ending just before the open edge. Make another cut starting from the open edge and ending just before the folded edge. Continue cutting the rest of the paper by alternating back and forth between starting points. Be careful not to cut all the way through (see image)! The narrower your cuts are the wider your end result will be.
3. Open the paper. Leave the top and bottom intact.
4. Cut down the middle.
5. Gently stretch out the paper.
6. Step into the circle it makes.

Say: How many of you didn't think I could step through a piece of paper? (*Children respond.*) This thing that looked impossible turned out to BE possible. The religious leaders in Jesus' time didn't believe that Jesus could heal. They asked the healed man to repeat his story many times! Even then they accused the man of pretending to be blind. They just needed to trust God. In our lives, we can trust God. **By faith, God shows us things beyond what we can see!**

Materials

- paper (several sheets for practice)
- scissors

OPTIONAL ACTIVITIES
FOOLING YOUR EYE

Preparation: Fill bowl halfway with water. Set bowl on a towel and have other towels nearby.

Directions: Choose a volunteer to drop small items into the water. Looking only through the side of the bowl, children take turns to retrieve an item. Then return items and have them look through the top of the water to retrieve items. Compare the two experiences.

Materials

- large clear bowl
- water
- towels
- small items (pebbles, blocks, etc.)

Say: Why is (Joey's) hand in a different place when you look from the side than when you look from the top? (*Children respond.*) Water bends the light so that we don't exactly see things the same through water. We have to search around a little to pick up things on the bottom. So we can't always trust what we can see. But we can trust God! **By faith, God shows us things beyond what we can see!**

WITHOUT SIGHT

Preparation: Place small items in a bag.

Say: How much do you need your eyes in order to learn something? (*Children respond.*) Let's see what we can learn without using our sense of sight.

Directions: Children sit in a row with hands behind their backs. Set bag behind person on the end. Sit behind the first child and place a small item in their hands. Keeping hands behind back, children touch and pass the item down the line. After item has moved down the line, children tell what they think it is. Show the item each time.

Say: How easy or hard was it to guess what those items were? Which was the hardest? (*Children respond.*) Sometimes, we can't see at all what God is doing. But we might sense it another way. The blind man in our Bible story must have been confused when Jesus rubbed mud on his eyes. But in faith, he followed Jesus' directions. He washed off the mud and was healed! **By faith, God shows us things beyond what we can see!**

> **Materials**
> - a variety of small items (coin, bobby pin, eraser, etc.)
> - bag

FOOL YOUR EYES

Preparation: Photocopy Polka Dot Spinner on page 227, making one copy for one child.

Directions: Distribute Polka Dot Spinner to children.

Child colors pea-sized dots with colored markers on the spinner circle. Laying a piece of cardstock behind the page, child cuts out both papers. Child glues spinner to cardstock. Child pushes pencil through center of spinner and spins it like a top. Talk about how the dots become rings of color when spinner is moving.

Say: We're going to make something that looks one way when it is still but looks very different when it is moving. It is another way our eyes can be fooled. But even when our eyes are fooled, we can trust God. **By faith, God shows us things beyond what we can see!**

> **Materials**
> - Polka Dot Spinner, page 227
> - scissors
> - cardstock
> - glue
> - colored markers
> - pencil (one per child)

POLKA DOT SPINNER

Faith shows the reality of what we hope for; it is the evidence of things we cannot see.
Hebrews 11:1

With colored markers, color pea-sized dots on the spinner circle. Glue spinner paper to cardstock and cut out. Push a pencil through the center of spinner at the dot. Now, spin it like a top!

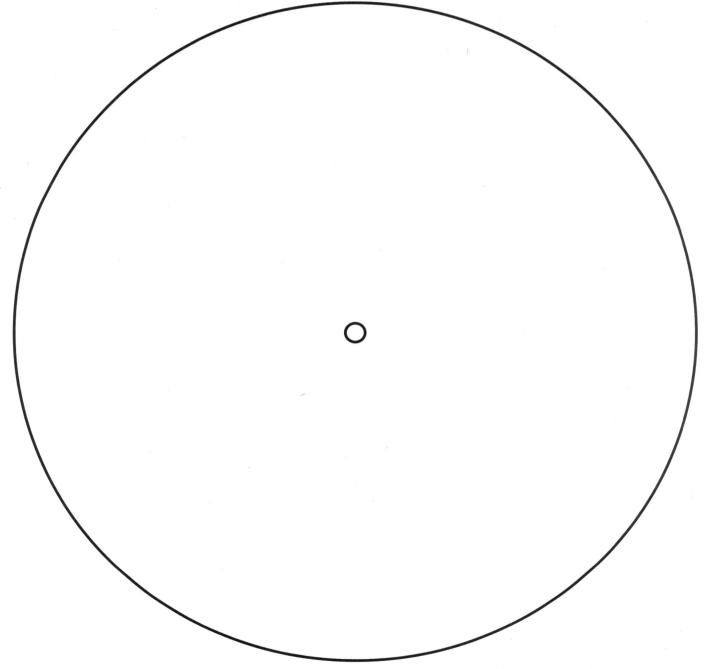

45. ARK OF THE COVENANT

2 SAMUEL 6:9-22

I will praise you with music on the harp, because you are faithful to your promises, O my God. I will sing praises to you with a lyre, O Holy One of Israel.
Psalm 71:22

BIG IDEA

THERE ARE MANY WAYS TO WORSHIP GOD

OVERVIEW

Directions: Children form pairs. Give each pair a rubber band. Each child holds up a finger and uses it to stretch out the rubber band, experimenting with the differences in tone the rubber band makes as it is stretched or relaxed.

Materials
• rubber bands

Say:

- What kinds of musical instruments do these rubber bands remind you of?
- How many of you have ever played a guitar, ukulele, banjo, violin, or other stringed instrument?
- What instruments have you tried?
- What instruments do you hear in church when there is a musical worship time?
- Are all those stringed instruments?
- What other kinds of instruments are they?

We sometimes think of worship as music that happens during church. But worship is more than music. We're going to learn more about that today. Because God is part of everything in our lives, **there are many ways to worship God!** (*Open with prayer requests, praises, and a time of prayer.*)

BIBLE STORY

Say: Let's hear what our Bible verse says about ways to praise God. (*Read Psalm 71:22 aloud.*) What are the instruments listed in that verse? (*Children respond.*) A harp and a lyre. Have you ever seen a lyre? (*Children respond.*) A lyre is another stringed

instrument. It is like a harp, but it is played a little differently. So those are two ways to praise and worship God. (*Children hold up two fingers.*) Keep on counting ways as we listen to this Bible passage.

When David became king of Israel, he built his palace in Jerusalem. The Ark of God, the big golden box that carried God's presence, was far away from there. David wanted to have this important reminder of God's presence with him in Jerusalem. But when people had tried to move the Ark, they had not obeyed God's instructions about the way to move it. Bad things had happened.

Even though David wanted to bring the Ark to Jerusalem, he waited. (*Read 2 Samuel 6:9 aloud.*) David understood that God had a right way for David to move the Ark. He wanted to obey God's way. So he waited until he knew just what to do.

Three months later, David was ready to bring the Ark to Jerusalem. He was SO HAPPY! How do you show that you are very excited? (*Children respond.*)

(*Read 2 Samuel 6:14–15 aloud.*) How did David and the people worship God? (*Children respond and keep track on their fingers.*) David danced. David wore a priestly garment to show respect. The people shouted for joy. And the people blew rams horns.

How many ways to worship is that? (*Children respond and hold up six fingers.*) Those might not be ways we worship when we are in church. But they are ways David and his people worshiped God and showed him their love and thanks! **There are many ways to worship God!**

OPENING GAME
A TELLING CIRCLE

Preparation: Choose a worship song familiar to the children and cue it up on your device.

Directions: Children form two groups. Group A stands in a circle with everyone facing outward. Group B stands in a circle around Group A, with everyone facing inward. While music plays, each group walks in a circle in opposite directions.

When music stops, children take turns to tell their partner their answer to the question you ask. Play then continues, asking and answering the next question until all the questions have been asked and answered.

Tip: Feel free to repeat questions a few times as children will have different partners each time.

Say:

- What musical instrument would you like to play to praise and worship God?
- What do you think is a good time of day to worship God? Why?

Materials
- music player

- What is a way you like to worship and praise God?

- How do you talk to God?

- What do you think is hard about worshiping God?

- What do you think is the best part of worshiping God?

- What is a way you might like to worship God that we haven't talked about yet?

There are many ways to worship God!

Alternate Idea: Invite children to move in a different way for each round—slide feet, tiptoe, hop, etc.—to increase the challenge.

OBJECT LESSON
STRING IT OUT

Preparation: Punch a hole in the bottom of each plastic cup. Cut string into 20-foot lengths for each pair of children.

Tip: Use a variety of string or line (twine, fishing line, nylon string, etc.) and invite children to tell which one seems to carry the sound best.

Say: How many of you have at least one cell phone in your family? (*Children respond.*) How many of you have a telephone at home? (*Children respond.*) Let's explore how our voices can travel on a string phone!

Materials

- plastic cups (one per child)
- scissors
- string
- measuring tape

Directions: Children pair up and complete the following steps.

1. Choose a string and tie a big knot in one end.

2. Slide one cup onto the string so that the knot is inside the cup.

3. Slide a second cup onto the string, so its opening faces away from the first cup.

4. Tie a knot in the other end of the string so that the knot is inside the second cup.

5. Partners stand so that the string is tight and straight between the cups.

6. One partner talks into the cup, while the other holds the cup to their ear to listen.

7. Children switch, so that each has chances to talk and to listen.

Say: How softly can your partner talk so that you can still hear? (*Children respond.*) Can you tell what your partner is saying? (*Children respond.*) If it is hard to tell what your partner is saying, ask your partner to count to ten. See if you can hear the counting.

What happens if you put your finger on the string while one of you talks? Why is that? (*Children respond.*) If anything touches the string, the vibrations go into whatever touched the string.

What part of you traveled over the string? (*Children respond.*) God gave you a unique voice. It is not like anyone else's voice. What's a way you can use your voice to praise God? (*Children respond.*) Tell your partner, using your string phone! **There are many ways to worship God!**

OPTIONAL ACTIVITIES

SHOEBOX LYRE

Directions: Instruct the children to do the following:

Use a cup to trace a circle around the top of a shoebox lid. This will be the sound hole. Cut out the hole. Insert six brads in either end of the box (use scissors if necessary). Cut rubber bands in half. Tie each end to the corresponding brad on the other end.

Encourage children to make some strings tighter than others. Insert a paper-towel roll under the strings, above the sound hole to lift the strings off the box.

Tip: The week before, send a notice home asking children to bring a shoebox to class. Bring extra in case some forget.

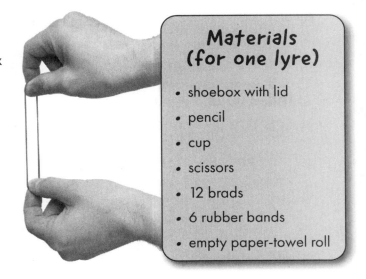

Materials (for one lyre)

- shoebox with lid
- pencil
- cup
- scissors
- 12 brads
- 6 rubber bands
- empty paper-towel roll

Say: Remember all the ways we can praise or worship God? We counted playing harps, bowing, dancing, singing—and what about speaking praise to God on a telephone? And what about playing lyres? You can make your own lyre from a shoebox! **There are many ways to worship God!**

SHORT STRINGS

Preparation: Invite a string musician to join your class.

Directions: Musician demonstrates how the instrument works, and how the pitch rises as musician shortens the strings. Children use plastic spoons to strum strings as musician holds instrument and shortens strings or makes chords.

Say: David was very excited to have the Ark of the Covenant back in Jerusalem. He organized a whole parade and danced and sang. We can also dance and sing for God today. What are some songs you like to sing? (*Children respond.*) Let's sing along with our musician! **There are many ways to worship God!**

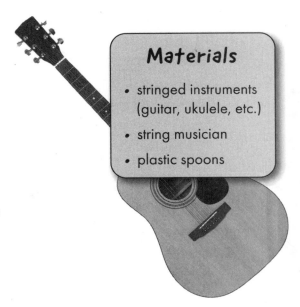

Materials

- stringed instruments (guitar, ukulele, etc.)
- string musician
- plastic spoons

WORSHIP GOD

Preparation: Photocopy Ways to Praise on page 233, making one copy for each child. Cut out activity.

Directions: Distribute Ways to Praise to children. Children help each other find as many words about worship as they can, circling words on the page.

Say: The Bible tells us some ways to praise and worship God. But since God is part of all our lives, we can worship him ALL the time! We can worship him with the way we live—by being kind, by listening well to others, by speaking kindly, and telling the truth. In our word search, see if you can find those words as well as the words we have found in the Bible! **There are many ways to worship God!**

> ## Materials
> - Ways to Praise, page 233
> - crayons or markers

WAYS TO PRAISE

*I will praise you with music on the harp, because you are faithful to your promises,
O my God. I will sing praises to you with a lyre, O Holy One of Israel.*
Psalm 71:22

Circle the listed words in the word search below. Then, on the back of this page,
draw a picture of you doing your favorite way to praise or worship God.

E	S	S	V	V	J	S	P	E	A	K	K	N	R	J
J	V	X	D	U	O	U	S	L	X	K	M	D	W	W
O	V	O	I	C	E	Z	Z	H	I	D	D	A	P	I
T	S	H	Z	F	X	K	R	A	Q	S	K	N	U	R
E	O	L	B	M	H	L	C	R	Y	J	T	C	H	Z
P	L	E	J	U	T	Q	Q	P	U	Q	W	E	K	O
E	G	A	J	H	L	T	I	J	J	J	H	D	N	S
A	F	P	J	P	T	H	M	L	H	H	C	T	Z	J
F	B	Z	F	P	S	J	U	F	Q	B	C	V	B	E
R	N	P	U	R	Q	K	S	I	X	D	X	Q	T	V
E	K	D	O	H	H	Y	I	J	R	R	G	U	L	A
N	P	W	H	I	O	V	C	Q	U	N	O	Z	Y	O
L	V	O	K	B	O	N	L	G	I	H	T	Y	R	V
A	O	I	G	A	F	V	O	S	S	K	G	N	E	X
H	G	Q	O	U	R	X	I	R	D	N	T	W	A	X

DANCE

HARP

HONOR

LEAP

LISTEN

LYRE

MUSIC

SHOUT

SING

SPEAK

VOICE

WORSHIP

46. JESUS HEALS A DEAF MAN

PSALM 19:1–4; MARK 7:31–37

The LORD, the Mighty One, is God, and he has spoken; he has summoned all humanity from where the sun rises to where it sets.
Psalm 50:1

OVERVIEW

Say: Is it easy or hard to give someone a message without saying words? (*Children respond.*) Let's play a game to see how well we communicate. Imagine you wanted to tell the person sitting on your right that you have candy and you want to share it with them. What ways could you communicate that without speaking words aloud? Ready? Go! (*Children take turns to respond or demonstrate.*) Good job!

Now, let your partner try telling you that you have gum in your hair—without speaking aloud. (*Children take turns to respond or demonstrate.*) Today, we're going to talk about listening to God. God doesn't always speak in a voice we can hear—but he is speaking to us all the time. **God speaks and wants us to listen!** (*Open with prayer requests, praises, and a time of prayer.*)

BIBLE STORY

Say: What are ways God might speak to us? (*Children respond.*) We know he speaks to us through his Word, the Bible. Nature speaks to us about God, too. (*Read Psalm 19:1–4*

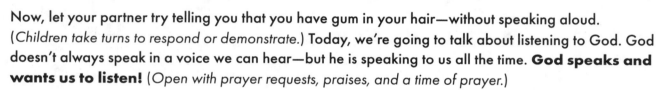

aloud.) It said that the heavens tell everyone about God's glory—and it's a message everyone can understand, even though no words are spoken. God speaks in many ways and he wants us to listen!

Today, let's find out how Jesus communicated when he helped a man who could not hear or speak! (*Read Mark 7:31–32 aloud.*) Jesus was in a part of Israel that was far from Jerusalem. People thought of it as the place where gentiles or foreigners lived.

Why do you think these people brought their friend to Jesus? (*Children respond.*) By bringing their friend to Jesus, they showed they believed Jesus could heal his deaf ears and his tongue!

Let's find out what Jesus did for the man. (*Read Mark 7:33–35 aloud.*) Why do you think Jesus led the deaf man away from the others? (*Children respond.*) Jesus cared about the man, but he did not care about everyone seeing him heal. That is something to think about!

What do people do today when they do a good thing? (*Children respond.*) Yes—they take a picture of themselves! They want everyone to know what they did! But Jesus did not.

Listen to what Jesus asked. (*Read Mark 7:36–37 aloud.*) Jesus did not want to get credit for what he did. He didn't want people to praise him for it. But because people were amazed that their friend could now hear and talk, they just couldn't keep quiet!

Jesus communicated love and care by healing the man. He led the man away from the crowd. He spoke only one word. This helps us see the ways God speaks to us: by leading us, by helping us, and healing us. **God speaks and wants us to listen!**

OPENING GAME
STRING HUNT

Preparation: Cut string into varying lengths. Ensure there are at least two strings per child. Hide the lengths of string in the area you designate for the game.

Directions: Children group into teams of four. Set timer for thirty seconds. Children search and find the pieces of string. After time is called, teams lay out their collected strings end-to-end to see who collected the most.

Play several rounds, with the winners hiding string for the next round. At the end, invite teams to work together to use the strings they collected to spell out the words "God speaks" or "listen."

Say: When we searched for the strings, we paid attention to what we saw. That is how we knew where the strings were. When we laid the strings end-to-end, we found out which team had the most strings. Sometimes when we are looking. Sometimes we are reading. Sometimes we are listening to a song or to words we hear. God speaks to us in many ways. God speaks, and wants us to listen!

> **Materials**
> - string or yarn
> - scissors
> - timer

OBJECT LESSON
HEARING THROUGH BONES

Preparation: Cut string into 2-foot lengths for each child.

Say: Today, we are going to think more about how sound travels. We know it travels through the air or you would not hear my voice! But did you know that sound also travels through solid things, like rocks and the earth— and your bones? Let's see how our bones conduct sound!

> **Materials**
> - string
> - scissors
> - masking tape

Directions: Instruct children to do the following:

1. Tape one end of your string to the table.
2. Stretch out the string so it is tight.
3. Pluck it so it vibrates and notice the sound.
4. Wrap the string around a finger several times.
5. Place finger in your ear.
6. Pluck again. Notice the difference in sound.
7. Place finger on skull behind ear.
8. Pluck again. Notice the difference in sound.

Say: What can you hear when you pluck the string in the air? (*Children respond.*) What do you notice when your finger is in your ear? (*Children respond.*) Why do you think this is so? (*Children respond.*)

The sound of the string is louder when you put your finger in your ear. That is not only because the string is closer, but also because the string is now attached to something solid—the bones in your head! The vibrations move faster through the bones in your head than they do through the air.

Now, try placing your "string finger" on the bone behind your ear. Pluck the string. Is it louder or softer? (*Children respond.*) Many people who have severe hearing loss have hearing aids which connect to this bone because it is a good place for vibrations to concentrate! There are many ways to hear vibrations or receive a message—**God speaks and wants us to listen!**

OPTIONAL ACTIVITIES
TAP TIME

Directions: Children form groups of four. Children make a list of objects around the room. Children estimate which objects will make the most sound when tapped, from loudest to softest. Children use pencils to tap on items and test their estimates from before, creating a new list of loudest to softest from what they found. Teams compare results.

Say: We're going to do more testing about how well sound travels through solid items.

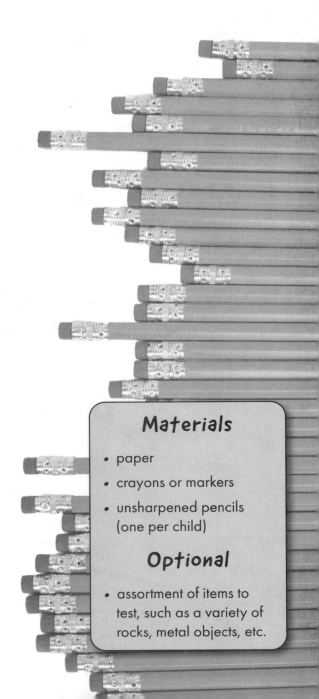

Materials

- paper
- crayons or markers
- unsharpened pencils (one per child)

Optional

- assortment of items to test, such as a variety of rocks, metal objects, etc.

Everything conducts sound, but some things conduct better than others. Why do you think trumpets are metal instead of plastic? (*Children respond.*) Because metal conducts sound better than plastic. Like these different sounds, God speaks in many ways. **God speaks and wants us to listen!**

Optional: *If you've brought items to test, show them and talk about them. If not, children use pencils to tap items found in the room or outdoors.*

STRAW KAZOO

Preparation: Make a sample kazoo following the directions below.

Directions:

1. Cut off bendy end of the straw.
2. Flatten the end of the straw with your fingers.
3. Cut the end of the straw into a V shape.
4. Place the V-shaped end into your mouth and blow or hum.
5. After you have tried this s few times, cut off part of the straight end of the straw. Note the difference in sound.

Say: In our Bible story today, Jesus healed a man who had never heard any sound before. When Jesus healed him, the news spread very quickly. The same way this kazoo catches attention, the healed man got a lot of attention, too. Sometimes, God speaks to us through sounds and music. **God speaks and wants us to listen!**

Materials

- plastic drinking straws
- scissors

SOUND REPORTING

Preparation: Photocopy Quiet or Loud? on page 238, making one copy for each child.

Directions: Distribute Quiet or Loud? to children. Children circle items that are quiet and square items that are loud. Children number the items from quietest to loudest.

Say: Jesus healed a deaf man and he was able to hear. Sometimes we are surrounded by so much busyness and noise that we cannot hear God's voice. **God speaks and wants us to listen!**

Materials

- Quiet or Loud?, page 238
- crayons or markers

Answer Key: Circle oranges, fish, bubble gum, brush teeth. Square dog, drum, alarm, airplane. Number images: (1) Oranges, (2) Fish, (3) Blowing Gum Bubbles, (4) Brushing Teeth, (5) Howling Dog, (6) Drum, (7) Alarm, (8) Airplane

QUIET OR LOUD?

Circle items that are quiet and put a square around items that are loud. Then, number the items from quietest to loudest (one is quietest; eight is loudest).

47. JESUS VISITS MARY AND MARTHA

LUKE 10:38-42

Come, my children, and listen to me; and I will teach you to fear the LORD.
Psalm 34:11

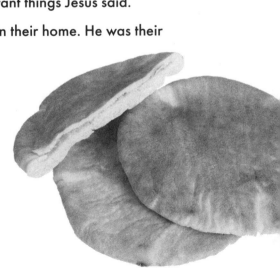

BIG IDEA

LISTEN WELL TO JESUS

OVERVIEW

Say: There are sounds all around us. What do you think are some very important sounds? (*Children respond.*) It's important to hear when a parent calls out, "Watch out for that car!" or "Stop there, so you're safe!" It's important to hear people say, "I love you" or "I think you're important!"

There is a difference between just hearing something, like noticing a fly buzzing, and really concentrated attention. But listening well can really help us! **Listen well to Jesus.** (*Open with prayer requests, praises, and a time of prayer.*)

BIBLE STORY

What are some things you know that Jesus said? (*Children respond. Repeat their answers and add these.*) Jesus said we need to believe he is God's Son. This is how we become part of God's family, so that is very important! He also said to love our enemies. He said to pray for people who are mean to us. He told us to be kind to everyone. Those are all important things Jesus said.

One time, two sisters, Mary and Martha, invited Jesus to rest and eat in their home. He was their good friend. Listen to find out what happened. (*Read Luke 10:38–39 aloud.*) Jesus was probably tired from walking. He and his disciples came into the house and sat down.

Usually the women would do all the work in preparing a meal, but what was Mary doing? (*Children respond.*) Mary sat at Jesus' feet and listened. Why do you think she was doing this? How do you think her sister Martha felt about this? (*Children respond.*) Let's find out!

(*Read Luke 10:40 aloud.*) Martha was angry! She was having a hard time getting everything ready by herself. There was so much to do to feed thirteen men! Martha wanted Jesus to tell Mary to help her.

Jesus had an interesting answer for Martha. What do you think Jesus said? (*Children respond. Read Luke 10:41–42 aloud.*) Jesus understood that Martha had a LOT of things to think about. He understood that usually Mary would help her get the food ready by setting the table and making everyone comfortable.

But Mary only wanted to do ONE thing when Jesus was around. She loved him and she always wanted to hear the things he said. She knew that if she was running in and out of the room, cooking in the kitchen, or going to the pantry, she'd NEVER hear what he was saying. To Mary, Jesus's words were the MOST important thing in the world! Listening well to Jesus was even more important than eating!

Jesus agreed with Mary. Sure, he was hungry. Of course, everyone wanted to eat. BUT there is nothing as important as listening to Jesus carefully. He was saying things that would change Mary's life. Jesus' words can change our lives, too, if we listen well to him! **Listen well to Jesus.**

OPENING GAME
LISTEN CLOSE

Directions: Play a game of Simon Says—but after the first few instructions, vary your voice with each instruction: whisper, speak softly, speak in a funny voice, speak through your hands, etc. Other adults might also speak or do other things to distract children from listening and responding. Children listen and do the actions "Simon" says to do.

Tip: If playing with younger children, when a child gets the direction wrong, acknowledge it but don't eliminate the child. For older children, increase the speed of the directions and the speed of your words to increase the challenge.

Say: The game was fun—but it was sometimes frustrating. How did it make you feel when you could not understand the words I said? (*Children respond.*) Do you think it would be harder or easier if I gave directions in another language? (*Children respond.*) Sometimes it is hard to listen! People may talk too softly or too fast. They say too many words at once. Other things may happen to distract us from listening. That's why it is a skill to learn to listen well!

To listen well means we do more than just hear the words. We must pay attention. Mary was a good listener when Jesus came to visit. Martha was listening, too. But she was so busy that she couldn't focus on what was said.

We have to ignore things that distract us. But it's very important that we learn to listen well. It helps us in school, it helps us in life, and most of all, it helps us gain good things from Jesus! **Listen well to Jesus.**

OBJECT LESSON
MUSIC FROM A GLASS

Preparation: Pour water into the glasses. Look at glasses at eye level: fill one full, one ¾ full, the next half full, the next one ¼ full. Leave the last glass empty.

Directions: Children gently tap the glasses, first in order, and then to see if they can make a tune by tapping on the glasses. Children take turns to tap on the glasses, listening to see the differences in the sounds.

Say: Not every glass sounds the same. Why do you think that is? (*Children respond.*) **What do you think causes the difference in the tones?** (*Children respond.*) **When there is less water in the glass, is the sound lower or higher?** (*Children respond.*) **With different amounts of water, the tones become lower or higher.**

What difference do you notice in the tone when you hit the glass with a wooden spoon? A mental spoon? (*Children respond.*)

Can you sound two notes at the same time to make a harmony? (*Children respond.*) **That might take some listening and experimenting. But it is good listening practice! Listen well to Jesus.**

> ### Materials
> - set of 6 identical glass water glasses
> - pitcher of water
> - large spoons (wooden, metal, plastic)

OPTIONAL ACTIVITIES
EARDRUM SIMULATION

Directions: Stretch the plastic wrap tightly over the top of the bowl. Tape the wrap on all sides so that it is tight, like a drum. Sprinkle some salt onto the stretched plastic wrap. Stand a few feet from the bowl. Hold the pan at the height of the bowl. Bang the pan lid onto the pan a few times.

Say: What do you see happening? (*Children respond.*) **Sound waves move through the air and hit the bowl. The plastic wrap moves, and bounces the salt, so that we can see the vibration's effect. This is the way our eardrum works inside our ears. It is a thin membrane that is very tight like our plastic wrap.**

When vibrations go inside our ears and hit our eardrums, the eardrums move. The eardrums transfer the sound to tiny bones inside our ears and on to our brains. Listening happens

> ### Materials
> - large bowl
> - plastic wrap
> - masking tape
> - salt
> - metal pan with lid

naturally, but listening well takes practice. Mary showed us how to be a good listener. She sat still at Jesus' feet and paid attention to every word he said. **Listen well to Jesus.**

LOOK FOR THE RED

Preparation: Gather Bibles with Jesus' words in red.

Directions: Children break into four groups. Each take a Bible and choose one of the Gospels. Children look through that gospel to find Jesus' words in red. Children read aloud what they found. List these words and references on the whiteboard.

Instead of raising a hand, change the method of "signaling" from wiggling fingers over the head to standing up and turning around, jumping twice, etc.

Say: Look at all the important things we found that Jesus said! Which one do you think is easiest to do? (*Children respond.*) Hardest? (*Children respond.*) Surprising? (*Children respond.*) Listening to Jesus is so important. Mary didn't even want to eat—she put all her attention on Jesus. Jesus said she had chosen something even better than eating dinner—because Jesus' words fed her on the inside! **Listen well to Jesus.**

> ### Materials
> - Bibles with Jesus' words in red
> - whiteboard
> - dry-erase marker

LISTEN WELL

Preparation: Photocopy the Oh My Ears on page 243, making one copy for each child.

Directions: Distribute Oh My Ears to children. Children color page and read fun facts. Discuss how to listen well.

Say: When we hear a sound, the vibrations are funneled into the ear canal. The vibrations hit the eardrum, which vibrates three tiny bones in the middle ear. Those vibrations are made into signals that travel all the way to the brain. The brain remembers the sounds and helps you know what you heard!

It's wonderful to have ears—but to focus and listen well with those ears takes some practice! If you are busy doing other tasks, like Martha, you won't be able to listen well. Mary knew how to limit her distractions by sitting at Jesus' feet and listening. Listening to Jesus is the best! When we **listen well to Jesus,** we feel at peace.

> ### Materials
> - Oh My Ears, page 243
> - crayons or markers

OH MY EARS

Come, my children, and listen to me; and
I will teach you to fear the LORD.
Psalm 34:11

Color the page and read the fun facts.

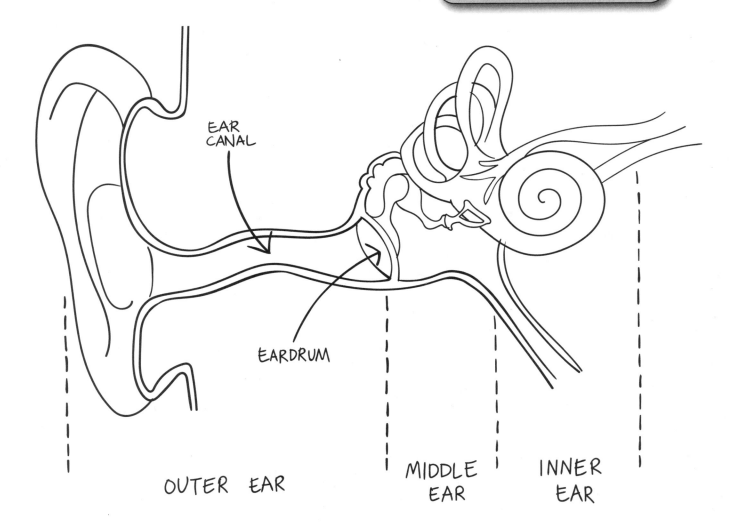

EAR CANAL

EARDRUM

OUTER EAR

MIDDLE EAR

INNER EAR

DID YOU KNOW?

The smallest bones are inside your ear. All three of them can fit on a penny!

Pores in your ear canal produce earwax.

Wearing headphones for an hour increases the bacteria in your ear by about 700 times.

48. JESUS RIDES INTO JERUSALEM

LUKE 19:28-40

BIG IDEA

JESUS IS WORTHY OF EVERY KIND OF PRAISE

Sing, O heavens, for the LORD has done this wondrous thing. Shout for joy O depths of the earth! Break into song, O mountains and forests and every tree!
Isaiah 44:23

OVERVIEW

Say: Let's see if we can make some sounds we hear in nature. Let's start with animal noises. Which ones shall we make first? (*Children respond. Make a variety of animal sounds together.*) Can we make sounds like the wind and rain? (*Children respond.*) You are very good at this!

Do you think that trees, planets, stars, and mountains make sounds? (*Children respond.*) Those sounds are sounds we can't hear. But just like the many kinds of light we cannot see, those sounds exist! That's truly amazing! Whether WE can hear the sound of the praise or not, we can learn to listen carefully. Maybe we'll discover new sounds and new ways to praise Jesus. **Jesus is worthy of every kind of praise!** (*Open with prayer requests, praises, and a time of prayer.*)

BIBLE STORY

Say: Sometimes there are things in the Bible that we think of as poetry. We might think that they are not literally true. But in our story today, listen to the end to find out what parts of nature praised Jesus. Listen for what Jesus said about rocks!

It was almost time for Jesus to die to pay the price for our sins. But first, there were things he had to do. There were prophecies—messages told long ago—about how Jesus would come on a donkey into Jerusalem. Why do you think there were prophecies? (*Children respond.*) Yes! When those words came true it proved that Jesus was who he said he is.

Jesus sent his friends to find a young donkey. They found the donkey just as Jesus told them they would. They laid a cloak on its back. Jesus climbed onto the donkey and rode into

Jerusalem. (*Read Luke 19:35–38 aloud.*) **Many people laid their cloaks on the road. They wanted to welcome Jesus like a king! They waved branches of trees and sang songs of praise to Jesus!**

This all happened so the prophecy about Jesus would come true. Jesus rode the donkey all the way into the city of Jerusalem and up to the Temple. Everywhere, men, women, and children were singing songs of praise to God.

The religious leaders didn't like this one bit. What do you think they said about all this praise to Jesus? (*Children respond. Read Luke 19:39 aloud.*) **The religious leaders told Jesus to quiet the crowds. They did not believe that he was God.**

Listen to what Jesus told the religious leaders! (*Read Luke 19:40 aloud.*) **If the people did not praise Jesus then the stones would! Jesus MADE this world. He knows how everything works.**

Jesus said that even though we can't hear the rocks, they would praise him just like the people who were singing praises to God! **Jesus is worthy of every kind of praise!**

OPENING GAME
LISTEN WELL

Preparation: Mark a start and a finish line with masking tape about ten feet apart. At the finish line, set four to six rhythm instruments.

Directions: Children form even teams. Teams line up at start line. Before first player runs to finish line, the Sound Master (an adult) makes a simple rhythmic pattern with their hands (five short claps, one long clap and three short, etc.). First player in each line runs to the finish line, repeats that pattern with an instrument, and then runs back to tag the next player. Play continues until one team has completed their run.

Tip: If playing this game with younger children, play a practice round first, and don't have teams compete.

Say: It's a challenge to remember the pattern and then repeat it. But you did a great job! That takes careful listening. Today, we're going to talk about listening and hearing. Listening gave us new patterns to imitate. Maybe listening can also help us learn new ways to praise Jesus. **Jesus is worthy of every kind of praise!**

Materials
- masking tape
- 4–6 rhythm instruments

OBJECT LESSON
HEAR THE PRAISE

Preparation: Cut plastic tubing or old garden hose into varying lengths between two to four feet long. Sterilize water bottle tops.

Directions: Provide enough materials that every child can experiment. Child tapes a funnel to one end of the tubing or hose. Child holds a water-bottle top to the other. Child blows into or hums into the water-bottle top. Child moves the hose to see if the sound changes. Compare the sounds each other's instruments make and talk about what makes them different.

Tip: This is an exploration as much as it is an object lesson. Expect lots of sound! If you are able, invite a musician in to play a short piece on their instrument to help children understand how the instrument works.

Say: Jesus said even the rocks can make a sound if he asks them to! Our Bible verse reminds us that the sounds of nature are praising God. Let's explore some ways we can make sounds with these tubes, funnels, and water-bottle tops!

Sound is a kind of wave. When we blow or hum though the tubes, those vibrations move through the tube and make a new sound. When we move our hoses, what happens? (*Children respond.*) **Why do you think your tube horn sounds different from someone else's?** (*Children respond.*) When the hose changes shape, the sound changes, too.

What is a song we could hum together through our horns to praise Jesus? (*Children respond.*) **Jesus is worthy of every kind of praise!**

Materials

- Bible
- plastic tubing or old garden hose
- plastic tubing cutter
- tops from sport water bottles
- plastic funnels
- duct tape
- other kinds of hoses (dryer hose, vacuum cleaner hose, etc.)

OPTIONAL ACTIVITIES
MUSICAL PLANETS

Preparation: Find video clips about the kinds of sounds that are made by the planets, such as "NASA Space Sounds."

Directions: Play short video clips. Children watch, and then describe the sounds they hear. As the videos play, children read the following verses aloud: Psalm 19:1, Psalm 66:4, Isaiah 55:12, Revelation 4:11, and Revelation 5:13.

Say: The Voyager spacecraft recorded many sounds of the planets, and many are unique to that planet. Did you hear some actual musical tones? (*Children respond.*) What other kinds of sounds did you hear? (*Children respond.*) When Jesus entered Jerusalem, the people praised him! But even if those

Materials

- Bible
- laptop

people were not there, Jesus said the rocks would praise him. The planets are made of different kinds of rocks. It turns out that they make their own kind of songs. **Jesus is worthy of every kind of praise!**

SOUND GUESSING

Preparation: Place small items of the same kind in a yogurt container. Use masking tape to secure the lid. Make five or six containers. Number the containers.

Directions: Children take turns to shake and listen to the sounds made by each container. Children guess what is in the container. Children write down their answers and describe the sounds. After everyone has guessed, open the cup to see whose guess was correct. Lead children in a song of praise using the shakers.

Say: We listened carefully to figure out what was in these containers. God made our ears to listen to many kinds of sounds. He also made it possible for us to make our own sounds. Let's pretend we are in Jerusalem and Jesus has just arrived. **Jesus is worthy of every kind of praise!**

Materials

- empty yogurt containers with lids
- small items (gravel, pasta, beans, paper clips, etc.)
- masking tape
- paper
- crayons or markers
- permanent marker

DO YOU HEAR WHAT I HEAR?

Preparation: Photocopy Sound Bingo on page 248, making one copy for each child. Plan to take children into an area where they are outdoors and can hear a variety of sounds.

Alternate Idea: If you are not able to go outside, play a sound clip of a busy town.

Directions: Distribute Sound Bingo to children. Children close their eyes and sit for about one minute. They report what kinds of sounds they can hear. Children move around the area, and listen again for about thirty seconds. Repeat in different areas, listening for the highest pitched sound, the lowest sound, the loudest, softest, etc. as they fill in their Sound Bingo card. Children fill in the blank space on their board with a surprising sound.

Materials

- Sound Bingo, page 248
- crayons or markers
- timer

Say: We have heard a lot of different sounds. Some are pleasant to hear, some are not so pleasant. Remember that when Jesus entered Jerusalem there were happy sounds of cheering and praising. But there were also bad sounds—the religious leaders told others to be quiet. They did not want Jesus to be praised. **Jesus is worthy of every kind of praise!**

SOUND BINGO

Look at each picture below. Close your eyes and listen to hear what you can. If you hear any of the things pictured, put a cross in the box. In the center box, write or draw a sound you heard that isn't pictured!

SURPRISE!

49. JESUS TEACHES ABOUT PRAYER

MATTHEW 6:6–15

If you forgive those who sin against you, your heavenly Father will forgive you.
Matthew 6:14

BIG IDEA

GOD'S POWER IS FOUND IN PRAYER

OVERVIEW

Directions: Make a list of things that use electrical power.

Say: What have you used today that needs electric power? (*Children respond. Write responses on the board.*) We've used phones, computers, hair dryers, stoves, refrigerators—all of those are powered by electricity, or partly powered by it. When do you think electrical power became something people could use? (*Children respond.*) In cities, many people had electricity by the late 1920s. People who lived on farms did not have electricity in their homes until much later. So one hundred years ago, most people lived without any electricity at all. That is hard for us to imagine!

But what is the strongest, most amazing power in the world? (*Children respond.*) It is God's power. How do you think we can "turn on" God's power? (*Children respond.*) **God's power is found in prayer.** (*Open with prayer requests, praises, and a time of prayer.*)

Materials

- whiteboard
- dry-erase marker

BIBLE STORY

Say: Jesus wanted his friends to understand what prayer is because prayer connects us to God and his power. Every person needs to know God and know his power! Here's what Jesus told them about how NOT to pray. (*Read Matthew 6:5–8 aloud.*) Jesus said not to pray loudly for a lot of attention. The attention will make others think you are very spiritual. But actually you just want attention.

Where did Jesus say to pray? (*Children respond.*) Jesus wants you to pray privately in your room. Why? (*Children respond.*) In your room you can concentrate on talking to God. You are not doing it for a show.

Jesus said not to keep repeating empty words. God knows what is in our hearts. We don't need to pray to impress other

people. We've talked about ways not to pray. Now, let's find out how we should pray. (*Read Matthew 6:9–13 aloud.*) These words are often called The Lord's Prayer.

- We pray to God—he is our loving Father. He is not some far-away person. This was a new idea to Jesus' friends.
- We pray about God's desires. We want to see his kingdom come. We want more and more people to hear the gospel. We want God's plans to come true. What God does is always the best!
- We ask for what we need—such as food. Food is as important as forgiveness. Jesus taught his friends to ask God to forgive their sins in the same way they forgave anyone who had hurt them.

Jesus asks us to do something hard. Forgiveness is not a feeling. It is a mindset. We may not FEEL like forgiving someone who wronged us. But if we don't forgive, then we hold a grudge. The grudge doesn't hurt the other person. It hurts us! Jesus wants us to be free from grudges.

(*Read Matthew 6:14 aloud.*) Jesus went on to make sure his friends understood forgiveness. If we will not forgive other people, that is like a broken power line! God waits for us to forgive others. When we do it, then he can forgive us. We pray like this so that we can be like electrical lines for God's power.

(*Read Matthew 18:20 aloud.*) Jesus also said that when we gather in prayer, he is with us. There is power in numbers. There is power in prayer! **God's power is found in prayer.**

OPENING GAME
ELECTRICAL CONNECTION

Directions: Children move around the playing area in any way they like (or may move as you direct—tiptoeing, hopping, etc.) Say "FREEZE," and name an appropriate body part (hands, feet, elbows, shoulders, etc.) Two players closest to each other must connect those body parts (elbow to elbow, for instance). Play continues, with children moving and then connecting other body parts.

Optional: Play music while children move. Stop music as a signal to listen.

Tip: If you have mainly older children, increase the challenge by calling out "Elbow to knee!" or "Shoulder to back!" and so on, giving children more difficult connections to make.

Say: How many of you have ever put together a string of holiday lights? (*Children respond.*) Those lights make a connection or they wouldn't all light up, right? When you all connected to each other, you were like connected electrical wires! Today, we are going to learn about God as our ultimate power source and prayer as the ultimate connection. The Bible says that when more than two of us are gathered in prayer, God is with us, too (*Matthew 18:20*). **God's power is found in prayer.**

> Optional
> Materials
> • music device

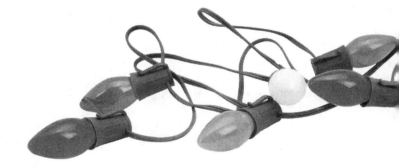

OBJECT LESSON
ELECTRICITY EVERYWHERE

Say: We know there is electricity in the light fixtures. We know there is electricity in our phones and devices. That electricity is contained in the batteries and fixtures. Let's find out if electricity is everywhere!

Directions: Scatter tissue paper confetti across a table. Blow up a balloon. Rub the balloon against a volunteer's hair or carpeting at least ten times. Hold the rubbed side of the balloon a few inches above the confetti. Observe. Confetti should rise to the balloon.

Say: What does the confetti do when we hold a rubbed balloon above it? (*Children respond.*) Why do you think this happens? (*Children respond.*) Everything is made up of little bits called atoms. The atoms have negative and positive parts. When we rub the balloon against someone's hair, the negative-charged bits called electrons, move between the two objects. That creates an electric charge on the balloon called static electricity. The charge attracts the confetti.

Directions: Pour a teaspoon of salt and a teaspoon of pepper in a pile on the table. Hold the balloon above the salt and pepper.

Say: Why do you think the pepper jumps up to the balloon? (*Children respond.*) The pepper is positively charged. So it is attracted to the negative charge of the balloon. Even with all this power around us, we can't use it unless we can somehow channel it. That is why we have wires and batteries! But when we need the strongest power in the world, what do we do? (*Children respond.*) We PRAY. **God's power is found in prayer.**

Materials

- tissue-paper confetti
- small balloons
- salt
- pepper
- measuring spoons

OPTIONAL ACTIVITIES
WORLD WITHOUT POWER

Directions: Children take turns to draw something that they would find in a world without electricity, nuclear power, gas power, etc. Other children guess the item. Drawing child may respond with "warmer" or "colder" as the others guess. Child who guesses correctly becomes the next drawing child.

Say: These were good illustrations! We rely a lot on electrical power. But what do we do to get the STRONGEST power? (*Children respond.*) We pray. Jesus told us that there are right ways and wrong ways to pray. You don't have to say the same words every time you pray. But be sure to be in a private place so that God knows you are only talking to him. **God's power is found in prayer.**

Materials

- whiteboard
- dry-erase marker

MORE POWER TO YOU

Preparation: Write Matthew 6:14 on the board.

Directions: Read the memory verse together. Children think of someone they need to forgive. Children draw an item that reminds them of that person. Children pray. Children color over their item to signify that God has it covered.

Say: If we need power, Jesus said to pray. Jesus also said that forgiving others keeps the flow of God's power and forgiveness coming into our lives. Take time today to think: Is there a person you need to forgive? **God's power is found in prayer.**

Materials

- whiteboard
- dry-erase marker
- paper
- crayons or markers

POWER TOOL EXPLORATION

Preparation: Photocopy Power Tool Exploration on page 253, making one copy for each child.

Directions: Distribute Power Tool Exploration to children. Children unscramble names of power tools.

Say: We use many kinds of power all the time. Some of the items pictured use electrical power for heat. Some make a machine go. Others use the power for light. We rely on power. But what kind of power do we rely on when we pray? (*Children respond.*) **God's power is found in prayer.**

Materials

- Power Tool Exploration, page 253
- crayons or markers

Answer Key:
wicahnsa (chainsaw)
rnasde (sander)
dllir (drill)
lnia nug (nail gun)
crluarci was (circular saw)

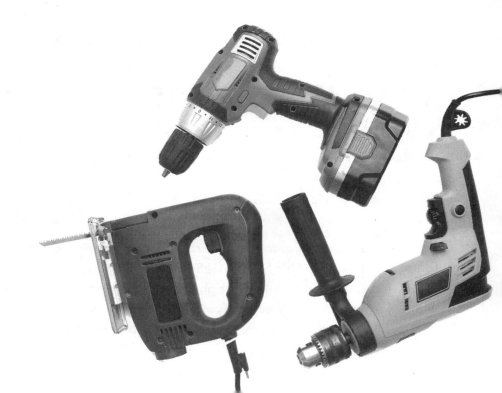

POWER TOOL EXPLORATION

If you forgive those who sin against you, your heavenly Father will forgive you.
Matthew 6:14

Unscramble the names of power tools. Write them on the blank lines.

wicahnsa

_____

rnasde

_____

dllir

_____

lnia nug

crluarci was

_____

GOD'S POWER
IS FOUND
IN PRAYER

50. JESUS HEALS A DEAD GIRL AND A SICK WOMAN

MARK 5:22-43

It is impossible to please God without faith. Anyone who wants to come to him must believe that God exists and that he rewards those who sincerely seek him.

Hebrews 11:6

BIG IDEA

FAITH IN GOD HOLDS GREAT POWER

OVERVIEW

Say: How does an electrical device work when it is not connected to a power outlet? (*Children respond.*) It uses batteries. (*Show several kinds of batteries.*) What do you know about these kinds of batteries? (*Children respond.*)

What are some of the ways you use this (9-volt) battery? (*Children respond.*) Each of these batteries is different. We use each one in a different way. But these batteries all have one thing in common. They store power! Faith in God is like that. When we believe that God will help us, we trust him to do what he knows is best. **Faith in God holds great power!** (*Open with prayer requests, praises, and a time of prayer.*)

Materials

- several kinds of batteries

BIBLE STORY

Say: Jesus often told the people he healed that their faith had made them well (*See Mark 5:34, Luke 7:50, and Luke 17:19*). What do you think Jesus meant by that? (*Children respond.*) Faith is having complete trust or confidence in someone. Because these people believed that Jesus could heal them, they were healed. Our memory verse tells us that we need faith if we are going to please God. When we believe that Jesus can help us, we have faith.

Let's read about some people who had great faith. (*Read Mark 5:22-23 aloud.*) Jairus's little girl was dying and he asked Jesus to heal her. But there was such a big crowd around Jesus that they could not move very fast.

In that crowd, there was a woman who had been sick for twelve years. She had spent all her money going to doctors. But instead

of getting better, her sickness got worse! Let's find out what she did when she saw Jesus. (*Read Mark 5:27–29 aloud.*) The woman came up behind Jesus and touched his clothes. She was healed instantly!

Now, Jesus knows everything. So even though he did not see the woman, he sensed that "healing power had gone out from him" (*Mark 5:30*). Jesus turned around and asked who had touched him.

Remember that Jesus was in the middle of a very big crowd. There were many people touching him. Why do you think he asked this question? (*Children respond.*) Jesus already knew who the woman was because he knows everything. He wanted her to come forward to show others how great her faith was. (*Read Mark 5:33–34 aloud.*) This woman's faith had healed her sickness! What a wonderful example of the power of faith!

While Jesus was still speaking to the healed woman, messengers arrived from Jairus's house. (*Read Mark 5:35–36 aloud.*) Jairus's daughter had already died. But Jesus did not worry. What did Jesus tell Jairus? (*Children respond.*) Have faith!

Jesus hurried to Jairus's house. He went into the dead girl's room and took her hand. He told her to get up AND SHE DID! Of course, everyone was AMAZED and happy! **Faith in God holds great power**!

OPENING GAME
MATCH IT

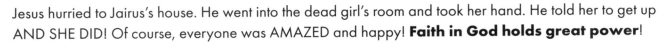
Tip: If you do not have colored buckets that match the small items, tape a sheet of colored paper to the bucket.

Preparation: Mark two lines about twenty feet apart with masking tape. Fill the big bucket with the small items. Set the big bucket at the finish line. Set out the colored buckets behind this bucket.

Directions: Children form two equal teams and line up at the start line. First child in line runs to the finish line and grabs an item from the bucket. Child places item in the bucket of the matching color. Child returns to the start line to tag the next player. Play continues until all have run on one team. Play several rounds.

Alternate Idea: To increase the challenge, expand the number of colors and colored buckets. Have runners move in a certain way (tiptoe, walk backwards, etc.).

Say: How could you tell which bucket was the right one to drop your item into? (*Children respond.*) The color matched. Imagine if you couldn't see the colors. What would be hard to do if you were color blind? (*Children respond.*) How could you tell if a traffic light was green or red? (*Children respond.*)

To play this game, we had to have faith in our eyes. We trusted that they saw the color correctly. We didn't even think about it, but we use faith in many situations every day! **Faith in God holds great power!**

Materials

- masking tape
- big bucket
- small items of various colors (balls, blocks, markers, etc.)
- colored buckets

OBJECT LESSON
STORED-UP POWER

Preparation: Cut copper wires to eighteen inches.

Directions:

1. Pick up the first wire. Attach one paper clip to one end and wrap the other end around a penny.
2. Pick up the second wire. Attach one paper clip to the end.
3. Pick up the third wire. Wrap the end of the wire around a penny.
4. Roll the lemons on the table to loosen their pulp.
5. Make two small slits in two places on the same side of each lemon.
6. Take the first wire and insert the paper clip deeply into the first lemon's slit.
7. Take the first wire and insert the penny deeply into the second lemon's slit. Your lemons should be connected with the wire in between.
8. Take the second wire and insert the paper clip into the lemon with the inserted penny.
9. Take the third wire and insert the penny into the lemon with the inserted paper clip.
10. Connect the two free ends of the wires to the battery terminals of the digital clock.

Tip: If the clock does not light up, then switch the wires.

Say: The steel in the paper clip makes a chemical reaction with the lemon juice. The copper in the penny makes a different chemical reaction. These two different reactions create power! The power travels along the wires and starts up our battery.

Faith is like a battery. Sometimes, we get sick or sad and lose faith. To recharge, we go to God in prayer. Jairus and the sick woman were able to go to Jesus! Jesus performed miracles because of their faith. **Faith in God holds great power!**

> ### Materials
> - scissors
> - 3 coated copper wires with exposed ends
> - ruler
> - 2 large steel paper clips
> - 2 shiny copper pennies
> - 2 lemons
> - paring knife (adult use only)
> - battery-powered digital clock (without batteries)

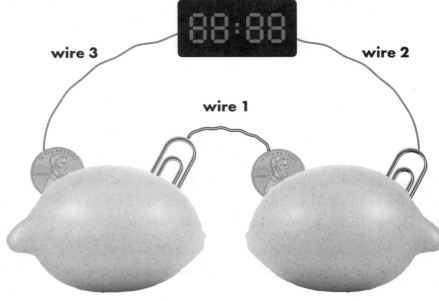

wire 3   wire 2

wire 1

OPTIONAL ACTIVITIES

AMAZING BATTERIES

Preparation: Choose several battery experiments or presentations for children to watch.

Directions: Play the videos. Discuss the amazing things that can happen with a battery. Remind children that you are watching these on video because they can be dangerous for kids to do.

Say: When we watch these videos, we see that by itself, a battery won't do much. It just sits there. But connected to something else, it starts a process of electrons flowing! Faith is like that, too. We can have faith in many things—the president, the weather, our popularity status. But those things are not the ULTIMATE power source.

Jairus and the sick woman knew that Jesus was the most powerful. The woman had faith that Jesus could heal her. Jairus had faith that Jesus could bring his daughter back to life. **Faith in God holds great power!**

FAITH CHAIN

Directions: Children do the following:

Cut paper into strips. Each strip represents a family member. Feel free to include extended family or friends, too! Write the family member's name on one side of the strip. Write a prayer for them on the other side. Take one strip and tape the ends together. It's your first chain.

Slip your next strip through the chain. Tape the ends of the strip together. Now the chains are linked. Continue this all the way until all your chains are linked. Hang the chain somewhere you look often. That way you'll remember to pray for your family often.

Say: We learned about two people who had amazing faith. Jairus believed that Jesus could heal his dying daughter. The sick woman in the crowd believed that Jesus could heal her long-lasting disease. When we pray to God, it shows we have great faith, too.

Like a battery, our faith needs to recharge. How do we recharge batteries? (*Children respond.*) We plug them into a power source. Our power source is God.

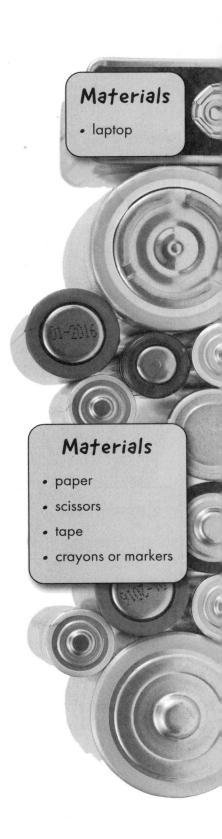

Materials
- laptop

Materials
- paper
- scissors
- tape
- crayons or markers

Use this faith chain to remind you of ways to trust God every day. When we pray, we trust God. We thank him for his answer—even before we see the answer! That shows faith. You will remember that **faith in God holds great power!**

BATTERY TALK

Preparation: Photocopy Battery Talk on page 259, making one copy for each child.

Directions: Distribute Battery Talk to children. Children color and interact with the page. On the picture with the working light bulb, children color the connection lines green and the light bulb yellow. On the picture with the off light bulb, children color the connection lines red.

Say: Faith is like a spiritual battery—it powers our belief in and obedience to God. Jairus and the sick woman had faith that Jesus was a powerful healer. Jesus performed miracles for them! We want to be faithful like them.

Without faith, our love can't shine. We're like a light without a battery! One of these light bulbs is working because it is connected to the battery. Can you tell which one it is? (*Children respond.*) When we pray, trust God and thank him for his answer—even before we see the answer, we show we have faith. **Faith in God holds great power!**

Materials

- Battery Talk, page 259
- crayons or markers

BATTERY TALK

On the picture with the working light bulb, color the connection lines green and the light bulb yellow. On the picture with the nonworking light bulb, color the connection lines red. Explain what needs to change to make the light bulb work.

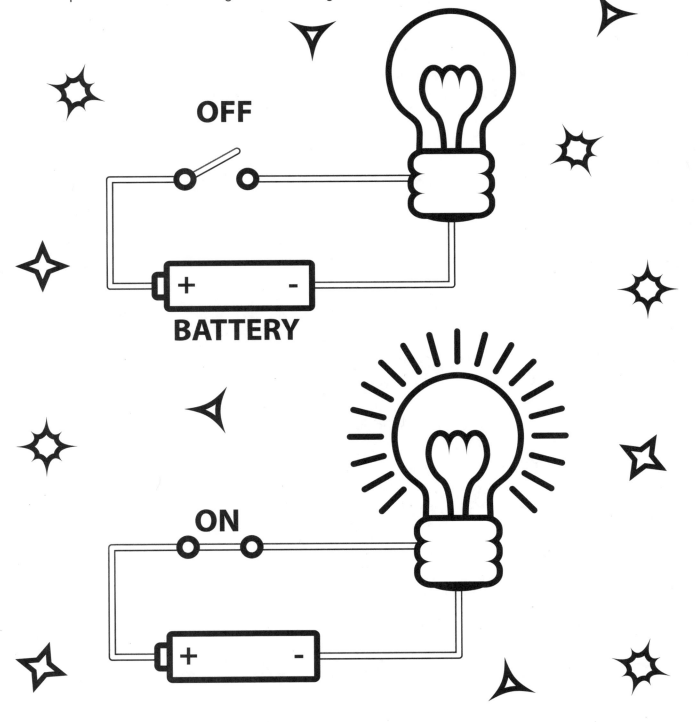

OFF

BATTERY

ON

BIBLE LESSON INDEX

OLD TESTAMENT

NEW TESTAMENT

MEMORY VERSE INDEX

OLD TESTAMENT

NEW TESTAMENT

Top 50
Teaching Resources

The Top 50 series aims to provide the top resources for children's ministries. Enjoy the quick and easy-to-use reproducible resources packed with lessons, activities, and crafts. Includes top lessons every child should know that are volunteer- and child-friendly.

256 pages each, Paperback, Black & White

Top 50 Instant Bible Lessons for Preschoolers	R50002	ISBN: 9781628624977
Top 50 Instant Bible Lessons for Elementary	R50003	ISBN: 9781628624984
Top 50 Memory Verse Lessons	R50010	ISBN: 9781628625059
Top 50 Bible Object Lessons	R50009	ISBN: 9781628625042
Top 50 Creative Bible Lessons	R38255	ISBN: 9781584111566

Find more great books by visiting **www.hendricksonrose.com/RoseKidz.**